Bread & Spirit
Therapy with the New Poor

A NORTON PROFESSIONAL BOOK

Bread & Spirit

Therapy with the New Poor

Diversity of Race, Culture, and Values

Harry J. Aponte

W. W. NORTON & COMPANY • NEW YORK • LONDON

Composition by Bytheway Typesetting Services, Inc.
Manufacturing by Haddon Craftsmen, Inc.

Library of Congress Cataloging-in-Publication Data

Aponte , Harry J.
  Bread and Spirit :therapy with the new poor : diversity of race,
culture, and values / Harry J. Aponte.
    p. cm.
"A Norton professional book" .
Includes bibliographical references and index.
ISBN 0-393-70176-X
1. Family Psychotherapy--Social Aspects--United States. 2. Poor-
-Mental health services--United States. 4. Anomy . 5. family psychotherapy-
-Moral and ethical aspects. I. Title .
RC488.5.A65   1994

616.89' 14' 086942--dc20
                                                              94-31002
                                                                 CIP

W. W. Norton & Company, Inc., 500 Fifth Avenue, New York, NY 10110
  W. W. Norton & Company, Ltd., 10 Coptic Street, London WC1A 1PU

              4   5   6   7   8   9   0

To Theresa, my wife,
The love and inspiration of my life;
To Maria, my dear daughter,
A beautiful and true heart.

Contents

Read last
was
good

Acknowledgments

Theresa Romeo-Aponte, my wife, has been my partner administering a clinic, healing patients, and toiling in the streets of the community. With my writing she has been my editor, creative inspiration, and toughest critic. With *If I Don't Get Simple, I Cry* (Chapter 7), she has shaped, focused, and brought a new life into my writing. She suggested the concept of this book; she is the *spirit* behind it.

This book also owes a grateful debt to the families who have shared their lives with me and who, in one way or another, contributed to every page of this book. Thanks to my students, who have taught me so much. My thanks also to the colleagues who have been my teaching partners; they have provided this book with clinical material and tested with me both concepts and methods, in particular, Joan E. Winter and Grace Hadeed at the Family Institute of Virginia, and Glenn Davis, Katy Pelz-Davis, Bennet Wolper, and Zona Scheiner, the Family Therapy Associates of Ann Arbor.

The book contains formerly published material as well as new writing. I have revised the earlier material where needed, drawing upon new clinical material, making more explicit the themes of diversity, culture, and values, and stressing the community and the ecosystem. The previously published material appeared as:

Chapter 1. Underorganization in the poor family (1976). In P. J. Guerin (Ed.), *Family therapy: Theory and practice* (pp. 432–448). New York: Gardner Press.
Chapter 2. Diagnosis in family therapy (1979). In C. B. Germain (Ed.), *Social work practice: People and environments* (pp. 107–149). New York: Columbia University Press.

I wish also to acknowledge my debt to my deceased parents,
Enrique and Juana Aponte, and to the friends, neighbors, and
mentors of my childhood from Harlem and the South Bronx who
are the deep context for my career and this book. The pain, struggles, and triumphs we shared became the inner bridge to the lives
of the families in this book.

Bread & Spirit
Therapy with the New Poor

Introduction

Man does not live on bread alone . . . (Dt 8:3)

This book is about doing therapy with the America's new poor, who are distressed more by the want of spirit than about the want of bread. Having written about the poor for years, I have here compiled a number of articles previously published. I have refreshed the originals and added new chapters. While the book represents a summation of a major interest of my professional career, it also speaks to my efforts to understand, claim, and discover meaning in my own growing up as a Puerto Rican in New York City. Writing it has been a labor of love. I hope it communicates something of both professional and personal worth to the reader.

Woven throughout the chapters that make up the book's fabric are the threads of my philosophy about working with the poor. Behind this philosophy are certain assumptions about poverty in America. Among them is that America's poor may be the richest in the world, certainly in comparison to the third world. However poorly patched together and ridden with holes, our social safety net does provide most people with the basics to sustain life. People certainly suffer deprivation, but I believe that at the core they suffer a poverty of *despair*. This is a poverty that robs people of their souls—of meaning, purpose, and hope.

THE NATURE OF
THE PROBLEM

America's popular culture seems to be about owning cars, looking fashionable, being entertained—and believing that it is all

1

owed us. There is in the air a philosophy that says we are entitled to feel happy and satisfied. If we are not, then somebody out there is depriving us and we have a right to be resentful, even vengeful. For the poor this translates into a pervasive sense of injustice, help-lessness, and rage.

The poorest in America, either through slavery (African Americans), conquest (Native Americans), or colonization (Puerto Ricans), have lost much of their original cultures. These cultures once told them who they were and gave them values that helped structure their families and communities. With these cultures there also came purpose, whether in mythology or religion. They had reasons for living and loving that were independent of economic achievement.

America's pragmatism and consumerism have since filled the space created by the loss of the original traditions and rituals of these cultures. The result has been tragic for minorities. Here's a current news story.

> On a recent sunny Sunday afternoon an 18 year-old Afri-can American man was gunned down. . . . Friends say he was shot because he dressed too well. (Marder, 1993, pp. A1, A10)

A local community activist commented:

> Nothing in their houses and everything on their backs. . . . It's all about low self-esteem. You buy how you feel. . . . So they get artificial stimulation from clothing. (Marder, 1993, p. A10)

The word on the street was that it was jealousy among neighbor-hood kids. They were measuring themselves by fancy jackets. Where were their own cultural values and traditions to give their lives worth even in the face of hard times and tough neighbor-hoods? What slavery had snatched from them!

In contrast, European and Asian immigrants to the United States, who were not subjugated, were accompanied by their cul-

tures into the American scene. Their ghettos, even with poverty
and discrimination, became nurseries that fostered identity, social
role, personal values. They contended with American society from
a core that affirmed who they were, what they were worth, and
why they should strive.

However, even white Americans are suffering from America's
loss of spirit. Today Appalachian whites, the descendants of the
original "18th-century Irish and Scottish pioneers" (Fleishman,
1994, A11) are losing their way of life, as the coal industry changes:

> The heartbreak of leaving seems unbearable. Almost no-
> where else in America do people feel so interwoven with
> their culture and their land. (Fleishman, 1994, A10)

Families are breaking up. There are now reports of suicide, alcoholism, marijuana abuse, and domestic violence. As the community comes undone, so do families and individuals. Social values
and structures break down. The men, in particular, are losing their
status and roles; adrift, they begin to get into trouble. The women
cannot depend upon them and have to rely on themselves. The
partnership withers. The children lose the closeness, safety, and
direction they had. They begin to wander off into trouble. A new
poverty develops, with its own culture of despair, self-devaluation,
and rage.

These Appalachian whites begin the slide to the dark valley of
the inner-city. Yet, these new poor, wherever we find them, look
in many ways much like the rest of America. They find themselves
in a society that lacks the identity, values, and structure to provide
direction, safety, and a foundation for esteeming self and others.
Upper-class America can camouflage its distress, but even there the
strain is showing.

America has become a society of stress, isolation, and distrust.
People are anxious about commitment in intimate relationships.
They are fearful of abuse and violence from their family, friends,
and neighbors. They are marrying less and divorcing more. More
children are living without both parents. They are learning early
about the instability of relationships.

Americans are becoming more alone. The numbers reflect the trend.

> Demographers predict . . . that 10% of young men and women today will never marry and that half of those who do will divorce. Some 37% of adults over 18 are single, and roughly one-fourth of all households consist of just one person. One child in four is born out of wedlock, and one-fourth of all children now live with a single parent. (*Business Week*, March 5, 1990, p. 20)

I believe the social isolation and fragmentation of American society, coupled with the vagaries of today's culture and values, have made us a vulnerable people. We do not connect with one another. We are anxious and angry. We lack a consensus of values and a common social structure to bring us together. On the contrary, America today leads the world in every category of violence, including murder, rape, and robbery.

> The nation's citizens committed a record number of killings in 1990—at least 23,300, or nearly three an hour— and record numbers of rapes, robberies and assaults. (Weiner, 1991, p. A3)

We all talk about losing community. People are progressively depending more on the electronic technology and less on one another. Telephones, television, and computers, which are media for communication, have also become an end in themselves, substituting for people contact. Community is no longer where we work, often not where we go to school or where we find friends and spouses. The neighborhood has less and less meaning. The society where we share life with our loved ones and raise our children is not in our neighborhood. It is beyond the reach of our personal influence. It is virtually without boundaries.

Television has probably become the most powerful influence on values in American society. Yet, like our society its message about values is fragmented and contradictory. Schools no longer represent a local community's priorities. Impersonal bureaucracies decide the values taught, which may be the notions of an educational reformer who may or may not reflect local ethnic, religious, or neighborhood values. School boards, not wanting to offend anyone, may decide to homogenize values taught in schools into an innocuous blend that reflects no one group's values—and thereby contradict every group's beliefs. Yes, we raise our children, but within a society that does little to support and much to oppose our cultural, ethnic, and religious values. The influence of families and communities over their children is radically attenuated by the larger society in which we live. When we cannot pass on our heritage to our own children, our spirit dies with us.

DIVERSITY

Just as community embodies our participation in and responsibility for each other's lives, diversity is the uniqueness of our identity. Our history, traditions, and values both join us and distinguish us. While we are losing community, we are losing ourselves among the contradictions of diversity. We do not seem to know how to respond as our society becomes progressively more diverse not only in ethnic groups, but also in values. For example, we are in the midst of a war between those who favor English as the official language and symbol of America's common heritage and those who advocate multiculturalism, which often translates into ethnocentrism that in its own way denigrates every other heritage. Then there is another values war between those who champion "traditional" values and those who see tradition as oppressive and unequal. One side does not recognize the evolution in society, while the other fails to acknowledge transcendent principles that speak to our heritage and our destiny. The effect of these ongoing conflicts is a cultural paralysis—no one's values are supported. We lack a national consensus that could also nourish cultural diversity. A paralysis over political correctness has us stuttering and unable to communicate across differences.

Whom does this hurt most? I think it is those groups who have the weakest grip on their cultures and do not have strong communities to support, guide, and protect them. These are often poor minorities who sink into discouragement, self-depreciation, and anger. Many give up on one another and avoid the risks of commitment and intimacy. Many try to kill the pain through drugs and alcohol. Many lash out for control through violence and intimidation. Many isolate themselves in fear and depression. With the breakdown of hope comes the collapse of the social structure.

> Increasingly, family structure is the chief determinant of whether a child will grow up in poverty. The children of single parents are five times as likely to be poor as children born to married couples. Today, more than half of all children living in single, female-headed households are poor. (National Commission on Children, 1990, p. 33)

The problems of children from single-parent families, who are largely female-headed, do not stop with poverty. According to the Report of the National Commission on America's Urban Families:

> Children from fragmented families are more likely to suffer emotional or behavioral problems than those who live with their own parents. (National Commission on America's Urban Families, 1993, p. 4)

The same report goes on to say that:

> About one-third of all children today live apart from their fathers. Father absence is an important predictor of problems such as juvenile crime, poor school performance, and adolescent pregnancy. (p. 9)

This social tragedy does not play out just in individual homes. It is tragically dramatized in the fractured communities that host fractured families. Yet, let us keep in mind that these communities nestle in the larger society. The plagues are endemic to American society. I would argue that the plagues began in the failures of the larger society. They became pestilential in vulnerable neighborhoods, which in turn became a source for an even more virulent strain spreading through the greater community.

AN ANSWER: A PHILOSOPHY

Is despair all there is among America's new poor? Of course not. There still is a spirit of love, courage, and hope in those communities, although it is often muted. You will witness some of that spirit among the people in this book. However, that spirit survives *in spite of* the social and cultural environment of today's America, not because of it. Can we, as therapists, make a difference? I believe so. This book will suggest some ways. We must begin by recognizing the power of that spirit.

I recently read a newspaper article about a book published in Japan that exploded into a best seller, *The Courage of Honest Poverty*. Its author, Koji Nakano, speaks to an issue that is very much American but seems to be spreading throughout the world.

Our image is that of a country that's good at making things but has no culture. Foreigners say Japanese lack character and dignity and think of us just as people with money. (Nakano cited in O'Neill, 1993, p. A22)

He urges his people to reach back into what defines the Japanese "essential culture."

Now is the time for things of the heart and the spirit, things that cannot be seen. These are what the Japanese of today have neglected most of all. (Nakano cited in O'Neill, 1993, p. A22)

If they worry in Japan about their national character, we should be wailing in America. The answer to America's new poverty cannot only be more jobs or even be more schooling—at least not what passes for schooling in the inner-city today. Certainly more therapy will not do it. It needs to be all the above, along with culture, values, and spirituality to give them meaning and purpose.

It is not as if no one has thought of this before. But there has been little commitment on a national level to cultivating the cultural values, social structures, and spiritual practices of racial and ethnic groups in America within a common American cultural frame. This would not mean embracing static, historical caricatures of cultures. I do not speak of either the insulation of ethnocentricity or the mummification of dead traditions. I refer to cultivating the growth and evolution of diversity of spirit within a common national character.

I introduce a book on therapy by talking about culture, values, and spirituality because therapy can be an enemy or a friend to spirit. The technology of therapy has attempted to replace tradition, ritual, and customs. Therapy has also often masqueraded as spirit. Sometimes it has pretended to give life through the power of technique. However, just as medication can only succeed when it cooperates with the healing powers of the body, therapy only works when it joins with the indigenous forces of culture and faith in people's lives. Sometimes therapy dresses as spirituality. However, therapy is a healing potion invented by doctors. It is not the spirit of the ages embedded in cultural and spiritual traditions. It can prepare the ground that suffers some damage, but it is not the seed of grain that has journeyed down through the generations.

THERAPY FOR THE NEW POOR

This leads us right back to the new poor, whose emotional and relationship problems require understanding within their socioeconomic and political contexts. The poor are dependent upon and vulnerable to the overreaching power of society. They cannot insulate themselves from society's ills. They cannot buy their children private schooling when their public school fails. They cannot buy into an upscale neighborhood when their housing project becomes too dangerous. When society stumbles, its poorest citizens are tossed about and often crushed.

Therapy with the new poor must address, in particular, the special issues of poor minorities and the sociocultural fabric of their families and their communities. As Lisbeth Schorr (1989, p. 13) has argued, programs that are effective with the poor "view the child as part of a family and the family as part of a neighborhood and community . . . [and] programs for those with the greatest needs [must] be clearly designed to take their special needs into account."

The poor about which we speak have all the personal and family problems everyone else has, along with the complications of a personal, family, and community (ecosystemic) constitution weakened by chronic social and economic problems. Therapy with the poor must have all the sophistication of the best psychological therapies. It must also have the insight of the social scientist and the drive of the community activist.

The benefit to all society is that, because the same social conditions that wounded the poor are also hurting everyone else in this country, finding a cure for America's poor may also heal the rest of society. Teenage pregnancy, single-parent families, divorce, alcoholism, drug addiction, domestic violence, etc., are not limited to the poor of America. However, tragically enough, the poor have become the miner's canary that dies first as a warning of the toxicity of the environment. How many of the poor must die to warn us of the toxicity of our social environment?

What have we learned about working with the poor? I have based my work on several assumptions:

1. *Options and power.* The poor need to feel control over their own lives. They must experience therapy as a place where they discover their inner potential to determine their lives' direction. Therapy makes this possible when the poor are not treated as helpless victims of the unconscious, of family systems, or of society. Therapy helps them believe in their ability to direct their own emotions, attitudes, and actions in the face of horrendous problems. From within themselves, they can achieve the freedom to exercise fully their ability to make attitudinal and spiritual choices, even if they are not able to change their economics. Outside themselves, they can make choices and changes about family, friends, and officials. They do not

have to stay put. With some backing they can expect more not only of themselves but also of the world around them.

2. *Purpose and meaning in life.* The poor need to work not only to solve problems but also to reach for purpose in life. This pursuit is rooted in their psychology, family history, and cultural and spiritual origins. From these sources they can connect with their traditions, rituals, and beliefs, as well as share in the meanings and goals of life common to their culture. To the extent that religion plays a part in their lives, they have a vision beyond themselves to help them face life. Culture and religion also form the foundation for their personal moral and social values. These values become the internal gyroscope that gives them an internal autonomy, personal identity, and sense of self-worth. In therapy the poor work to solve their problems in accord with who they were, are, and want to be.

3. *The personal ecosystem's multilevel structural organization.* Chronic deprivation of socioeconomic resources and cultural supports to an ethnic group undermines the infrastructure of its communities, families, and personal psychology. These crippled communities do not have positive and well-defined identities. They have difficulty choosing leadership and organizing behind it. Families lose their cohesiveness; their members fail to develop roles and relationships that work or healthy internal psychological structures. They feel incompetent, lack self-confidence. These individuals, families, and communities need help organizing among themselves. Solving personal emotional and relationship problems among the new poor calls for mobilizing the full bread and spirit resources of their ecosystems.

When looking at the dispirited new poor, it is easy to be overwhelmed by the magnitude of their social and economic problems. It is easy to be dragged down by the emotional and family devastation, the educational failures, criminal convictions, domestic abuse, etc., that so often pervade poor families that are losing or have lost hope, meaning, and purpose. Solving specific personal or family problems seems impossible when we cannot envision mending the psychological, familial, and community fabric of people's lives. Building and rebuilding that foundation of body and soul becomes the central challenge with the new poor.

This special goal requires not just a reemphasis of focus but also new tasks. Repairing a roof, leaking because of age and wear, on an otherwise sound building is quite different from repairing a roof set on a faulty foundation that caused structural damage throughout the structure. Our cost conscious society would like to treat all roof leaks as minor repairs. However, the new poor need help to restore the basic structures of their personal and community lives. At the same time the spirit of their traditions, rituals, and beliefs must be revived. Efforts aiming short of the double goal of restoring a structural foundation *and* revitalizing spirit will be costly because they will ultimately fail—and the malady of spirit will spread throughout society.

Undertaking this intensive effort does not mean replacing families' personal ecosystems with new services and thinking. It means working in partnership with the community that exists; the mandate for service providers is to *serve*, not colonize. People and families come into being, develop, and are sustained by their personal traditions, structures, and beliefs—not by services.

Service providers who try to substitute their personal political and social views for a community's views about moral behavior and family relationships stifle the souls of communities. In today's politically correct atmosphere, many therapists and professional associations have determined that they should be the source of solutions for today's social problems. They insinuate their social and moral values into therapy, so that therapy becomes a new culture, a new religion.

Some service providers attempt to increase services instead of building up and enriching communities from within. In their best of all possible worlds they would devise new social structures, overwhelming the existing ones. They would bring in new money. With the new money would come control from outside. They would create a leadership around their own services and funding, becoming the social conscience and infrastructure of the community.

In the poor, professionals face a diversity of racial, ethnic, cultural, and religious values that may well contradict their own core beliefs about family structure, sexual mores, and social hierarchy. This is not to say that therapists should not have their own convictions; it does mean that therapists need to work in a partnership that recognizes the boundaries and limitations of what it means to be a service provider. A family owns its life and its soul no matter how much help it needs from a therapist.

THIS BOOK

As therapists we can best relate to the weave of the personal, family, and community lives of the poor by working with them on the specific, concrete problems they present. The poor live in the struggles of daily life. They come to us seeking palpable solutions to palpable problems. However, even though their social stresses may feel overwhelming, the poor, above all, are *people with problems*, not just victims of problems. There is a soul in each client that calls for nourishment, support, and yes, even challenge. This book hopes to speak to both bread and spirit in the work with the new poor.

I have attempted to present a balanced, cohesive, and comprehensive perspective on doing therapy with the new poor. However, this book on the America's new poor is not just about the poor. We all live in the same social and cultural environment. What hurts the poor hurts the rest of America. America's poor can teach us all how to repair human life in America.

1. Underorganization in the Poor Family

To write about therapy with the poor we must answer the question: What is special about working with the poor? The answer, as I see it, is that the poor bring with their personal problems two distinct factors: (1) difficult social conditions, and (2) the destructive effects of those conditions on their lives. Not all the emotional and relationship problems the poor bring to therapists are special to the poor. However, when their problems converge with the complications of poverty, their personal struggles become inextricable from their social troubles.

To work with the poor may be to contend with social issues about money, housing, and crime-ridden neighborhoods, as well as racial, ethnic, and cultural discrimination. It may entail dealing with the people and institutions linked to these issues, such as public assistance, protective services, public housing, public schools, and the justice system.

Moreover, working with an underprivileged family may also mean coming up against the scarring and eroding effects of these socioeconomic forces on the psychology and relationships of the poor themselves. In America poor people who come into therapy are more often than not laboring under the burdens of American society's failures. The effects of society's failings are often seen in the most intimate corners of their lives. Poverty combined with the disruption of the social ecosystem, as we are seeing in this country, results in devastating psychological effects, demolished family relationships, and destroyed communities.

Yet, at the other end of the continuum, people can be poor

economically and still be emotionally, familially, and socially healthy—at least as healthy as anyone else. With their communities and cultures intact, the poor can maintain their identity, self-esteem, and sense of belonging. They have their trust in family and friends, as well as in their social network—public institutions and economic infrastructure. Instead of withdrawing in despair or becoming predatory in anger, they take care of themselves, their families, and their neighbors. The intactness, order, and connectedness of the social ecosystem is reflected in personal living.

People with intact communities and cultures also know power in a healthy, natural, and benign form that allows them to assume a society that will respond to their voices. They feel they belong to a society that gives to them and to which they want to give. They can endure material deprivation because the spirit is nourished with self-esteem, caring personal relationships, and trust in the community. There is a sense of meaning and purpose at home and in the community.

In real life, we do not see people who are totally at one extreme or the other, but we do see communities, families, and individuals that approach these extremes. When the poor come to therapy, insofar as they approach the cohesive end of the spectrum, they present personal problems contained within their personal psychology and in their personal relationships. Their poverty needs no special attention. Insofar as they are closer to the devastated extreme of society, their personal problems become synonymous with these extreme social conditions. The personal problems of poor people then become problems of poverty, and their therapists face a different task. Henceforth, when I refer to therapy with the poor, I am speaking of the poor from the social ruins of our society.

POVERTY AND THERAPY

The first challenge to the therapist is that the problems of the poor, especially of poor minorities, are so pervasive and horrendous. Understandably, many people do not want to identify the devastation among the poor for fear of both blaming the victim and devaluing the already discouraged. Yet, if we do not have the courage to assess frankly the damage to the socially disadvantaged, we cannot repair the harm. We also run the risk of patronizing them and of underestimating their readiness to name the problem and engage the fight.

This brings us to a specific phenomenon that is, I believe, central to understanding what it means to do therapy with the poor—*underorganization*. Social destitution *in the absence of a strong sense of self and cohesive familial and social network* can injure the fundamental structure of the individual's psychological development, the formation of family, and the vitality of a community. Individuals may fully develop neither their intellectual and emotional capacity, nor the ability to form intimate and committed personal relationships, nor their potential to perform effectively in society. Families may fail to serve as stable, safe, nurturing nests for their members. People may not learn to live in community where they learn to depend upon one another. Life becomes difficult, painful, and even frightening.

For the therapist, it is vital to diagnose the extent to which poverty's injuries have handicapped the poor person or family seeking help. Poverty attacks people's sense of self and their familial and social network, which I view as their emotional and social immunological defenses. Once poverty breaches these defenses, people are vulnerable to all sorts of personal problems. However, the results of society's failings are not exclusive to the poor. While money can hide failure, people in the moneyed classes are also hurting. We are seeing today in America the undermining of society's basic social structures—from the individual to the family to the community. Depression, alcoholism, drug abuse, and violence are not exclusive to the poor; loneliness, divorce, and the alienation of generations from one another are part of everyday life. Pain, stress, and fear belong to everyone.

Speaking about the interdependence of people and society's institutions, Bellah and his associates state that:

> in our life with other people we are engaged continuously, through words and actions, in creating and re-creating the institutions that make that [social] life possible. (Bellah, Madsen, Sullivan, Swidler, & Tipton, 1991, p. 11)

They refer not only to how society through its institutions provides the political, economic, legal, and human service support system for family life, but also to how it maintains the moral structure of the community and its citizenry.

> This process is never neutral but is always ethical and political, since institutions (even such an intimate institution as the family) live or die by ideas of right and wrong and conceptions of good. (Bellah et al., p. 11)

Through these institutions and their moral framework, society provides the social context for us to define ourselves and our relationships with one another. Bellah continues:

> [society's institutions] are the substantial forms through which we understand our own identity and the identity of others as we seek cooperatively to achieve a decent society. (p. 12)

The structures of our relationships, our identities within society, and our morality root deeply in the soil of society's own structure, identity, and morality, as manifested in its institutions. The family is where we most palpably see the effects of society on our personal lives.

THE UNDERORGANIZED FAMILY IN THERAPY

What happens when society does not provide that supportive and defining context described by Bellah and his colleagues? We find broken families and broken people. Families coming for therapy present one problem after another. One problem improves and another worsens. In the more extreme cases, families do not seem to have within them what they need to attack their problems. Their social immune systems can no longer fight off social disease. It becomes endemic in their lives.

Many families come for treatment because a crisis has forced the issue, or an agency or court has mandated it. Motivation is uneven. They come a few times and then do not return. When they continue in therapy, they show up irregularly, mostly when new crises erupt. In sessions, they have trouble presenting their stories coherently. They seem in disarray as they talk over one another or talk hardly at all. Often workers feel they cannot do enough to make a difference and become discouraged.

Some have described these families as *disorganized* (Minuchin, Montalvo, Guerney, Rosman, & Schumer, 1967); I prefer the term *underorganized*. Underorganization suggests not so much an improper or randomly chaotic organization as a lack of organization, a structure that has never fully developed. These structures have not achieved the *constancy*, *differentiation*, and *flexibility* they need to meet the demands of life. Underorganization is part of the family environment in which children grow up and, like an indigenous infection, shows in the undeveloped psychological structure of the family's individual members. Underorganization characterizes the communities—destitute and dangerous—in which these children and families live and develop. Underorganization runs through the entire ecosystem.

Yet, this underorganization is not a single entity. There are degrees and varieties of underorganization, and not everyone in the ecosystem is equally affected. Moreover, there is potential for change in everyone. The therapist who looks finds these strengths even in the most underorganized family. However, curing an infection presumes both addressing the debilitated immunological condition (the underorganization) and attacking the specific location of the infection (the family problem). The entire ecosystem is host to the infection, but we begin with the family that comes for specific help.

Structure in the Family

A family organizes itself around its life functions. Family members develop roles in the family and pattern their relationships to bring in the family income, manage finances, discipline and nurture children, maintain cleanliness, repair the house, etc. Everyone has a flexible number of roles and every relationship a variety of structures to meet life's assorted demands. A family develops its own unique structure. People in families make their choices about these patterns influenced by the make-up of the individuals, their feelings toward one another, and the familial, cultural, and religious frameworks within which they operate.

In today's society these sociocultural frameworks are particularly complex, as we go through a period of intense and controversial revision of both social morality and social and family structure. For the chronically disadvantaged living in socially and economically devastated neighborhoods, today's guidelines for personal relationships offer little guidance and support. Society at large with its own problems is a big part of the problem facing families, and the poor know this better than anyone.

Alignment, Force, and Boundaries

A poor family, like any other family, works with certain structural dynamics to organize itself; these are *alignment, force*, and *boundary* (Aponte & Van Deusen, 1981), the basic building blocks of a social relationship. While these form the structural framework of relationships, they do not of themselves give any more meaning to a relationship than a steel frame gives to a building. They take on meaning according to the purposes through which people relate to one another.

In a family, *alignment* refers to the joining or opposition of one family member to another as the family carries out an operation. *Force* (or *power*) defines the relative influence of each member on the outcome of an activity. *Boundary* tells who is included and excluded from the activity in question, and what each person's role is in the operation. Since these three structural dimensions are inherent to every transaction, you cannot say you fully understand a social transaction until you can speak to its three structural components in relation to the action's goal.

To understand structure in action it is best to look at how family members carry out their tasks vis-à-vis one another. Different tasks may require different structural patterns in family relationships. This makes for the complexity of structure in families.

Nevertheless, a family will have patterns that dominate and characterize most of its interactions. Diagnosing a family's problems means discovering how its patterns of relating are failing to meet the demands and challenges of life.

Underorganized families present tremendous challenges when it comes to identifying structures. They appear chaotic. People talk over one another. Roles are neither clearly defined nor consistently assigned. Family members do not team up easily to solve problems. The same few approaches to solutions repeat even when they do not appear to work. Relationships lack a constant, coherent, and flexible structure.

With *constancy*, family members trust what to expect from one another. With *coherency*, they have patterns of relating that have an internal compatibility, patterns that reinforce one another and enable family members to work together successfully. With *elaborateness*, a family has available a flexible repertoire of ways to cope with life's expected and unexpected tasks. These are the fundamental mechanics of an organized family structure.

Yet, one cannot say a family is well-functioning just because it has a workable structure. These are only mechanics. The spirit of the family is what breathes meaning into that structure. The goals and motivation of the family members go beyond carrying out functions. Executing the most mundane of tasks potentially has purposes for the family, which can range from exploitation to love to spiritual fulfillment. The role in a family structure of a mother's supervising her children has significance beyond gaining compliance. Her supervision as the executive parent signifies protecting her children, guiding them, and teaching them. She makes choices that accord or not with her values, which may be high-minded or ill-conceived, and she follows through on those choices with wholehearted or indifferent effort.

In a family that is underorganized, alignments, force, and boundaries may be unreliable, poorly defined, limited, or rigid to varying degrees. The spirit that motivates a family's transactions may be more demoralizing than inspiring. At the heart of it all, underorganization represents the arrest of both functioning and spirit in a family. It comes in many forms.

The underorganization may be narrow in scope or broad

based. A mother may be able to care for young children who do not challenge, but not with older youngsters who test limits. Another mother who cannot connect easily because she is blocked emotionally may be at a loss with younger children. She may be better with older children, who can relate more as peers. She may vacillate between laissez-faire withdrawal that allows disorder and violent imposition of control. At an extreme she may want to parent but feel so inept that she seeks refuge in a narcotic stupor.

The male counterpart may dream of being paterfamilias but keep failing at it. He may be able to be the nice guy but not the authority. Another man may be just the opposite—authoritarian without heart. One may be an affectionate lover but not a committed partner. Another may commit but be shut down emotionally. One knows only hustling, another only driven work. The patterns vary, but the constant is that something is missing, something is not fully present. They may want to, but they do not have it in their experience and within themselves to take care of themselves and those they love.

The children from these relationships long to attach but fear to trust. They look for safety but live in fear. They naturally incline to openness but close up. They want to love but live with anger. They look for social cues about family life but face confusion. They try to make it outside home but home is not there to give them a start in learning and coping. The world outside, in the neighborhood and the school, is difficult and dangerous. The adults in their lives seem to care but somehow keep letting them down.

The umbrella of the term underorganization speaks of those who did not perform because they never fully developed the potential. These are not failures that flow from neurotic defenses against conflict at home or outside. Their families and communities did not nurture, teach, or form in them the mechanics or spirit for successful family relationships. Making the family work would take a supreme effort on their parts, and usually, some extraordinary support from others.

Diagnosis here is important, because the cure for what is blocked by conflict and neurosis is different from that for what is stunted or lacking. Of course, there is little that is purely just one or the other. Problems come mixed and require intervention that considers the nature of the failure. Strategic interventions are effective with neurotic entanglements. They outmaneuver defenses to free potential. Structural interventions break down old structures and build new ones, or help build structures where they did not exist. Most underorganized families need both kinds of interventions, more of one than the other depending on a family's story.

Work with seriously underorganized families will take place through talking and doing. Talking may do for relatively well-organized families who can take for granted the basics of the human relationship that allow them to abstract and generalize. Those who do not have these basic structures in their lives tend to struggle from life task to life task. They do not have the experience within them from which to build new understanding and new potential. They see, feel, and trust the palpable experience.

In therapy, the underorganized family needs experience from which to learn—not only talking about life, but living it in a different way. Therapy needs to offer transactions that embody how they experience life. Thus, therapy with underorganized families takes place within *enactment* (Aponte & Van Deusen, 1981), where families live out an issue in a therapy session through an encounter with one another that approximates their experience at home. The therapist lets people experience the old to see what is not working and then creates with them a new and better experience.

Therapists who work in this mode participate actively in the enactment to help supply what may be lacking in the family, personally motivating, articulating, connecting, etc. They also actively attempt to secure what is lacking in the family's social context, whether it be other family or friends or community institutions. All this reconstructive work combines with the disentangling work of therapy. It is active.

AN UNDERORGANIZED
POOR FAMILY

The following are excerpts from an initial interview conducted by the author with a family that in many respects is underorganized. The family is African American, and consists of a mother,

Mrs. Cass, and four children: Charles, age 12, Marge, 11, Joe, 9, and Dennis, 5. This family lives on public assistance. A pediatric hospital's social service department referred them to a child guidance clinic for a consultation. The mother was complaining that her 12-year-old son was incorrigible. The mother had been seeing the hospital's worker with some regularity for about two months. The worker called the guidance clinic in desperation, saying she could not get beyond the mother's insistence on placing Charles. The boy was resisting his mother's discipline and controls, but was in no way delinquent. He was, in fact, a mild, shy youngster. The clinic agreed to see the family with the worker for a consultation.

As the family and worker sat for the session with the consultant, all the children clustered around the mother except for Charles. He took a chair in the corner and sat with his back to her. Knowing that the mother wanted Charles out of the home, and having observed the seating arrangement, the consultant's first challenge was to see whether he could make the boy experience himself as part of the family for the session. Structurally, Charles had no one in the family who appeared aligned with him. He seemed powerless, and he was on the periphery of the family boundary. His mother was about to exile him from the family.

The consultant began by asking Charles where he lived, and the directions to his house. The boy haltingly tried to give the directions to his house. However, his sister, Marge, immediately answered for him. Charles fell silent. The consultant's first move had been to align himself with the boy. He wanted Charles to feel included within the boundaries of the interview and know the power of having his voice heard. Marge's response defeated that move, and the mother immediately followed up with, "Charles, he doesn't like his sisters and brothers." Her move sealed his exclusion at that moment. The family enacted the old pattern.

The consultant would not be able to maneuver subtly. The mother's power could overwhelm his efforts, as had happened already with the hospital's worker. The consultant decided to interpose himself as a gently restraining boundary between the mother and the children over the next several sequences, concentrating on the children and their relationships with each other. He wanted to see whether, if mother were on the sidelines, Charles' siblings would still exclude him. If they did not, it would suggest that it was the mother who was locking Charles out because he was too much to handle. If so, the consultant would subsequently focus on ways to support her in managing him.

What follows is a verbatim account of this segment of the interview. What the transcript cannot convey is the amount of noise and confusion that ensued whenever the mother was not actively on top of the children directing all their interactions. They interrupted and talked over one another. The consultant repeatedly attempted to call time out so that people could hear one another. They enacted their underorganization.

The Interview

MOTHER And Charles, he doesn't like his sisters and brothers.

CONSULTANT Oh, is that true?

MOTHER He's just evil around them and just as cross and fretful as he can be.

(*Marge and Charles attempt to talk at the same time, even as mother is talking.*)

CONSULTANT (*To the children*) Okay. Wait a minute! Charles, do you realize what she just said? Is she right? You don't like your sisters and brothers?

CHARLES Yeah, I like them. I didn't say that.

CONSULTANT You do like them?

CHARLES Yeah.

DENNIS He likes me.

CONSULTANT He likes you?

DENNIS I don't know why he doesn't like the rest of them.

CONSULTANT Okay. Charles, do you like Dennis?

CHARLES Yeah.

CONSULTANT You do. All right. (*To Marge*) What about you, Marge? You and Charles. How do you two get along?

MARGE Terrible. I help him with his homework.

CHARLES You do not. You never help me with my homework.

MARGE I have homework and I don't know how to do it, and he won't even show me how to do it, but I show him how to do it.

(*Marge and Charles start shouting at one another.*)

CONSULTANT Wait! Wait! Wait!

MARGE He doesn't like for me to look on his paper.

CONSULTANT Is that true?

CHARLES Yeah.

CONSULTANT Why not? (*To Dennis, who was talking over everyone else trying to help*) Wait, Dennis! You're very good, but I want you to wait . . .

MOTHER (*Addressing Charles in an attempt to help the therapist*) Now you turn around and look at people when they're talking to you.

CONSULTANT (*To Charles*) Why don't you like her [Marge]? What does she do to you?

CHARLES She tells lies on me all the time.

CONSULTANT Who does she tell? She tells on you? She tells your mother on you?

MARGE (*Jumps in*) Everything they do and I see—(*Joe and Dennis argue, drowning out Marge.*)

CONSULTANT Wait! Wait!

MOTHER Didn't you hear him say wait? One at a time. (*They quiet down for a moment.*)

CONSULTANT I want Marge to talk.

MARGE Everything that they do and I see that my mother don't want them to do, I tells on them.

CONSULTANT I see. That's why you don't—(*To Joe, who again interrupts*) I will let you talk in a minute. (*To Charles*) That's why you don't like Marge. Because she tells on you?

CHARLES She tells lies on me, and every time Joe does something she blames it on me.

CONSULTANT (*Because Charles only has Dennis on his side, and is in danger of alienating Joe, the therapist moves to that relationship. To Joe*) What about that? Is that true what he just said?

JOE ~~Yes.~~

CONSULTANT Really?

MARGE It is not.

CONSULTANT Wait a minute Marge. Now it's Joe's turn.

JOE When she hits me, she says I hit her. She cries and then makes me get a beating.

MARGE I do not.

JOE You do.

MARGE Them two right there (*Charles and Joe*) they tell lies on me. Like if my mother goes somewhere—they tell lies.

(*Marge inadvertently pushes Joe toward Charles, and then Dennis again starts talking over her.*)

CONSULTANT (*To Dennis*) Okay. We'll get to you.

MARGE They tell lies on me, and them two they are always fighting, and me and him (*Dennis*) we don't fight as much as them two. (*She tries at least to bring Dennis back to her side.*)

CONSULTANT Okay. But wait a minute. (*To Joe and Charles*) But right now, Joe and Charles, the two of you say that Marge tells on you. (*They indicate agreement.*)

MARGE They say I'm a tattletale.

CONSULTANT They say you're a tattletale? (*To Dennis*) Does she tell on you, Dennis? (*Testing Dennis' loyalties*)

DENNIS Yeah. When she gets mad at Charles, I get mad at her.

CONSULTANT Because Charles is your friend, right?

DENNIS Yeah. I like them two. (*Pointing to Charles and Joe*)

CONSULTANT I see.

JOE I like them two.

CONSULTANT You like which two?

JOE I like them two. (*Pointing to Charles and Dennis*)

CONSULTANT So you three guys are all together here, and poor Marge is all by herself.

When the boys isolate Marge, the consultant makes a gesture to support her. He then explores the family reaction to her isolation by pushing it further. When it becomes apparent that Charles has allies among the boys, the consultant invites the mother back in. He wanted to look at the mother-daughter coalition and its effect on the boys, Charles in particular.

CONSULTANT Are you the family tattletale?

MARGE No, I'm not.

DENNIS Marge and Mom. (*Pointing to them, suggesting collusion*)

CONSULTANT That's it? Okay. All right. Now I understand. (*To Mother*) Is that the way it is?

MOTHER Well, I carry her with me a lot.

CONSULTANT Yes—

MOTHER And I leave the boys a lot.

MARGE (*Mother and Marge now begin pulling together.*) And they get mad at me, because most of the time I go to New York and we have been up here going on five years in September, I think. Is it, Mom?

MOTHER Yeah, I think so.

MARGE September and—

MOTHER I believe it's four years.

MARGE We came in 1970.

MOTHER I think it's about five years. I have it written down.

MARGE And I've been going to New York ever since then. I've been to New York about ten or fifteen times and they've been only about two times.

CONSULTANT Is that true? (*Dennis begins talking and the others jump in talking over one another.*) What are you talking about? Stop! (*To Mother*) Mrs. Cass, does this happen at home?

MOTHER Well, I don't know what he's talking about. We were on one conversation—

CONSULTANT No, I'm talking about—do they all talk at the same time?

MOTHER Well, that's the way they do. I tried to beat it out of them. I can't beat it out of them to save my life. And Charles carries on so bad that he gives me a headache, and I really have a headache for two or three days.

CONSULTANT Oh, really—

MOTHER I think that causes me to be cross like I am. Charles is the worst one. He's the main one. And he don't like Philadelphia and wants to go down south.

CONSULTANT Actually, all the boys, the three boys, are coming together and causing noise, and causing some trouble?

MOTHER Yeah.

The consultant ends this part of the interview by trying to group the boys together in their mother's eyes. If she can see Charles as one of three troublemakers, he will not stand alone in her view. She may not need to extrude him from the family. As is evident, when she is not actively controlling all the transactions among the children, there is little order in their communications. When she is in control, she targets Charles, who is the oldest male and her biggest headache. However, when the therapist checks her control, the boys unite against the Marge-mother coalition and dump on the easier target of the two, Marge. There is no hierarchy of seniority or respect (boundaries) among the boys. So, when on their own, they are disorderly. The problem of constantly forcing order is too much for the mother. She has chosen to extrude Charles to relieve the strain.

Following this portion of the interview, the consultant tried several times to realign family members to get Charles re-included in his family, but could not succeed. The longest effort was one in which the consultant tried directly to draw the mother and Charles together. The mother brought this sequence to a painful end when she openly said, "Yeah, unwanted, that's right, unwanted. I don't want him." Charles cried. It was difficult to witness.

The consultant had been reaching for some positive feeling between mother and son to salvage the situation. His hypothesis was that the mother cared for him, but had lost touch with these feelings in the face of her failure to get the boys under control. Her recourse was to eliminate Charles as a force among the boys.

Nevertheless, by connecting with Charles the consultant made room for him to acknowledge he loved his mother. The consultant then elicited from the mother an admission that she would feel differently about Charles were she to feel more in charge with him.

"Yeah, I would feel better towards him. You know, you can't love a sassy big one." Her referring to him as the "big one" suggested that what makes him intolerable is Charles' age. She had more trouble with an older male. The younger boys faced trouble ahead.

With the mother's admission that if she could manage him she could tolerate Charles, the consultant felt he had gone as far as he could in one interview to bring mother and son together. So, he chose another structural maneuver and tried to align Marge, the mother's closest ally, with Charles. The clue to this possibility was in Marge's complaint at the beginning of the interview that Charles would not help her with her school work. The consultant started toward his goal by spending a bit of time talking with Marge about her perception of her problems, attempting to align more closely with her. He had already gained Charles' confidence, and the mother was also feeling he understood her.

MARGE He don't like for me to be in the same room with him. My mother tells me to try to help him when we have something new in the classroom, a new subject in the classroom, and he don't know how to do it and I know how to do it. I show him how to do it. And when we get another new subject and I don't know how to do it, he don't even want to show me.

CHARLES When we get something new, the teacher always shows us because I stay after school. She [Marge] didn't never show me nothing. I know how to do my own work.

. . .

CONSULTANT (*To Marge*) Okay. Wait a minute. (*To Charles*) Are you good in arithmetic?

CHARLES Not that good.

CONSULTANT Are you better than she is? Or are you worse than she is?

CHARLES I'm better than she is.

MARGE I'm smarter than he is in spelling.

(*They both want some validation.*)

CONSULTANT Is that true? She's smarter than you in spelling?

CHARLES I have trouble. I can't pronounce the word out.

CONSULTANT Oh, I see. (*To Marge*) Do you get homework every day?

MARGE Every single day.

CONSULTANT . . . Gee, that's a terrible thing what's going on between you two and the homework, because you're (*to Marge*) so good in spelling and I don't know why you're not helping him, and (*to Charles*), you're so good in math and I don't know why you're not helping her.

CHARLES She's telling a story.

CONSULTANT What story is she telling?

CHARLES (*Defensively*) She's telling a story about she's smart in spelling and I'm not smart. Only thing I can't do is I can't pronounce the word out correct.

CONSULTANT But can she pronounce the word out better than you can?

CHARLES (*Afraid that a parent figure cannot value both Marge and him*) I don't know.

CONSULTANT Can you, Marge? (*She agrees. To Charles*) Well, maybe she can do something a little better than you can, and maybe you can do something better than she, right? There's nothing wrong with that. I'm terrible in math. . . . I used to have to get others to help me with my math.

MARGE When I was in the third grade and I didn't know my tables as good as he did, he would pick at me and say, "You old dumb thing, you don't even know tables."

CONSULTANT You would have done the same thing to me, Charles, because I would have been an old dumb thing who didn't know his tables. . . .

MARGE Now I know them. I know them now. (*They compete for the consultant and he tries to pull them together through himself.*)

CONSULTANT Well, what worries me is what's happening with this homework. I think it's a terrible thing. You know, do you (*to both*) think you could come over here to the clinic to do your homework together?

CHARLES (*Tentatively*) Yeah—

CONSULTANT Well, when do you do your homework?

CHARLES At night.

CONSULTANT Uhuh!

CHARLES Sometimes in the day. Sometimes I stay after school and do it in school.

CONSULTANT . . . How about if I could get the two of you to come over here right after school, and just spend half an hour and somebody [a tutor] here would help you to do your homework together? . . . Would you like that, Charles? (*Charles again nods in agreement.*) Would you like that? (*Marge, smiling, says she would.*) Because we have some tutors here, special teachers. . . . They could help you to do it together.

MARGE I wanted to go to tutoring. Some other girls in my classroom, they go to tutoring, and I don't know why I can't go.

CONSULTANT You can go to tutoring. You can go to tutoring here with this guy (*indicating Charles*), right?

CHARLES Yeah.

CONSULTANT Hey Mom, what do you think about that? (*Soliciting Mother's okay, thereby including her, and acknowledging her authority*)

MOTHER Well, it will be all right. . . .

Mother agreed, but did not let the interview end without again expressing reservations about Charles. The consultant assured her that he heard her concern, and that this was only the first step in the hundred steps they would need to solve their problems. The interview ended with the mother agreeing to continue with her worker, and to send Charles and Marge together to the clinic's tutor.

The consultant never did receive a follow-up, but some months later, while visiting a library in the Cass family's neighborhood, someone tugged at his sleeve. It was Charles, with a big smile, who was obviously still living at home.

Discussion

In this case the most challenging task was to help the mother consider keeping Charles at home. The family was underorganized, and this single mother found it painfully difficult to supervise her male children by herself. Speaking structurally, she did not know how to exercise the power to handle the boys. She withdrew from them and sought companionship in her only daughter, thus violating hierarchical parent/child boundaries. She aligned with her daughter in a positive way and negatively against her oldest son. The result was that for the moment this son had become the scapegoat for all the boys. She was about to lay the sins of the tribe upon him and exclude him from the tribal camp, like the biblical scapegoat.

To prevent this outcome the consultant would need to find a way to shore up the mother's ability to deal with Charles. The consultant attempted to align all the children within the boundaries of the sibling subsystem, allowing some distance from mother without losing her. That generational space between the mother and her children would permit the consultant to support her in her parental role. Were the consultant to continue working with the mother, he would need to think of helping her find support and companionship among the adults in her family and community. In the meantime, the clinic offered concrete supportive services, so the mother could provide for her children what she personally did not have. Without supplying some resources they lacked, we could not hope to help them with life's tasks, which seemed daunting to them.

We need to note, however, that these structural maneuvers were meant to make it possible for the mother and children to make a shift in their relationships. In the end, they still had the option of accepting the opportunity or not. Therapy opens possibilities; people make choices.

2. Assessment in Family Therapy

The assessment process is as essential to the therapy we do as our change-inducing techniques. An intervention exists in a vacuum if we do not truly understand the people we are treating, their issues, and their process behind the issues. Moreover, until recently our focus has been so exclusively on the family unit that we have given only cursory attention to the assessment of social context, including race, culture, and socioeconomic conditions. We cannot treat poor and minority families without understanding their social and economic contexts.

ASSESSMENT RELEVANT TO THE POOR

Low-income and poor minority families, in particular, may come to therapy with all kinds of personal issues connected with the social forces in their lives. These social dynamics add complex dimensions to the assessment, requiring consideration of a range of factors, from urgent economic issues to subtle cultural and racial factors.

More often than not, the most extremely socioeconomically stressed families come to therapy looking for relief *now*. Both assessment and intervention need to address present urgencies, understand the past in the context of today's need, and speak to how to help *today*. The work is done in an environment oriented toward results in the present.

Therapists working with the poor must pursue the problem in

front of them. However, this *now* focus has also led many professionals, particularly in strategic and brief therapies, to give less attention to assessment than to intervention. We can become so intent on solving today's problem that we underestimate the complexity of *today* for the poor. The concreteness of their social and economic issues often obscures the depth of their emotional involvement. The inarticulateness of some of the poor about their psychological distress can lead therapists to underappreciate the profoundness of their emotional pain. The strangeness to a therapist of the race, ethnicity, or culture of minority family members can also hide from the therapist the complexity of their personal and relationship dynamics. Therapists need to understand the poor's *today*.

That current reality contains the existential decisions people face today that grow out of yesterday and will determine tomorrow. The concrete and urgent issue of the moment has dynamic roots in today's practical circumstances as well as in the transcendent meaning and purpose of everyday issues in people's lives. The complete meaning of today's issue goes beyond anything we can begin to grasp. The meaning of bread becomes complete in the significance of spirit. This is as true for the unsophisticated as for the most educated. Working in the true fullness of the present is not about superficiality. It involves concentrating on a point of reality—the fullness of people's lives in relation to the focal issue. The immediacy of the poor is as complex as anyone else's. The poor hurt as deeply as anyone else. The poor are as spiritual as anyone else.

AN ECOSTRUCTURAL APPROACH TO ASSESSMENT

This book's framework for the treatment of the poor is the ecostructural model. It expands structural family therapy (Minuchin, 1974) to include both the individual and the community. The ecostructural approach to assessment with the poor attempts to take into account the present issue, the ecosystemic context of the issue for the client, and both immediate and long-term goals.

The therapist:

1. Rivets on the present reality of the client by negotiating a *focal issue(s)* for the therapy;
2. Includes the *complex ecosystem* of the client (from personal to social) in the field of assessment, anchoring all in the focal issue;
3. Assesses through a change-promoting approach to therapy based on the focal issue, the goals of therapy, and the client's potential for self-determined choices relative to change.

Therapist and client determine the focus—the problems to be addressed. It must include the primary concerns of the client. However, therapist and client must also formulate the issue in a way that points to the possibility of making a real difference. Clients' pain that is ensconced in their complaint is always legitimate. However, they may look at the cause and, therefore, the solution in a way that leads them away from hard choices. The formulation of the problem and its causes is the first step toward its solution.

The formulation of an issue for therapy needs to take into account:

1. The agreed-upon achievable goals;
2. The parties involved, the dynamics of the problem, and the resources relevant and accessible to solving the problem;
3. The control the client has and does not have, with or without professional help, over what goes into the outcome.

This last is critical for poor families because it recognizes that there may be actions with the community in which the professional helper must join for clients to attain their outcome. However, it also means that, regardless of who does or does not cooperate with them, they are not helpless victims. They always have choices that will make vital differences in their lives.

From the formulation of that focal issue flow the diagnostic hypotheses and therapeutic strategy. The diagnostic hypotheses speak to both the structural conditions underlying the issue and the functions of or reasons for the structural dynamics. The structural hypotheses describe the "what" or status of current ecosystemic structure in relation to the focal issue. This means the structural configuration of relationships (alignments, boundaries, and forces) among the parties within and outside a family in relation to the problem.

The functional hypotheses speak to the historical and contemporary reasons for the current conditions creating the problem. The functional hypotheses offer explanations, the "whys." Together the structural and functional hypotheses tell us what we are trying to change and why. We need only know then what resources (ability and motivation) exist in the client and among all other parties involved to work toward change. For the poor, the assessment considers both the personal and the social forces relevant to solving the personal issues a family presents. The "presentation outline" in Table 2.1 sketches the place of a therapist's hypotheses in relation to the focal issue (problem) of a family and the therapeutic goals.

The entire process of assessment serves to facilitate therapeutic change. It scans all information likely to throw light on the problem, the parties involved, and the purposes of the therapy. Assessment takes direct aim at outcome and selects the data most relevant to determining strategy, interventions, and therapist posture in the therapeutic relationship.

Hypothesizing for the Poor

Hypothesizing examines how each component of the ecosystem organizes itself within and between levels in the ecosystem. The community has its own structure—its institutions and laws. A family has its own unique structures of internal and external relationships, which color everything done by the family. Each individual has his or her own unique psychological structure, which is continually evolving through its interdependence upon family and community. An action of a family or of any subsystem

Table 2.1
PRESENTATION OUTLINE

ssue(s)

.ist and client negotiate the issue(s) that will be the focus of ther-
.hese issues have to do with the current concerns for which the cli-
.ndividual or family, seeks help. Therapist and client will formulate the issue(s) in a way that points to the potential for change—having
achievable goals and recognizing what control the client has over what
goes into the outcome.

(*The rest of the outline, including diagnostic hypotheses and therapeutic hypotheses flows from the focal issue(s)*.)

2. **Diagnostic hypotheses**

Diagnostic hypotheses are tentative explanations of the sources and nature of the problems the client faces.

A. **Structural hypotheses**

The structural hypotheses describe the "what" or current status of
the client's ecosystem in relation to the focal issue. Their definition
identifies the systems in the client's life within which the issue(s)
are rooted, and the structure of relationships in those systems
around the focal issue(s). The structure of those relationship break
down into:

(i) **Boundary**

Boundary represents the people and institutions within the ecosystem that are involved in the issue. Boundary also speaks to
what *roles* they play in the problems at issue.

(ii) **Alignment**

Alignment describes the alliances and coalitions and the opposition among people in an ecosystem that contribute to generating the problems at issue.

(iii) **Power (Force)**

Power talks about influence in the ecosystem in relation to the
issue(s). It speaks to who is influencing, and how, the transactional patterns that generate the problems at issue.

B. **Functional hypotheses**

The functional hypotheses will speak to the *meaning* and *significance* of that current structure of the ecosystem vis-à-vis the focus issue. They offer explanations—the "whys"—based on history, social
conditions, culture, family relationships, individual psychology,
motivation, etc.

(i) **Value hypotheses**

The value hypotheses present the principles that give meaning
and purpose to the focal issues and their underlying dynamics.
These values have to do with the ethnicity, culture, race, gender, religion, spirituality, and any other influence on principles, standards, morality, and priorities giving personal significance to life and its problems.

(*continued*)

36

Table 2.1
(continued)

(ii) **Motivational hypotheses**
Motivational hypotheses tell why people do as they do based on social conditions, family relationships, and individual psychology. These hypotheses include the agenda of social institutions, the needs of families and the drives and defenses involved in the personal motivations of individuals.

(iii) **Historical hypotheses**
The historical hypotheses describe sources and antecedants based on the past—social, family, and personal. This history includes dates and events, as well as the personal drama of family legacies and of the emotional struggles of individuals.

3. **Therapeutic hypotheses**
Therapeutic hypotheses are the premises upon which therapists rest their therapeutic strategy. That strategy takes into account the focal issues(s), the goals of therapy, resources available for change in the ecosystem and the client's potential for self determined change. It also includes the person of the therapist and the relationship of the therapist with the client.

A. **Hypotheses about issues**
Therapists hypothesize about what key issues need addressing to help clients resolve the problems they face. They negotiate the identification and formulation of the issues with their clients. These focal issues dictate the goals of therapy. Hypotheses about the focal issues and therapeutic goals are the bases for developing a therapeutic strategy.

B. **Hypotheses about client**
Developing a strategy requires hypothesizing about the resources available to the client to resolve the problem. Because the therapeutic contract is with the person(s) who define themselves as clients, formulation of strategy also depends upon their motivation, commitment, and internal freedom to change.

C. **Hypotheses about the person of the therapist**
Finally, the strategy that will fit any therapy depends as much on the therapist as on the client because it is a joint plan of action for therapist and client. Therapists need to understand something of how the client and the issues affect them at a personal level, given their personal background and current life circumst⸻⸻ Moreover, because strategy is effected through the therapeutic therapists need to be able to hypothesize about th⸻ tial nature of their relationships with clients.

(Therapy is a constantly evolving, dynamic proce *this outline is to help therapists organize their thinkin* *tionships within that process. The outline is meant to* *ally with the gathering of new data and the testing o*

37

of the family, including an individual, is the product of the transactional convergence of the various levels of systems—community, family, and individual. Personal power and responsibility lie with each unit's choices. Structural convergence is the linkage of circuits; people's choices are the switches. For a therapist the relevant convergence and choices relate to treating a client's problem. The goals of therapy determine the paths of exploration.

Hypothesis Building

Ecostructural therapists work toward achieving results with every client transaction. From the very first transaction between the therapist and client, every action of the therapist seeks not only to understand the people and problem, but also to facilitate a solution. Assessment serves intervention, and intervention follows assessment. Diagnostic probes are incorporated into therapeutic interventions, so that therapeutic and assessment efforts are intrinsic to the same therapist action.

In this approach each intervention in a session flows out of a progressive series of diagnostic hypotheses. The process goes hand in hand with the progression of interventions that build one upon the other from intervention to intervention. This building of hypothesis upon hypothesis progresses through the entire course of treatment. Each transaction, each session, each phase of treatment is a unit of exploration driven by its own hypotheses. Treatment evolves into an intricate, complex, but single, continuous tapestry of interweaving multicolored threads of probing transactions that follow themes as they progress through various life contexts into a whole experience.

Working in the Present

The therapist conducts all this work in the present under the premise that the forces creating the problem are all active in current behavior and transactions. Within the session, every transaction among the family members and between them and the therapist is a product and representation of the forces underpinning the lives of those in the session, including the therapist. The therapist explores through these current transactions, and intervenes in the immediacy of their happening.

The therapist attempts to create a context in which family members will reexperience and reenact with the therapist some of the principal dynamics underlying the client's focal issue. The therapist becomes a participant in the reality of the clients as well as an observer of their lives. From that intimate connection with their reality the therapist hopes to understand and influence the course of their lives. The assumption is that the experience in session is at the heart of the reality of the client, so that choices and changes made there give shape and direction to people's lives outside.

However, what therapists actually witness is the life experience of their clients in the context of therapy. Therapists actively and passively co-create the experience in the session. Therefore, all hypotheses about what is happening among people in their presence must consider what therapists put into that experience. This means that therapists need to hypothesize about themselves in that experience even as they hypothesize about their clients. They need to consider how their clients' issues and their personal feelings about their clients affect their relationships with them; then they need to look at the impact of their attitudes on how their clients are with them. Therapists' hypotheses about their clients filter through themselves.

Step by Step

Assessment is an active and ongoing process throughout therapy. Within the transactional process of the interview the basic steps of assessment are:

1. Identify the issue of the moment;
2. Consider it in terms of goals, resources, and choices of client;
3. Collect and consider relevant data, reported and experiential;
4. Develop diagnostic hypotheses (structural and functional) in relation to immediate goal;

5. Decide on intervention;

6. Note client's point of decision and effect of intervention on choices client makes;

7. Confirm or discount hypotheses about accuracy of diagnostic hypotheses and effectiveness of intervention.

With the last step, the cycle begins all over again, taking into account the sequence that just ended. Some excerpts from a clinical consultation will serve to illustrate the process.

THE ASSESSMENT IN A CLINICAL SESSION

This is a blue-collar family of Mexican ethnic background, and the consultant is a Puerto Rican male. In the nuclear family are the parents, who are in their early forties, and five children, three boys and two girls: Fred, 16, Aida, 14, Esteban, 13, Aldo, 11, and Elena, who is four. The family has been in treatment for some months. The family's two therapists are Latina women. They reported that, because the family has so many problems, they were having trouble finding a focus for their work. They told of considerable conflict between the parents, but were enthusiastic about the mother, whom they described as motivated and active in the therapy. Although she worked outside the home, she was totally involved in the care of the children. They were pessimistic about the father, whom they viewed as peripheral both to his family and to therapy. Although there were problems with the other boys, the original problem was Aldo's inattentiveness in school and "childish" behavior at home and in school.

On the basis of this brief description, the consultant hypothesized that the mother was the high profile parent at home. He wondered whether the power struggle between the parents had pulled the children into the middle between them. Considering the problems of the identified patient and the other boys, the consultant also wondered whether the mother, although bright and motivated, lacked effective control over the boys. His initial structural hypothesis was that, somehow, the boys' problems flowed from the parents' power struggle, the mother's centrality, and the father's peripheral position in the family.

The consultant had no information upon which to base any substantial functional hypotheses to explain the story behind these current family dynamics. Nevertheless, the description of the father as peripheral might well have been associated with a commonly held image of Latino males. Moreover, the therapists, who were female, spoke of the father as uncommitted to the therapy. Yet, he was attending sessions regularly. Was he just quiet and resentful, giving the impression he did not care? Many a therapist has assumed that a man (often a minority male) is not involved when he does not speak readily. A related question had to do with Aldo, the identified patient. What was his relationship with his father in this triangle with his parents? It was likely that he had his mother's attention since she was so active. Was he looking for his father? These questions had to do with some classic triangulations in a family, but they also touched on gender in the context of culture. The cultural backgrounds and gender of the therapists and consultant would not be irrelevant in this case.

It was this kind of speculative hypothesizing that determined the consultant's first action with the family. As they came into the room, he asked the father to switch chairs with Aldo so that he, the father, would sit next to the consultant. The consultant wanted to connect with the father and to draw him into the center of the happenings in the session. He wanted the father to have the opportunity to be more active. Implicitly, the consultant wanted to see how the rest of the family would behave were the father to assume a central role in the process. The consultant followed up the seating plan with a request to the father, Mr. Gonzaga, to introduce the family to him, again further centralizing the father and linking him with the consultant. (The group sat in a semi-circle. Counterclockwise there sat the consultant, the father, Aldo, Esteban, the mother, Elena, Aida, and Fred.)*

*This clinical session, like most of the other transcripts in the book, has been heavily edited for the sake of brevity and readability. No words have been changed; nor did we alter the sequence of the dialogue. However, we did not put in ellipses with every omission of material to avoid chopping up the flow.

CONSULTANT Why don't you switch chairs so you will be next to me. (*Aldo and Mr. Gonzaga switch chairs.*) Okay. Introduce your family to me.

MR. GONZAGA (*Pointing to the boy next to him*) Aldo.

CONSULTANT Aldo. How old is Aldo?

ALDO Eleven.

CONSULTANT And him? (*Pointing to the next boy*)

MR. GONZAGA Esteban. (*Skipping over his wife*) Elena.

MRS. GONZAGA (*Interjecting spontaneously*) Elena is four.

MR. GONZAGA (*Continuing*) Aida, Fred.

CONSULTANT (*To Mr. Gonzaga*) You've been coming for a couple of months, right?

MR. GONZAGA Six, seven months.

MRS. GONZAGA Three months.

Mrs. Gonzaga's interjections quickly reinforced the consultant's hypothesis that she was the more aggressive of the two. Her spontaneous, quick, and accurate responses to the consultant's questions tended to draw the consultant toward her. She was more engaging. The father was reserved and quiet. The consultant risked not gaining the mother's alliance by not responding to her at the time. He chose to stay with the father for the present.

CONSULTANT (*To Mr. Gonzaga*) I listened to [the co-therapists] describe a little bit about what's been going on. It was so complicated that I couldn't keep up with it.

MR. GONZAGA That's right. (*Laughing*)

CONSULTANT . . . . but there seemed to be so many things that you fight about and so many things that you are worried about. You two have got problems, and Aldo has problems. Anyway, it just seemed like so many things, that I already got confused. . . . So, if you could pick just one thing, just one problem, that we could concentrate on during this hour out of all the things that you have talked about, then we could try to do something about it. . . .

The consultant wanted to focus on one issue. Only by doing so could he structure the session in a way that would allow him to follow a clear line of exploration. He also stayed with his strategy and put the agenda in the father's hands.

MR. GONZAGA What would you like to talk about?

CONSULTANT This is your family. . . . You just pick out one thing and we'll work on that.

MRS. GONZAGA Well, we came here for Aldo. That's why we came. Everything else was discussed along with Aldo, but we still haven't solved Aldo's problem, why he behaves the way he does at times, why he gets behind schedule in his work, why he hasn't been keeping up, why he acts babyish—

CONSULTANT Among all these problems that you have, you would rather talk about Aldo?

MRS. GONZAGA Well, the other children are fine, and . . . we just keep going round and round, my husband and I. He thinks one way and I think another way, but we are getting to understand each other better now because we know it will never change. You know, it will be that way all the time. (*Laughs*)

CONSULTANT That's one way to solve a problem (*laughs*) all right.

MRS. GONZAGA He thinks one way and I think another way. We can't change that. . . . We work to understand each other but we respect each other. Like he thinks he's the boss and I let him think he is the boss. (*Laughing*)

Mrs. Gonzaga has taken over defining the issue for the family, as Mr. Gonzaga has withdrawn into silence. While Mrs. Gonzaga could be an effective channel through which to help Aldo, the consultant had wanted to stay the course. In fact, Mrs. Gonzaga has already changed the direction the consultant had set. The consultant returns to Mr. Gonzaga, giving him another chance to have a say about the focus issue.

CONSULTANT (*To Mr. Gonzaga*) Which means you're not [the boss]? (*Laughs*) But . . . of all these things, which one do you want to talk about during this hour. . . .

MRS. GONZAGA I always talked so let him talk. (*Motions to Mr. Gonzaga*)

. . .

MR. GONZAGA Well, whatever you want to talk about. I don't have too much of a big problem. I know what I am supposed to do. Her problem or Aldo's I guess. We worried about Aldo because he was behind too much in school.

. . .

CONSULTANT Aldo. So you've both decided that it's Aldo? Okay, and you [Mrs. Gonzaga] have already described what you've thought was going on with Aldo. I think you said that he was acting immature, like a baby and he wasn't keeping up in class. I don't remember what else you said.

MRS. GONZAGA He hasn't kept up all these years and I have always been after the teachers because they ignore it and say, ''He's just going through a stage.'' They always say that but that's been going on every year. . . . Or he just acts silly. He thinks somebody is looking at him, but it's not funny. Marie and Joan [their therapists] said, ''Time him. Time him and see how long he'll take. . . .'' Well, we keep on doing that and it still doesn't work.

The consultant tries joining father and mother together in their agreement about their focus—Aldo. However, once he reincludes Mrs. Gonzaga, she again runs away with the session. The fact is that she is insightful and articulate. It would be easier for the consultant to engage with her than to return to Mr. Gonzaga. The consultant reincludes Mr. Gonzaga with a question that gives room for him to disagree with his wife. Mr. Gonzaga responds by trying to one up her. We see another side of him.

CONSULTANT . . . (*To Mr. Gonzaga*) Do you see it exactly the way your wife's describing it . . . ?

MR. GONZAGA No, I see it the same way. It's just like she says. [But] he acts up more when she's there. When I'm around, he doesn't act like that.

. . .

I think it is probably like I told her. You let him slide too much or something.

. . .

All she does is holler and holler but she don't do nothing.

CONSULTANT So that's easy. Never mind timing him. If she were just a little tougher with him then you wouldn't have a problem.

. . .

MRS. GONZAGA That's his view, not mine.

. . .

He's been very strict with him all the time. So, strict is okay, but not when you scare him.

CONSULTANT You think he's too strict with Aldo?

MRS. GONZAGA He's strict with all of them.

. . .

CONSULTANT Okay. (*To Mr. Gonzaga*) Find out from Aldo if he's scared of you.

Mrs. Gonzaga counters her husband's criticism of her with her own, which feels like a plausible hypothesis to the consultant. He follows her lead on this and, diagnostically, sets up an enactment between father and son—let them talk about a hot issue between them. Inherent in this exploration is an intervention to encourage father and son to interact.

MR. GONZAGA Are you scared of me?

ALDO No.

MR. GONZAGA Are you afraid of me? (*In a threatening sounding tone*)

ALDO No.

CONSULTANT (*Joking to Aldo*) You'd better give the right answer or he'll punch you in the mouth. (*Mr. Gonzaga and the consultant both laugh.*)

MR. GONZAGA . . . Is there anything that you're supposed to be afraid of?

ALDO Of hitting.

. . .

MR. GONZAGA That's your problem, and your mother—she don't hit you. That's what I think it is.

. . .

MRS. GONZAGA They never get—

CONSULTANT (*To Mrs. Gonzaga*) Wait. Wait. This is between them.

MR. GONZAGA She keeps on telling him, ''Don't do this.''. . . . and he keeps on going and going. . . . He just keeps on doing it.

CONSULTANT You believed him though, when he said he wasn't scared of you?

MR. GONZAGA In a way I do and in a way—he's not really scared of me. It's just a problem that he has, respect in a way that if he don't do things the way he's supposed—if I tell him more than three or four times, I'm going to—

CONSULTANT He's going to get it.

MR. GONZAGA That's right.

. . .

CONSULTANT But do you think he's said enough now [so] that you believe what he said to you just now that he doesn't live in fear of you all the time?

. . .

MR. GONZAGA He plays with me, you know. We joke with each other and I don't see that makes him afraid of me because if he can joke with me then he, he shouldn't be afraid of me. . . .

CONSULTANT Check it out with him.

MR. GONZAGA Do you agree with me or don't you—what I just got through saying?

ALDO Yes.

CONSULTANT Did he understand you?

. . .

MR. GONZAGA What did I say?

ALDO You said that if I don't do the thing right and you tell me about five times then you'll hit me.

MR. GONZAGA What else?

ALDO That I ain't afraid of you because I always joke with you. . . .

CONSULTANT You know what the real test is of whether a kid is afraid of you or not?

MR. GONZAGA What is it?

CONSULTANT Whether he can disagree with you.

MR. GONZAGA On his own?

. . .

CONSULTANT That's the test.

MR. GONZAGA He doesn't have too much to say. He never disagrees with me. He goes along with whatever I say.

. . .

(*To Aldo*) Is there anything that you can disagree with me— you think I am wrong?

ALDO No.

MR. GONZAGA That you don't agree with me. Then anything I say is right. . . .

ALDO Not anything.

MR. GONZAGA Okay. What is it you don't like or—

ALDO When you force me.

MR. GONZAGA Oh. How do I force you?

ALDO Like you say, "go, go read" even after I did it.

MR. GONZAGA Then what?

. . .

ALDO Then I just go do it.

MR. GONZAGA Oh, you don't want to go read. Is that it or what is it?

ALDO No, cause I already did it.

MR. GONZAGA Oh, it's when I send you again to go read—you read when I am not home right? Then I tell you to go read again.

ALDO Sometimes.

MR. GONZAGA That's when you don't agree with me. How come you didn't say anything? You just proved to me (*silence*)—I guess because you are afraid of me. . . . Is that right?

ALDO I'd (*pause*)—

MR. GONZAGA (*To consultant*) And then you were right about me. He goes along with me whether he likes it or not.

. . .

CONSULTANT They have to learn how to be able to say—like, you know—I'm sure—what kind of work do you do?

MR. GONZAGA I'm a packer.

CONSULTANT I'm sure you have somebody over you, a foreman or somebody. . . . You disagree with the person . . . you know how to say, "Hey that's not the way to do it," or "this isn't the time," without it becoming a big problem. . . . If he doesn't learn how to do that, he won't grow up.

. . .

MRS. GONZAGA May I say something? Fred's about the same like Aldo, but Fred's older. He grew up the same way as Esteban. He's almost like Aldo but thank God, at a different point he snapped out of it. He said he was being picked on by children in his class, by the teachers along with everybody and I'm not like that. So I used to tell him to fight back, argue back, ask questions, uh, talk back to them. . . .

CONSULTANT (*To Mr. Gonzaga*) Want me to tell you what I think is going on in your family? It's that he or they may learn how to respect you, but you are not teaching them how to disagree with you in a respectful way. She tries to teach them how to disagree [with you], Mrs. Gonzaga, and that doesn't work. It can't be her teaching them to fight back and you teaching them to obey [through fear]. . . . They've got to get the same thing from both parents, because otherwise the two of you are like lawyers on two sides of the same case. So, teach them how to disagree with you now.

(*Mr. Gonzaga is silent, groping for what to say*)

. . .

CONSULTANT . . . see, and I don't want her [Mrs. Gonzaga] to help. So, then you are back to the same old thing. I want you to solve that one with him [Aldo].

. . .

MR. GONZAGA (*To Aldo*) Is there anything else that you don't want to do that I say . . . that I ask you to do besides reading?

ALDO No.

. . .

MR. GONZAGA It's the same I guess. (*Silence*) That's all I guess. . . .
   (*To the consultant*) What am I supposed to say?

CONSULTANT You're both stuck. . . . You haven't solved it, man!
   You're both stuck.

MR. GONZAGA We need help Esteban.

The consultant is still expecting the father do to something
with Aldo. Interestingly, he turns to another of his children, Esteban, who is sitting on the other side of Aldo. The father is not so
proud that he cannot solicit assistance from another son, who he
probably knows will speak up to him. Esteban will respond. He
becomes a resource for father.

ESTEBAN (*To Aldo*) My father, what he means is, do you like it
   when he tells you to do stuff. Like, this morning, he told you
   to look for your shoes. You couldn't find them. You looked in
   the same place two times, three times. Did you get mad?

ALDO No.

. . .

ESTEBAN He gets upset easily. Like, if they tell him to do something
   he gets mad because he goes—(*demonstrates gesture of annoy-
   ance*) like that.

. . .

MR. GONZAGA He makes a face. . . . I guess that makes him angry
   . . . because you can tell . . . they change their expression.

CONSULTANT But if he had been able to say to you something like—

MR. GONZAGA He would have said it right there.

. . .

CONSULTANT . . . So, Aldo's problem isn't that he fights you. His
   problem is that he doesn't fight you.

. . .

MR. GONZAGA He holds it inside.

. . .

   (*To Aldo*) Okay. I guess we'll have to work on that.

ALDO Yeah.

CONSULTANT (*To Mr. Gonzaga*) You know you're the only one in the family who can solve that problem for him, because if he's going to learn to be a man he should learn how to be a man from you. . . . Well, we didn't solve that problem but at least we know it's your problem . . . right?

The father is getting it. Removed from the power struggle with his wife, he takes responsibility for the problem, and the consultant holds him to it. The consultant is sensitive to the cultural expectations of manhood and respect. He calls on the father to teach his son to disagree in order to help him be a man in his own image. That the therapist is also male and of similar age allows him to approach the father with a feeling of comradery. A therapist with a different personality, gender, or background would, of course, have to find avenues toward the same goals that were congruent with his or her circumstances.

MR. GONZAGA I thought it was his problem but it's my problem. (*Laughs*)

CONSULTANT It's your problem. Absolutely.

MR. GONZAGA Okay, Aldo. It's my problem. I guess you're right about that. I have to start someplace. It better be me, I guess.

. . .

Yeah. Right. It's my turn. (*Pats Aldo on the shoulder*) We'll work it out.

CONSULTANT Okay. So we did as much as we could with that one. Let's have another one.

ESTEBAN AND ALDO Freddie. (*Everyone laughs.*)

CONSULTANT It's up to the two adults. Okay now, Aldo and Esteban want to talk about Freddie but it's got to have your okay. . . .

(*Mr. and Mrs. Gonzaga both say yes.*)

. . .

Esteban and Aldo join together to point the finger at Fred. The effect, however, is that they are drawing Fred into dealing not only with them, but also with their father. The girls are not jumping in. They are staying with their mother, who has for the moment opted to remain out. The consultant has hypothesized that the father's involvement has special significance to the boys. They are confirming his hypothesis. The consultant's diagnostic probing is also serving as an intervention to reinvolve the father with the boys.

ESTEBAN Ah, like when we're seeing TV and comes a commercial, he starts beating me up and then Aldo jumps in [to help Esteban]. . . .

. . .

If we hit him too hard, he'll really hit us. That's when I get mad and I try to protect Elena. She's not doing nothing. Freddie messes around you know. He knocks down [her] blocks or do something like that. . . . Then he gets mad and beats me up again. Then Aldo helps me, and it keeps on going like that.

CONSULTANT Aldo, you speak up now.

ALDO I think he does it because he's mad, he gets mad at my mother or something, and then he takes it out on us.

ESTEBAN Because my father tells him to do something. . . .

. . .

CONSULTANT So you're both saying that when he gets mad at both your parents—right?—then he takes it out on the rest of you?

. . .

FRED Well, I do get kind of upset sometimes when my father and mother say anything to me but—okay—I'll be upset at my brother in the room. He'll look at me like I'm stupid or something. . . . I ask Aida a question or something and she says, "I got homework to do." Okay, I can understand that but then she says it *that* way. She just shouts at you, "I got homework."

. . .

Esteban comes out with something that he thinks. He knows too much, you know. He thinks he's older than me I guess. You know cause he says, "I'm better than you." . . .

. . .

CONSULTANT So why do you knock her [Elena's] blocks down?

FRED Things will pop up in my head like—okay—I've been sitting down looking at my brothers and sisters doing something, and

I'll go, man I don't have nothing to do. Then I come out with something like—and I wonder how my sister will look if I pull her hair (*laughs*). You know, like mess around, you know.

The consultant helps the boys deal with their problems without depending on the mother, who increasingly looks like the mediator in the family. Drawing the boys together will also serve to bring in the father, whose approval they clearly seek. The sequence also reveals a Fred who is feeling lonely and quite inadequate. His reaction to his parents further confirms and elaborates the hypothesis that these boys are strongly reactive to their parents. They are unable to talk things out with their parents, who cannot negotiate much because of the tension between them. The consultant's attention to Fred will also give Fred a place of his own in the session, so that he has the experience of being included.

CONSULTANT Okay . . . let me check something out. When your mother and father get mad at you, Freddie, why do you take it out on them [the siblings]?

. . .

FRED Ah, it's that I'm lazy just once in a while. They tell me something and then that's when I really get mad.

. . .

When I am arguing I don't like to talk back to my mother and father. My mother once in a while, we get into some pretty heavy arguments.

CONSULTANT Yeah?

FRED And I say, forget it. I just—right there I start throwing things or I'll go to my brother and I'll punch the wall or something, you know, and then—

CONSULTANT What about with your father?

FRED Oh, my father, I can't say nothing to him. If I do, you know, right across my face and that's what I'm thinking, you know. . . . I can say a couple of things [to his father] but then, right then and there my mother will jump in or else she'll say, "Don't talk to him," and I'll say, "Okay." I'll just go in the other room.

CONSULTANT You mean she tries to protect you from your father?

FRED Yeah. That's right.

CONSULTANT Why can't you settle it with your father? Why can't you talk with him without her getting in the middle of it . . . ?

FRED I guess anger gets in my head before I can even say anything. . . . He says a certain word that I don't like—you—you know, he'll say, "it's a lie." . . . Right there, that one word, "lie."

CONSULTANT Don't you think he cares for you?

FRED Yeah. I think he cares for me. He brings home certain things that I want. . . . He even told me that he loved me and everything, you know. He says, "all of us are different" and he talks with us and jokes around.

CONSULTANT So, if he uses the word, "lie" . . . you can't get over that fence. . . . Right?

FRED (*Long silence*) I don't know.

(*Aldo tries to speak.*)

CONSULTANT No, not yet. . . . I want to go back to the old man over here because he looks so mean and bad after these kids talk about him. I've got to just find out what's going on. We got the same problem right back.

MR. GONZAGA Same problem we already had.

CONSULTANT Same problem.

MR. GONZAGA My fault?

CONSULTANT That's right.

. . .

FRED It's just that I don't like to get hit, hit in particular from him. I don't like it! I don't want him calling me a liar or hitting me or any of these things, you know.

Fred continues to add to the picture of a boy who is afraid of his father but needs his approval. The father loves his son, but does not know how to connect with him. What was his relationship with his own father? Does he believe that he ever made his father proud? It would not appear so. One can also speculate about whether the father's minority status in an alien culture may have made him feel a loss in status, fueling his overcompensating aggres-

siveness at home. He puts too much pressure on the less scholasti-
cally adept boys to succeed in school. On top of the father's cultural
disadvantage, the consultant further hypothesizes that the father
feels he cannot measure up to his wife's mental and verbal quick-
ness. He pushes too hard for control over her. The consultant begins to view the father and Fred as hurting from a painful sense of
inadequacy.

CONSULTANT (*To Mr. Gonzaga*) . . . I don't want them to talk this
way about you because you wouldn't be talking to them the
way you talk to them if you didn't care about them, right?

MR. GONZAGA Yeah. I think you're right.

CONSULTANT . . . I want them to respect you, you know, but I also
want them to be close to you. That means they have to learn
from you, not from me, and not from their mom.

Here the consultant links himself up with the mother as a person who must stand by and give father room to connect with the
boys in his own way. This move hopefully serves to help the
mother not feel excluded as the consultant moves to link the boys
with their father.

CONSULTANT . . . Am I coming down too hard on you?

MR. GONZAGA No, no. You're coming on pretty good.

CONSULTANT Okay.

. . .

MR. GONZAGA It's the same problem.

CONSULTANT . . . [Fred] is looking at you. He's waiting for you to
say something to him.

MR. GONZAGA What can I say?

CONSULTANT I don't know.

FRED You want me to disagree with you?

MR. GONZAGA Yeah, go ahead. Say whatever is on your mind.

. . .

FRED (*To his father*) . . . Well, what I am saying is it's like when
you put me down, when you say I'm a liar. . . .

CONSULTANT Okay. . . . You don't want him to put you down?

MR. GONZAGA Well, I guess I'm going to have to start all over again.

CONSULTANT Yeah, you got to have the responsibility of—

MR. GONZAGA Start a different way—well, you [Fred] have to improve yourself too, not only me.

. . .

CONSULTANT . . . He needs to improve himself, but he needs to feel that you have respect for him too, and that you care. He has to think that, "In my father's eyes I'm somebody, somebody who's worth listening to, somebody who's worth caring for," because if he doesn't feel that you respect him, then what does he know—does anybody respect him if his own father can't respect him?

MR. GONZAGA Yeah, you're right. I got a father too.

CONSULTANT . . . You're the most important man in the world to these kids. (*Long silence*)

. . .

MR. GONZAGA . . . What he's really saying is . . . that is the important thing to communicate between him and me, talk it out and get it out.

We get a hint about the father's own history—his relationship with his father. It was a poignant moment when he could see himself in his son, Freddie, as he thought of his own father. He softened. It was as if he could give his sons the understanding of their struggles that he never received from his own father. In his relationship with the therapist, the father behaved like a man who felt it was safe to acknowledge his failings and vulnerabilities. He had a choice, to continue protecting himself or to open himself up, showing his confusion, inarticulateness, and guilt. He chose the pain to gain the connection with his sons.

Yet, there is still much work to do. He needs to reconnect with his wife. She felt anguish about his harshness with the boys, but she chose to make room for him to relate to the boys in the session. She need not have. She had plenty of reason to challenge her husband and the therapist for not addressing more directly her husband's acceptance of physical intimidation. Because she chose to suspend criticism, the consultant's work with father and sons could proceed.

In restraining herself about her husband's treatment of her children, she was also likely being silent about the pain in her marriage. It is probable she misses her husband's appreciation and affection. Chances are she voiced her own hurt by complaining about his hardness with their sons. She needs his acceptance of her, as he needs her to value his input at home. The marriage calls for more exploration, and more work. The adults need it, as do the children.

Whatever work continues will need to take into account the cultural context. This is a family of Mexican descent trying to be a family in America. There are issues around power, authority, and respect between husband and wife. Let me share some of the consultant's unspoken speculations. The mother cannot be vulnerable with her husband because he does not make it safe for her. She cannot easily show her competence because he feels threatened. She wants intimacy, but has to be guarded and aggressive because she is on her own. She cannot experience herself fully at home, both strong and tender, independent and dependent. As a Latina woman she has a strong sense of obligation toward her family. She wants to give her love, as well as her competence, to her family. Right now she can be affectionate with her children. She must be strong with her husband. In therapy, she can only relax her vigilance if she can trust that the therapists will not only validate what she sees but also help her husband to lay down his shield and sword.

The father knows himself to be a minority in America—not only racially (he has strong Indian features), but also in terms of his nationality, values, and culture. He feels he has low status in society because of his job and relatively poor earning power. He is not highly educated, nor does he have a high status job. At home his wife is much more articulate than he, better able to relate to the children. He could appreciate, enjoy, and even learn to take advantage of his wife's skills if he felt worthwhile as a man. This means something to him, especially given his Latino culture. He does not feel like much of a man outside or inside his home. He takes refuge in the persona of the quiet, tough, "I don't need anyone" image. Yet, there is a tender heart beating within. Given how he has been conducting himself at home, all these factors may well have resonated with experiences in his own family of origin. He does not easily feel valued, think himself entitled to respect from his family, and give affirmation to his family. In therapy he needs to experience himself as safe, valued, and having power.

There were also questions about cultural values—corporal punishment. The father's attitude about discipline felt culturally familiar to the consultant. Another professional might have resorted to looking upon the father as socially deviant, a physical abuser. Reporting this man, who surely was only talking and doing with his boys as he had learned, would have been to criminalize a cultural norm. The consultant treated the physical intimidation as an extreme that reflected the father's inarticulateness, emotional distance, and feeling of powerlessness. He could challenge the father's behavior with an understanding ease.

It is evident that the family's emotional and relationship struggles become more understandable in light of these cultural issues. The gender and culture of the therapists obviously play a role. The original therapists were both Latina women. They identified and were comfortable with the mother; the consultant felt at ease with the father. It made a difference in how they each perceived the family (their assessment), in how they related to the family members (the use of self), and ultimately, in the strategy they each adopted with the family (and the interventions they used).

3. Family Therapy and the Community

Today there is growing awareness of the effects of economic, social, and political conditions on the psychology of people. We hear more about how society's attitudes toward cultural identity influence the everyday functioning of people. There is greater recognition of how the disappearance of "community" is affecting the American family. Therapists increasingly move beyond the boundaries of the family when defining the dimensions of an emotional or relationship issue. If the personal conflicts of life and our choices in confronting them get their meaning and significance from the total context of life, how can we limit our vision to the individual or the family?

Furthermore, today's information-driven society is so saturating the boundaries of the family that the family can no longer pretend to be the main socializing force of its members. Today's society is increasingly assuming traditional parental functions. Schools are getting into the sexual mores of the community, offering youngsters advice and devices for "safe sex." States grant minors the rights to abortion without parental knowledge and consent. Television programs depict life and offer values driven by forces often unrelated to the values of families and their communities. At a time of allegedly unprecedented personal freedom, the family's ability to guide and direct family life is diminishing.

Moreover, mental health professionals and social service agencies are gaining increasingly more influence in children's lives. Therapists and counselors advise judges about whether parents are fit to raise their children. They tell schools whether a child should stay in school. They direct parents on disciplining their own children. In the interest of protecting children, they assume ever greater power over families. This influence by professionals over families is especially evident in the lives of the poor, especially minorities.

PROBLEMS OF CONCEPTUALIZING A FAMILY-COMMUNITY MODEL

The conceptual and technical challenges for therapists center around how to include these societal forces in the therapy with families. Specifically, the question is how to view and work with discrete clinical issues within a broad social context. By itself, with all its component systems, the family is an extremely complex social system. The family as contiguous with the community appears that much more complex.

In the clinical situation, therapists funnel their vision through the symptom, problem, or issue presented by the patient or family. Psychoanalysis focuses on the individual and intervenes in the transferential relationship. However, a family therapist cannot seal off the family and its members from their social network. Family members have too many vital roots outside the family—jobs, schools, friends—for the family to cut off these realities from the therapy. Families tend to draw the world into the therapy and to pull therapists out into their world.

Yet, the nature of families is not enough to force therapists to broaden their perspective if their therapeutic models insist on not seeing beyond the interviewing room. Therapists need therapeutic approaches that teach them how to do their clinical work within a broader social context. The vital questions for therapists are how to understand the problem in the relevant aspects of its ecosystem—individual, family, and community—and how to intervene in that complex.

THE COMMUNITY IN THERAPY: DIRECT REALITY AND ITS ANALOGUES

Therapists cannot practically comprehend the entire world impinging on a client's problem. However, they can reach out for the parts of that world that (1) most directly affect the issue and (2) are accessible to therapists' interventions. Clinicians have the technical problem of determining how to unravel the threads of the ecosystem's dynamics that *converge* into the problem. They must first unravel the "what," "how," and "why" of this convergence; they must then determine how *practically* to work with these influences.

As noted in the previous chapter, the discovery process begins with clearly identifying the focus issue. From there, therapists explore links to the various levels of the client's ecosystem. These systemic links behind a client's issue can be virtually *absolute*, so that a change in one system necessarily creates a new outcome through the entire ecosystemic chain linked to the problem. On the other hand, the systemic links can be associated in such complex ways that intervention on multiple levels is required. It is the difference between solving a child's school performance problem, in one instance, by resolving the single source issue of his parents' conflictual marriage, or in another instance, by working on multiple issues converging adversely in his life—the parents' marital problem, his school's failure to teach, and an atmosphere of violence in his neighborhood.

Once therapists know where to look, they may intervene in the ecosystem's complex linkages by working either *directly* or *indirectly through the analogue*. Therapists intervene directly when they work hands on with the various subsystems linked to the problem. They intervene in the analogue by going after a *dysfunctional structural pattern* in one or more logistically accessible, personally workable, and/or little defended subsystems to affect one or more related subsystems of a client's ecosystem. "Logistically accessible" means the therapist can contact them; "personally workable" says that because of who, what, or from where the therapist is, he or she can understand, relate, or otherwise have leverage with a particular party in the client's ecosystem; "little defended" means that the client and other parties feel less vulnerable in a particular area of their lives and will allow the therapist entrée. A direct attack on the problem is not always the shortest route to a solution.

AN EXAMPLE OF WORKING
IN THE ANALOGUE

The mother of an eight-year-old boy who refused to cooperate in school held the opinion that her son's teacher could get her son to work—but only if she used the mother's approach. The mother was a young, African American single parent living on welfare. She had no confidence that the teacher would listen to her and would not dare approach the teacher with her ideas. In a family session, one of the therapists went behind a one-way vision mirror with the mother and asked her to instruct his co-therapist on the other side. The co-therapist was to supervise the boy on an actual homework assignment. The mother was hesitant, but after several tries and some encouragement from the therapist she coached the co-therapist, through the telephone connecting the observation room to the interviewing room. She guided the therapist in being firm but engaging with her son, learned how to articulate her experience to another person, and experienced the power of directing a professional. Perhaps most importantly, she knew success. The mother walked out of the session confident, and subsequently she successfully talked with her son's teacher. The context in which the mother instructed the co-therapist was structurally analogous to the mother's relationship with her son's teacher. The therapy room was accessible to the therapist, the therapist had complete leverage there, and the mother and son were less anxious and consequently less protected. Success was more likely.

A FAMILY DEALS
DIRECTLY WITH SOCIETY

This case exemplifies intervening directly in an individual child's problem, which was rooted both in the family and the school and in the relationship between them. The therapist worked directly in the family and then with the family and school. The African American family came to a clinic because 14-year-old Robert was beyond his mother's control. He was skipping class and staying away from home overnight. His mother did not complain about the 17-year-old, Tina, or about 11-year-old Kenny or nine-year-old Cindy, who accompanied her and Robert to the first interview. In her request for an appointment, the mother depicted Robert's behavior as so awful that the therapist had to acknowledge the problem. Then, however, he asked about related concerns at home. He wanted to see the broader picture before deciding what to do with Robert. The mother responded by telling about her own hard life. We start with the mother's personal story 20 minutes into the session.

MOTHER   He [her second husband] said he wanted to take care of me. . . . Now, I'm talking about his father (*points to Robert*). Then after I moved into another house, then he started constantly, constantly beating me. But I said maybe he'll stop it, you know. . . . Then, after I got married, I came to Philadelphia and I was pregnant with him [Robert] and didn't know it. I had him in '64 and I didn't know what to do—none of my family up here and nobody to talk to. So I was constantly beat and then I heard that he was with the girl he was with before me. . . . My kids were seeing all of this. I tried to take up for myself. I tried to take up for my children the best I knew how. . . . I would never hit him back. He hit me with a lamp—that's how I got that right there (*she points to scar under left eye*). I got this (*she indicates a large scar on her back near her neck*).

THERAPIST   How did you get that?

MOTHER   That's where he cut me. That was before he stabbed me ten times. . . . So, then, his son came up, his older son. He came up when he was, like, 23. My oldest daughter [now out of the home] just had turned 12, and he got her pregnant. I didn't do nothing about that. I was scared.

THERAPIST   It's almost too much for me to take—what you are describing. I don't know how you survived.

. . .

MOTHER   (*Turns to her children*) Now you all have heard this [about her childhood] and so, therefore, it is nothing new to you. . . . (*Back to the therapist*) I would get hit with one across the back or across the head because of my father. He wanted to have a relationship with me and there was a beating every day. Every day I would run and the neighbors would make me come back home. . . . This went on from 9 until 17 and that's the life that I had to live and, right now, I still think about it. (*She later told how she had run away from home to the man who became her first husband.*)

. . .

MOTHER You know, like right now I am having financial problems. I know that's bugging me. Still, when I'm not having financial problems, it still seems something just keeps my head hurting all the time—tension. Then I feel like I just want to burst out and just cry and cry and just don't stop crying. . . . All the weight is like falling on me.

Could one think of trying to understand her and her children without taking into account the whole story?

The more the therapist heard, the more disheartened he became, making him wonder whether the children themselves felt overwhelmed by their mother's pain, past and present. The story disturbed the therapist. He hurt for her, but also felt blocked out by her powerlessness. He felt powerless to help.

The therapist had observed in the session that Robert was more attentive to his mother's unhappy story than the other children. Unlike his siblings, he volunteered answers and explanations to move her story along. Considering his own reactions to the mother, the therapist wondered whether Robert was feeling responsible for his mother and frustrated by the lack of opportunity to make a difference.

The mother was crying as she told her story. Her distress as she recounted her experience was real. On the supposition that the children's taking on more responsibility in the family would help the mother and further their differentiation, the therapist suggested the mother obtain help from her children with the household. The therapist urged her to ask more of her family in the session itself.

THERAPIST Do they know what you are going through right now?

MOTHER I tell them, but sometimes I tell them I don't have no money and they make a face or get mad. I try to explain it to them. I sit them down and try to talk to them. Sometimes they'll listen and sometimes they won't. . . . It seems like I don't have no help.

THERAPIST Okay, why don't you ask them now for some help. . . .

MOTHER (*To the therapist*) What would help me is like—what I have I don't mind giving, but when other children come in and they eat, it takes out of their mouths. I tell them don't give food away and they slip and do it. . . . (*Therapist gestures for her to address the children directly.*) Okay. . . . It is going to make me upset thinking that any meal . . . will be taken from you all and when I be telling you all I don't have no money. . . . I'll be trying to think of what the next move to make. That's my problem. That's my problem not having nobody else to talk to. That's a problem.

THERAPIST You are asking them for something, but they are not answering you. This conversation is just going one way.

MOTHER I done told them this more than once, and so I sometimes—

THERAPIST Get an answer. You have a young woman here [the 17-year-old, Tina] and you have a young man [Robert] over here. The others [Kenny, 11, and Cindy, 9] are listening to you also. You have people who can certainly answer you.

MOTHER First, do you all understand what I am saying? . . .

CHILDREN Yes.

MOTHER You understand? Well, what do you think about what I am saying?

ROBERT I think about it a lot.

Robert made an attempt to say something. His life was out of control so long as his mother could not manage the family. His wish to help was compelling, but frustrated, leaving him anxious and stressed. His mother was alone without family or friends. She was dejected and felt that her life was rudderless. She complained to her children. They were without direction. Robert, struggling to survive, was feeling pressure to do something at home. Was it surprising that he had withdrawn emotionally from school?

To help Robert and the rest of the family, the therapist decided to encourage the other children to assume appropriate responsibility in the household. Their mother was operating as so many mothers of underorganized families do. She was giving up because she did not know how to organize and delegate. Tina, as the oldest, emerged as a key issue for mother.

It became apparent that the mother was forever remonstrating with Tina for not helping at home. She was not giving Tina and the other children the emotional nurturance or the organizational help they needed to work together with her. The relationship between the mother and Tina was key to this effort. The therapist asked the mother to solicit Tina's cooperation in the session itself. The therapist was intervening in the session around the issue of the mother asking her children to help shoulder the family responsibilities. A change in how the family negotiated this issue in the session would hopefully carry over into the real world of home.

THERAPIST As I hear it, you are not giving her the chance to take some of the burden.

MOTHER I don't know what burden—what would she take? What would she do?

THERAPIST Ask her.

. . .

MOTHER Okay, like when I tell you to clean up, I can tell you to clean up, I can tell you to cook, tell you to, say, clean the bathrooms—not only you, but some of the rest of them, but, you being the oldest you should see that Cindy do it. When I come home—okay, what happens? The radio be on, the crowd be at the house, you be dancing. And how do you think I feel when I come in the house and I already upset? Don't you think by your being 17 years old that you should have a responsibility for seeing that Cindy do her work and telling Robert to do his, and if he don't do his or Kenny don't do his, that you are supposed to tell me?

THERAPIST Hold on, now. Give her a chance to answer.

. . .

TINA Yeah, but they hardly don't listen. So, if they don't listen to me I don't want to be bothered with them.

. . .

THERAPIST You would like to do the cleaning of the house and get them to help?

TINA Yes. Sometimes I have been in the house all by myself and go ahead and clean up everything and Mom come home and she just goes up in her room and go lay down. But, sometimes, when they make me mad, and don't listen to me, I don't do nothing.

THERAPIST Who doesn't listen to you?

TINA None of them out of these three don't listen to me.

THERAPIST Okay. Your mother has just talked about Cindy a minute ago. Why doesn't she listen to you?

TINA I don't know. I don't know why she don't listen to me.

THERAPIST Find out.

TINA Cindy, why don't you listen to me? (*To therapist*) I can't ask her no questions.

THERAPIST Why not? . . .

TINA It seems funny because I have never done anything like that. . . .

THERAPIST Ask her now. Your mother has said that you can ask her. Ask her about why she doesn't listen to you.

TINA Why you don't listen to me when I tell you to help clean up?

CINDY You be hollering at me a lot.

THERAPIST (*To Tina*) Talk with her about it. . . .

TINA Why when I tell you to do something you always saying, "You ain't watching me," and you gonna tell Momma when she gets home that I told you to do different things?

Neither the mother nor the children are accustomed to negotiating with one another. The therapist directed the mother to her oldest, Tina, who told how she could not help because she, herself, could not get the younger children to respond to her. Cindy only takes direction from her mother.

The mother, overwhelmed by her own troubles, does not know how to give more of herself to the children. The children feel like a heavy responsibility to the mother, and she tends to withdraw emotionally from them. The therapist tries to be supportive of her at the same time that he encourages her to hearten her children. He is trying to create a bridge between the mother and the children, and at this point he chooses to work through the relationship between the mother and Tina, instead of Robert. Robert's troubles appear symptomatic of a general breakdown in the family that is evident in what is happening between mother and Tina.

The therapist draws out Tina to talk about how hard her life is for mother to hear. Her daughter's pain is not unlike her own. The girl told how she, too, suffers and how she, too, does not expect others to help to her. What the girl reveals is news to the mother.

We rejoin the therapist and Tina as they talk about how Tina keeps her worries to herself.

THERAPIST . . . Tina, I feel bad for you. Do you want to be lonely?

TINA No. I just don't like telling nobody nothing.

. . .

THERAPIST What grade are you in?

TINA Eleventh.

THERAPIST In your eleventh year and you don't like [school] anymore? Since when don't you like it?

TINA About two months ago I started not liking it. I used to go every day and go on time every day. Now I don't even do that no more because when I was in school there used to be a lot of activities. The principal just is stopping everything.

MOTHER Well, you're just about out of school now. Think about your education. . . . Don't think about that principal.

THERAPIST Okay, let's understand what it is. What activities did they have before?

TINA Well, they had a lot of contests and I like won queen of ninth grade and I used to help raise money for a lot of people in school and in the neighborhood. I was in the student council, and I was like in choir and stuff like that.

THERAPIST In school? And you are not in that now?

TINA No.

THERAPIST Why not?

TINA Cause it ain't like it used to be. It is all boring. . . . Cause at school the only thing we do is sit around. The teachers make jokes.

THERAPIST Don't you learn?

TINA When I first started going to school . . . when I first knew my English teacher, I went and told my counselor that I couldn't get along with her. There was something, something that I didn't like about her. I couldn't really tell what it was, but it was just like her ways, like students would ask her something and she would look at us like we should know. She would like roll her eyes at us and stuff like that and I told him that I was uncomfortable with that teacher and they just left me in there anyway. They didn't take me out of there. I think I got an F or an E in her class. I do her work but it seems like I still don't make any effort at all.

THERAPIST So, really at school even the teaching part of it is just not making you happy. (*To mother*) Did you know all this?

MOTHER All I knew is that last part of last month they wrote me and told me that Tina had missed a lot of days out of school and that's when I went to school and that's when I heard everything.

THERAPIST But you didn't hear this . . .

MOTHER I just told you she don't never talk anymore.

THERAPIST But she just did. She just did.

Tina spoke like so many other youngsters from the inner-city—how the system has given up on her, and how she, herself, had given up. Between home and school, it was too much for Tina. No one was recognizing her efforts. No one was helping her. She stopped trying.

The therapist wanted to give Tina her mother. However, that would require empowering the mother, who herself was giving up. The place to start was with Tina and her school. The therapist thought he could make a difference there more quickly than at home. It would be an opportunity to bring mother and daughter together, perhaps with a successful outcome. The therapist concluded that first session with an agreement with Tina and her mother. They would go to the school with him and meet with the girl's counselor, the vice-principal, and her teachers, if possible.

This would be an attempt to intervene directly in the school context. The therapist would approach the school in a way consonant with the family goals of having mother more in charge, drawing the mother and daughter closer together, and assisting mother to help her daughter succeed in school. Through all these changes, the therapist hoped to give Robert a mother who not only was more in charge but also felt the support of responsible children, starting with her main lieutenant, Tina. Mother could then be available for Robert to relieve his anxiety, stop his acting-up, and help with his problems at school.

The meeting with the school officials took place a week after the family interview. In the session, the counselor and vice-principal reflexively began to organize the meeting as a review of Tina's poor performance in school. They put mother and daughter on the defensive, visibly eroding what little confidence they had about their right to challenge the school. The therapist interrupted the staff to ask that mother and daughter be given a chance to present their case. Because of the therapist's involvement, the school officials made room for them to speak. The therapist encouraged the mother to say her piece and also support Tina in talking for herself. He wanted the mother, not himself, to give Tina this backing, which she did.

Tina and her mother were able to convince the school of the girl's genuine interest in her classwork and her need for more positive support from the school. The counselor and vice-principal agreed to look into the mother and daughter's complaints and to meet with both of them again. The mother walked out of the session saying she would never again allow herself to be intimidated by an institution like a school. Tina spoke energetically to her mother about the meeting and her revived hopes.

These two sessions, with family and then with school, set a strong foundation for the rest of family work that Robert, Tina, and their mother needed. The work with the mother around Tina's school put the mother back in charge of her family. That set the stage for her to help Robert, and she could set personal goals for her own life distinct from her role as mother.

CONCLUSION

In the two families discussed here, the therapist worked with the families and with their relationships to the community, represented by the school. In both cases the therapist focused on a specific issue. He looked to define the field of intervention, the parts of the family's ecosystem that had a part to play in generating the problem and potentially in solving it. He identified specific outcome goals related to the focal issue, as well as structural goals in relation to these outcome goals. He sought changes in the relationships within the family and with the community necessary to sustain the family's personal goals. Because this was personal therapy, all goals related to the community reflected the family's personal goals.

The two cases exemplified the ecostructural approach to families and their communities. They took into account the individuals, their families, and the segments in their communities they were contending with at that time. There was direct work with the families and direct work with the schools. The work with the families had implications by analogy for their relationships with the community. The work with the community had implications for the personal relationships at home. All the work had in common solving the personal problems the families presented, along with their underlying structural issues. It was all part of an ecosystemic whole that linked home to community through the structural themes of the family's relationships with all parts of the ecosystem.

4. Home/Community-Based Services: The Two-Tier Approach

This chapter presents a two-tier model for work with high-risk families combining community-based intervention with home-based family therapy for individual families. The chapter discusses this home/community-based service model within an ecostructural conceptual framework. A case example illustrates an application of the model.

HOME-BASED SERVICES

Those who counsel high-risk families find home-based services an effective tool in working with families who do not respond to traditional in-office services (Tavantzis, Tavantzis, Brown, & Rohrbaugh, 1985). Home-based services are not merely "home visits." They represent a philosophy and a practical model in which therapists choose to work with families in their natural environments. They bring care "home" to families who would not otherwise use services or who may be better helped in their homes than in the office. The model attempts to empower the socially weak and isolated and to mobilize the underorganized.

Home-based services have been particularly effective with high-risk, underorganized families who lack internal resources and motivation. Home-based therapists provide a high impact intervention, often with several professionals working with a family for many hours per week and available 24 hours a day (Bryce

71

& Lloyd, 1981). They work for practical solutions to a family's problems, mainly through short-term services (12 to 16 weeks) focusing on the immediate and concrete. They create momentum toward positive change by building on families' strengths. This is a resource-rich approach for resource-poor families.

The articulation of home-based services has focused primarily on work with individual families in the home. However, in practice those working with these high-risk families also spend a great amount of time helping with money, housing, health, the justice system, and other community-linked issues. Models for home-based family therapy are already out there. The need is for perspectives on home-based work that conceptually and technically incorporate community work with family therapy.

THE ECOSTRUCTURAL PERSPECTIVE

Families receiving home-based services are usually low-income, often minority, and frequently single-parent families. They represent the most resourceless of our society. According to the National Commission on Children (1990), about 20 percent of children live in poverty in America today; the majority of these children live in single-parent families. Regarding families referred for home-based services, their "problems tend to be multi-generational, severe, and ongoing" (Brosman, 1990).

All evidence tells us that what is happening to the individual family in America has its roots in a society-wide phenomenon.

As recently as 1960, 91 percent of white children and 67 percent of black children lived with two parents. In 1988 the white figure had dropped to 79 percent and the black figure to 39 percent. (Rich, 1989)

This same society is also racked with violence, drug addiction, and alcoholism at rates that far outstrip our own prior records. Our communities are losing their cultural identities, moral constraints, and the security of social bonds (Wilson, 1993). The breakdown of our society and our communities inevitably infects families (Knitzer, 1982). The problems of America's families are not just personal reversals, but also societal failures. These personal problems have roots in society and spill over into the family's life in the community. Today, the field searches for models of therapy that reach beyond the family and include the social context, especially the communities of the most wounded victims—America's poor and minorities.

The ecostructural model is an example of a family/community approach that tries to speak to this need. As the name implies, the ecostructural model has two components—ecological and structural. Grounded in ecological (Auerswald, 1968) and structural theory (Minuchin, 1974), the ecostructural model broadens the reach of therapists working with an individual family in the home environment. The ecological perspective of the model targets the relationships among individual, family, and community. The structural base of the model looks at the relational framework common to all levels of the ecosystem, the structure. The model speaks of family and community in the common vocabulary of boundary, alignment, and power (Aponte & Van Deusen, 1981), emphasizing the meaning that culture and values give human experience.

The ecostructural model assumes that the family is not alone in the problems it brings to treatment. Ecostructural therapists work within the framework of the ecosystem, the individual, family, and community. They see personal issues as planted in the soil of the ecosystem, and toil with their interventions in that multileveled and complex environment. However, while viewing the entire ecosystem, they work for change at the most personal level of people's experience, targeting the convergence of the forces that generate the issue (see Figure 4.1). Therapists take aim at the linkages among systems that manifest themselves in people's lives. Not just *problems* lie within and among the individual, the family, and the community as they converge to shape the lives of our clients; the resources, the *solutions*, lie buried in this rich context as well. The ecostructural therapist enters that world.

The internal organization of each relationship will reproduce in some form what happens in the larger ecosystem. For example,

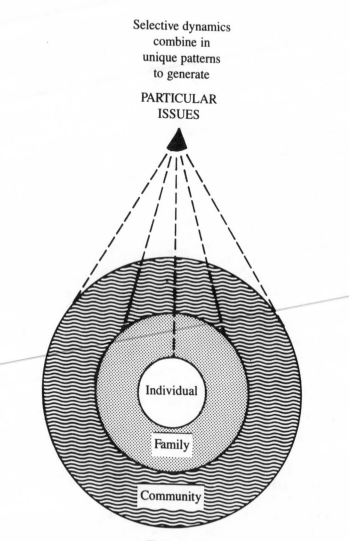

Selective dynamics
combine in
unique patterns
to generate

PARTICULAR
ISSUES

Figure 4.1.
Ecostructural Convergence

it is axiomatic that children are individual mirrors for both the contentment and the distress of their families. The harmony or disharmony in the family as a whole will also affect every relationship within the family, facilitating or impeding connections among family members. Moreover, the social conditions of a community will support or undermine families and their individual members. The ecostructural therapist sees these micro and macro forces in an ecosystem *converging* in a family to generate a problem. The therapist intervenes in the balance and configuration of these forces to free and strengthen people to make the choices that are good for them.

THE UNDERORGANIZED FAMILY

The poor families most likely to receive home-based therapy are the underorganized. They are the families who are less able to take charge of their personal lives and develop a stable network of community support. They are least able to benefit from weekly one-hour therapy sessions, which require a cohesive living situation that permits a focused, discrete intervention to take root in a family. Underorganized families need workers to help rebuild their lives from basic family relationships to their contacts with the world outside.

With their poverty as well as all their personal problems, these families often fail to function successfully on their own. They become dependent upon a multiplicity of helping institutions. Family boundaries become porous to the institutional environment in the form of agencies that assume responsibility for and care of these families. These social welfare agencies, mental health clinics, and other community institutions become part of their daily lives. Unfortunately, the service provider network usually does not coordinate its efforts with families and often becomes another disorganizing force in their lives. In its eagerness to help, the network of agencies more often than not also drains away the control families and communities have over their lives. The institutional network inadvertently substitutes its policies for a family's and its community's values, and its bureaucracy for their social structure.

THE FAMILY AND
ITS COMMUNITY

The ecostructural model encourages coordinated and integrated work with the individual, the family, and the community on behalf of individual families. It also supports efforts to solve community problems and enhance neighborhood resources to strengthen the social foundation of family life. In a fully developed ecostructural approach, an agency both focuses on individual families in the community about their particular needs and actively works to improve the general health of its clients' community.

The ecostructural model proposes a two-pronged agency thrust. Along with a clinical team to work with families, an agency creates a staff component to work directly on their community's social conditions. A community action team works on an ongoing basis in partnership with local neighborhoods and other agencies to better social conditions in the community. It also strives to generate avenues of linkage between community action and therapy with individual client families. For an agency, the model offers an ecologically integrated and coordinated approach to families and communities.

THE TWO-TIER
HOME-BASED MODEL

At the level of serving the particular family, this ecostructural perspective applies to home-based therapy by systematically integrating the community into the treatment model. It starts with the premise that, when families receive services in their home, they are receiving them in their communities. The two-tier approach combines family therapy with an ongoing community-based intervention. That community-based intervention can take many forms so long as:

1. A client family is working regularly on its particular issues with its personal therapists;
2. The family simultaneously participates in a community-based group to address both personal and common community issues;

3. The agency coordinates the two efforts primarily to benefit the individual families;
4. The agency also actively works with other local institutions for the community as a whole.
5. The agency's community work becomes a resource for the work with particular client families.

We are actually describing here double levels of tiers:

1. Family work:
    (a) Therapy with individual families, and
    (b) A community component (e.g., with community-based multi-family groups).
2. Community work:
    (a) General community interventions, and
    (b) Family related community interventions.

This chapter discusses working with the two tiers (Figure 4.2) of particular family work. It views home-based therapy as having an individual family-based component and a community-based component related directly to the work with individual families. This community component grows out of the work with individual families and primarily benefits them. It empowers them as families vis-à-vis their community. It helps them with their personal issues through their work with the community. The agency's general community work is a separate effort, which also links up with individual client families.

At the level of particular family work, an example of integrating a community-based intervention with family therapy is a multi-family community group operating as part of a home-based family preservation program. In the two-tier home/community-based model, individual families work at home with a treatment team (tier 1), and the families meet as a group for personal mutual support and to solve community problems common to all or to particular families (tier 2).

In the first tier, an agency offers families home-based family preservation services. The agency assigns families therapists to

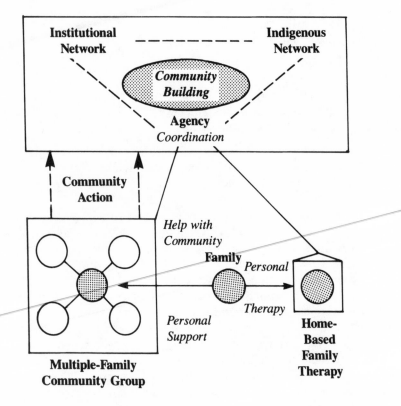

Figure 4.2.
Two-Tier Home- and Community-Based Model

work with them in their homes. The two-tier approach does not advocate any particular model of home-based services (Kaplan, 1986). It emphasizes time-concentrated interventions with a family by a team. It also pursues psychological and relationship change through the resolution of concrete problems. Most home-based models share these principles.

In the second tier, the agency organizes these client families into multi-family groups based on the model developed by Peter Laqueur (1973). The seed of Laqueur's model is planted in the community to enlist the families in the home-based therapy to join together to help one another. The groups are open, with families joining and leaving as therapeutically indicated. Being in active therapy is a requirement for entering the multi-family group. Agencies insure that the families have some sense of community, organizing the groups by neighborhood whenever possible. Families meet in the home base of their neighborhoods, preferably in a location that is not the agency. Their meeting place belongs to the community, like a church or a "Y."

The multi-family group has three basic purposes:

1. To provide mutual support to member families in pursuing their respective personal goals (Cassano, 1989; Paul & Paul, 1985);
2. To help individual families in their dealings with community agencies;
3. To act collectively as an advocacy group around issues common to all of them (Raasoch, 1981).

The agency assigns teams of at least two workers to the multi-family group. The use of co-therapists lends flexibility to the therapeutic team as it faces the complex task of relating to both personal family goals and community objectives. They maintain close ties with the therapists of individual families and with the staff in their own agency responsible for community relations. They move in two coordinated directions at once.

The group's workers make a special effort to share power with the families without blurring roles (Yalom, 1985). Because so many of these families are underorganized, they need help with empowerment to feel in charge of their own lives and to navigate their communities with a citizen's sense of entitlement. The workers support families' empowerment vis-à-vis other families, the workers themselves, and the outside world. In home/community-based work, agencies and workers actively provide organization, support, and direction. It is essential that they also respect the boundaries of responsibility for self and self-determination.

Implementation

Therapists encourage but do not compel families to join the multi-family groups. They invite families who have passed the peak of their personal crises, so that they can both accept support and offer help to others. Typically, families in the program enter the group during the third or fourth week of family treatment. By this time, they have some trust in their therapist and have gotten a handle on their original crisis.

The group meets at least once per week for two hours each time. A family's therapist and the group may encourage family members to participate more actively or not depending on what is happening in the family and in the group. The personal goals of a family take priority in deciding the level and kind of participation. A family, with the group's support, may also invite its personal therapist to attend a meeting to help the family articulate its needs in the group. The group attempts always to balance the needs of individual members with the process of the group.

The group leaders encourage each family to present its situation to the group and to speak to the support it needs. Group members advise, confront, and encourage one another. They offer practical help outside the group. However, they inform the group and their personal therapists of the contacts they plan outside with other group members. Their extra-group contacts need to fit with their own counseling and the group's internal process. Group leaders help insure the continuity and focus of the group while encouraging individual initiative and self-direction.

The group pursues bridges to its community. Officials from public agencies and community organizations are invited to meetings by the families. By inviting the community to meetings, families have an opportunity, with group support, to deal directly with outside agencies about issues of concern to individual members or the group as a whole.

A CASE EXAMPLE

The Waugh family consists of a single-parent mother and two children, a 13-year-old son, Dan, and a 10-year-old daughter, Lisa. Mrs. Waugh requested the home-based family therapy program to avoid placement of the boy, who was having severe school-related problems, both academic and disciplinary. He had been caught stealing and been arrested. Recently he had begun to abuse his mother physically. Since the father's unexpected death eight years earlier, Mrs. Waugh had been a passive parent, unable to take charge of the children.

Therapy focused on strengthening her hand in the family. Following an explosive argument between mother and son around household chores, the Waughs' primary therapist arranged for two paraprofessionals from the agency to coach the mother and the children in their interactions. In one intervention, a coach, herself the parent of a teenage son, instructed Mrs. Waugh in the supervision of Dan's room cleaning. When Dan defeated his mother's efforts, the coach offered her alternative ways of remaining in charge. The other coach supported the boy as he struggled with his reactions to his mother. This coach also helped keep Lisa out of the mother-son scrimmages. With help from the coaches, these tussles did not escalate out of control. Mrs. Waugh and Dan began negotiating their relationship. The family was then able to move out of its crisis status to join the multi-family group.*

The family group accepted the Waugh family after the third week of home-based work. Five families belonged to the group. They had been meeting for about three months. Apart from mutual personal support, the group also dealt with a number of common concerns of the families. They worked on parenting in gen-

---

*As a later follow-up intervention, Mrs. Waugh, with the help of the workers, made contact for her son with the man who headed the school's wrestling team. He eventually arranged for the boy to assist in the local YMCA junior wrestling program.

eral, the special issues of single-parenting, children's behavioral and academic problems, illegal drug sales in the community, and the high rate of neighborhood vandalism. In the process they generated a sense of community among themselves, identifying common values, rules, and structures for family and community life.

The Waughs used the multi-family group in several different ways. On an individual level, the children responded to the advice of other parents, accepted confrontation from peers, disclosed feelings about friends, and shared their grief over the loss of their father. The mother received praise from other parents for her efforts raising her children alone. Because of the group, she was also able to see her children more positively. She then could acknowledge before everyone the children's good efforts at home, which the children liked. The group became a community that shared some responsibility for the well-being of their children by validating values and providing emotional encouragement.

The Waugh family also participated in some group community actions that brought notable results. With funds donated by a local corporation, the group started a neighborhood cleanup operation. The families also successfully lobbied the juvenile court to arrange for teens who damaged property in their neighborhood to be assigned to a community task force doing repair work.

For a period of time, personnel from a community drug program attended every other meeting to offer education for both parents and youngsters. Parents also held negotiations with school personnel to establish a program in which the parents could learn how to tutor their children. This latter program also served to link individual parents to their children's schools—to their children's advantage.

5. The Family-School Interview: An Ecostructural Approach

This chapter describes the family-school interview, an intervention with a child, family, and school that illustrates the ecostructural paradigm. The model offers a practical method to address a client's problem in the context of the individual's psychology, the family's relationships, and the social forces of community and the larger society.

The family-school interview takes into account the dynamics of each unit in the social ecosystem and the structural relationships among them relative to a client's problem. The multilayered structure of the client's ecosystem forms the therapist's framework. In Piaget's words that framework is "the structure *qua* whole or system is defined" (1970, p. 7).

THE CONTEXT FOR THE FAMILY-SCHOOL INTERVIEW

A family-school interview includes the child with his or her family and the school personnel related to the child's problem. The school staff—the teachers, counselor, and school principal (in a high school usually a vice-principal)—have the most to say about the child's life in the school.

Because of the size and complexity of the group involved, co-therapists usually run the session. The child is a citizen of two systems, the family and the school. Each system has its agenda and its particular dynamics related to the issue on the table. A therapist wants the process to respond to the needs of all involved even as they focus on the child's problem. A single therapist would be hard put to relate to all parties personally and to the needs of each, while balancing all their differences around a single issue. Co-therapists offer that potential and flexibility.

Preparing for the Family-School Interview

This interview model was developed as part of an experimental effort at the Philadelphia Child Guidance Clinic to conduct first interviews in schools with the families and school staff of the children who were the clients. Our hope was to keep the issue in the hands of family and school, with the therapist serving as a consultant. Only when the family-school session(s) were not enough to do the job would the clinician engage the child in the clinic.

In our experience, the family-school interview, as an initial intervention, is most successful when the school initiates the referral. The school still owns the problem. It is most disposed to undertake the difficult scheduling task of convening all relevant personnel. The family, for its part, is likely to respond to the expectation of the child's school to participate. The session is for the child and is related to school problems, not to mental health issues.

From the point of intake, the usual sequence begins with a mother calling to ask for an appointment for her son or daughter, most often the former. When asked to describe the problem, she often explains that the school has prompted her to get help for her son. In the cases that invariably gain the parent's acceptance of the family-school interview, the mother states that, although the school is complaining about her son, he is not a problem at home. The intake worker then asks her whether the boy and the family would meet with the school staff to find out more about the school's concern. When the mother agrees, the worker calls the school counselor to arrange the interview. The counselor is usually willing, but occasionally questions freeing the teacher(s) from class or imposing upon the principal's time. The worker might then call the principal personally, to explain that the family is not experiencing the problem as the school is. The school knows the problem firsthand. It would help the family get started if the school personnel could offer the family a full picture of the problem at an initial meeting in the school. We are willing to wait until the relevant school personnel are able to arrange to attend the interview.

We have found that, when we compromise and have the first interview with the child and family without the school, we meet with greater resistance to a school interview from both family and school. Our leverage diminishes with everyone once we take ownership of solving the problem. This is not to say that such interviews are never held after treatment has begun at the clinic, just that they are then more difficult to arrange.

The Goals of the Family-School Interview

The family-school interview, as a first session, is intended to discover the exact nature of the precipitating problem, the relationships among all involved with the problem, and what is needed to achieve change. What works best is to:

1. Work in the initial session toward agreement on common goals that speak to the concerns of both school and family;
2. Build during the session on the positive assets of both school and family to create momentum toward a solution;
3. Aim at a positive and practical outcome in the first session that contains implicitly the long-term goals of all involved.

School personnel often perceive the results of tests and examinations from mental health professionals as of little practical help with the immediate problem. For them to stay engaged with the family and, if necessary, with the therapist, they need to experience the practical advantages of their participation. This means that they understand *how* their involvement gains them the results they seek. They need also to remain *in control* of their role in the partnership with family and therapist. The therapist helps them experience themselves as *active*, not passive, partners in the process. If the interview is conducted properly, they will want to participate.

The interview is for the family as it is for the school. The therapist looks for what will lead to good, practical results, but in line with the deepest understanding of the case and long-range goals for both family and school. The therapist needs to formulate the child's issues so as to reflect the concerns of both school and family. Each participant—family and school—needs to view achieving the articulated joint goals as reaching its own goals.

Practical Questions of Strategy

A delicate issue requiring attention from the very start is the relationship of the school to the therapist vis-à-vis the child and family. Teachers request help with their pupils, but they do not expect to become clients. On the other hand, if therapists enter as colleagues of the school, they cannot also be consultants to and intervene directly in the relationship of school to family and child. In the ecostructural model, the therapist implicitly negotiates with the school its role with the family throughout the process. To do this, the therapist maintains a narrow focus on the issue and the goals of the work. The therapist's formulation of the problem and the goals is not primarily educational; rather, it is aimed at the emotional well-being of the child. However, the psychological goals clearly take into account the school's educational aims. The therapist offers solutions that the school can accept, modify, or reject in line with its mandate to educate the child. Therapists lead the effort by exerting the power of accurate analyses and practical solutions to a child's emotional problems. They support and do not usurp the school's role, and succeed to the degree that they come up with solutions that meet the child's, the family's, and the school's needs.

This is a difficult spot for therapists, particularly when the interview takes place on school grounds, often in the principal's office. However, the task for a therapist is clear. The therapist is not a parent or a teacher, and certainly not a principal. The therapist must acknowledge the primacies of school and parent in their respective contexts while at the same time taking leadership of what is essentially a clinical interview. The therapist assumes leadership by calling the session, organizing its structure, and working with all parties to set the goals of the session.

THE ILLUSTRATION: JERRY'S SCHOOL PROBLEM

The mother of 10-year-old Jerry called the clinic to ask for an appointment. She said Jerry was fighting in school and not doing his assignments; however he was not troublesome at home. She was agreeable to meeting with the school the next day but was reluctant to include her husband, since he had a "bad heart." His attendance would depend upon how he was feeling. The therapists wanted him present if it were at all possible. The therapists did not know whether any of the other children would have something to offer to the meeting, but told the mother they would be happy to have them in the session. She said it would be too hard for her to bring them. The therapists agreed on Jerry and the father.

The therapists called the school counselor who had referred Jerry's mother to the clinic about setting up the family-school session. She thought our request for the participation of the principal, Jerry's three teachers, and the counselor herself was unusual. However, she was worried about Jerry and would try anything. Her main question was whether the clinic's purpose was to try to change the school or help the boy. She said the staff of another mental health center had tried to do therapy on the school every time the school had referred a child for treatment. The clinic assured her that the goal was to solve Jerry's problem. The therapists wanted to find out how well everyone concerned—school, family, and clinic—could work together to help Jerry. The counselor agreed and called back to confirm that the principal and all of Jerry's teachers would be there.

The family and the school personnel assembled at the school the following day. The principal snatched the initiative by asking the therapists if they knew about the language Jerry had used with his homeroom teacher the previous day. They did not, but wanted to get to know Jerry better personally before plunging into what he had done. One therapist sat back as the other chatted casually with Jerry until he relaxed a bit. The second therapist then turned to the parents and asked what Jerry was like at home with them. The mother spoke for both parents as she related that he was not a serious problem. He was a good athlete, did not talk much, but could be stubborn. He did not pay too much attention to her requests, but was not disrespectful. The mother said that it was her job to take care of the children (there were six), and that the father helped her if she asked. However, he had not been working since his last heart attack a year ago, and she has not wanted to burden him with worries about the children.

The father spontaneously interjected that he would gladly help. He was up to it. As the therapists probed for information about the other children, both parents admitted that it was not just Jerry who was inattentive to his mother. None of the four boys paid much attention to her orders, but this did not cause her to worry because they never did anything seriously wrong. Jerry did have a problem with his three older brothers, who often picked on him. He would fight back. If things really got out of hand, the mother could always turn to the father who, with a word, could get any of the boys in line. When alone with his parents, Jerry was affectionate and responsive. Jerry agreed with all they said about him.

Only after having heard the family's story did the therapists turn back to the school staff. Jerry's homeroom teacher presented written notes about the racial slurs he had directed at her. She did not want to voice them. (Jerry is white and his teacher black.) The parents knew from the counselor's call the previous day that Jerry had called his teacher names, but did not know what he had said. The parents wanted to see the notes. One of the therapists passed the teacher's report to them. When they read the notes, they became visibly embarrassed. They were further upset to learn that this was not the first such incident.

Responding to the parents' surprise, one therapist asked the counselor (who is white) about what she had told the parents about Jerry's behavior. The counselor said she had told them that

Jerry was giving his teacher trouble, but had not spelled out what he had done. She had been trying to counsel Jerry herself and did not want to get him in serious trouble with them. The teachers did not know the parents had not been told the full story.

Jerry's homeroom teacher focused on Jerry. She was overtly indignant about his language. She added that he had also been fighting with the other children in class and was not doing his school work. He was out of control in the classroom. As she filled in the details of her relationship with Jerry, it became evident that the teacher had been having difficulty handling Jerry for a long time. The clinicians questioned each of the other two teachers (also black), who said they had had no trouble from Jerry; they liked him. When asked the size of their classrooms, one said she was giving Jerry individual tutoring. The other had him in a small, special make-up class. These teachers were part of the counselor's and principal's efforts to give Jerry added help. At this point in the session, the homeroom teacher had to return to her class. Before she left, the parents apologized to her for their son. Jerry was silent.

The therapists talked aloud in the presence of the family and staff about how Jerry did indeed have school problems. However, they noted how well he did with individual attention from the latter two teachers, and even at home when alone with his parents. Competitive situations with his classmates and siblings seemed to bring out the worst in Jerry. For the moment, it seemed that the immediate remedy was to give Jerry more individual attention and supervise him more closely.

At home, Jerry needed his father's protection from his sibs and more supervision with his school work. It seemed that only his father had the power to make that happen. The parents agreed that the father would take over with Jerry at home. Jerry liked the idea. Moreover, the school could well use the father's support helping Jerry get his assignments done. The school staff was pleased with the therapists' suggestion that Jerry's father become involved, and he was glad to do it. He said that he would have done more had he known what was happening. The therapists suggested to the principal that Jerry be excused from his homeroom for a while. The father could receive assignments through the counselor and tutor Jerry at home. The principal readily consented.

The therapists wanted the counselor to be the link between the school and the family. They arranged for her to consult daily with the teachers and relay to the father Jerry's school assignments. Since Jerry would be bringing his work home, the father would not only be coaching him academically but also helping him learn better study habits. Jerry was ready to work with his father. The mother would try to ensure that the other children did not interfere when he and Jerry were working. However, the parents recognized that the home lacked organization. Mother's getting the children under control would take some doing. Father would help her.

The two special teachers agreed to continue with Jerry. The principal liked the plan. Everyone agreed to meet again at the school in two weeks. As the session ended, one therapist asked to speak with the principal alone. The other sat with Jerry, the parents, and the counselor to detail how they would carry out the home program. The principal needed no persuading to remove Jerry permanently from his main teacher's room. There was now too much bad feeling between them. Moreover, Jerry needed a teacher for the larger class who could maintain better control. The principal knew the teacher who could handle Jerry once Jerry returned to regular class.

Every two weeks for a few sessions the therapists worked on the continued mutual-support program between the school and the family. The family needed much help to change the longstanding pattern of the mother trying to manage the children without the father but with little ability to discipline them herself. The father needed to become actively involved. The therapists also met separately with the school personnel to help them plan how they would work with the parents. At the clinic and in their home, one of the therapists worked with Jerry and his entire family. The parents helped Jerry negotiate with his older brothers for more territory at home. The overburdened mother was encouraged to visit friends and to take some recreation time with her husband.

As these changes took place, Jerry's school performance and behavior improved rapidly.

JERRY'S ECOLOGICAL CONTEXT

A boy having trouble in school is not having trouble alone.

> A child's behavior is caused by many factors. Some are
> "inside" the child. . . . "Outside" the child are factors like
> his parents, his siblings, his family socioeconomic status,
> his house, his school (teachers, peers, and curriculum), his
> neighborhood, his neighborhood peer group, and the hue
> of his skin, television, and others. (Minuchin, 1970, p. 41)

Minuchin ties together various elements in the social ecology of a
child, from his individual personality to his community. In the
family-school interview, the therapists consider the entire world of
the child, from his individual personality to his family to his
school, and try to work with them. Let us look at some of the
systems in Jerry's ecosystem and their structural organization.

The Individual

The boy in our example has internalized ten years of life experience. Freud described the inner world of psychological structures
in terms of the ego, id, and superego. Fairbairn talked about internalized objects. Piaget described the internal learning process. Regardless of our chosen vista, we know that Jerry has a complex of
internal psychological structures generating forces that are simultaneously in harmony and at opposites. These psychological forces
are a vital context of Jerry's world.

In spite of Jerry's bravado, we could see that he was shy and
awkward. His parents confirmed that this was Jerry most of the
time. His specially assigned teachers had seen it, too, but his main
teacher had only experienced the irascibility of a lost and anxious

boy. When I talked with Jerry in the interview, it was evident that, although distrustful and fearful, he also wanted very much to be liked. Jerry was a boy who did not think himself likeable and fought for recognition. This distrustful, shy, tough, but responsive personality was part of Jerry's context. It helped us to see the vulnerability behind the tough mask. For the therapists, it drew a sympathetic reaction and made it easier to relate to him. It was important for the school personnel to see Jerry as a complex person.

Schools are reluctant to include children in family-school interviews. They want to protect them. However, to keep the child out denies the youngster the chance to help him or herself, and deprives the session of a key resource. Nevertheless, the school has a legitimate concern. The child is vulnerable in that context and needs the adults to remain aware and connected to what he may be experiencing. Had the therapist allowed the session to begin with an indictment of Jerry for his misbehavior, however bad, the interview might well have turned into a tragedy rather than a triumph for Jerry.

The Family

Jerry's family is a second context for his being and becoming. The family is not only a collection of complex personalities, but also in its own right a living organization with rules and dynamics. Family members define who is and who is not a member of the family. Outsiders reciprocate with their fences. There are boundaries within the family itself, delineating groupings related to roles within the family. Family members align with and against one another according to the issue or task the family faces at any particular moment. Some family members will exercise more power than others at home. The family thus structures relationships among its members. Moreover, the family has its own culture and values, which give meaning to their relationships.

As related earlier, the therapists talked first with Jerry individually and then addressed the parents. They learned that Jerry's mother could not control him. In fact, she could not handle any of the boys, although she had assumed almost total responsibility for them to protect her husband's health. In fact, neither the father nor the mother saw child-rearing as the father's job. That was the culture of this working-class Italian family. They saw little role for the father at home now that he was disabled.

Moreover, the mother was protecting her husband because of his heart condition. She was playing out her role as mother as she knew it. The problem was that she just was not a good organizer and disciplinarian and the boys were out of control. Jerry, being the youngest and most vulnerable, lived frightened and angry. He became out of control in school.

Even so, Jerry's family context had the potential of being both loving and organized. The parents cared about one another and about their children. Father was happy to be useful at home by helping his son. Mother felt relieved of a burden she had trouble carrying. A basically healthy family responded quickly to an encompassing intervention.

The School

Jerry's school is a third social context for Jerry's life. That context is the teachers, counselors, and principal, as well as student peers. For Jerry, the school represents the world outside the family. It is a scary world for him. For Jerry to grow up successfully, he needs to make it in school.

After the therapists engaged with the family in the family-school session, they turned their attention to the school. Each teacher and classroom provided a subcontext of the school for Jerry. His experience was different in different classrooms. He took to the smaller classes where he received more teacher attention. He was anxious and disruptive in the large class, where he felt lost among his peers, just as he did at home among his brothers. Had the therapists included in the session only the complaining teacher, they would have lost a critical diagnostic opportunity, the chance to see the contrast in Jerry's behavior in the different school contexts.

Each social context has its structural organization with alignments, boundaries, and power distribution. Jerry's father had the potential of playing the authority in Jerry's family. The school principal was the final authority in the school setting. With that kind of power, both the father and the principal were vital to the interview. Without them, therapists could not have effected the changes that took place. The father took over the supervision of Jerry, and the principal excused Jerry from one class and allowed him to substitute home tutoring.

The school counselor, in her role, was the conduit for communication between family and school. However, she had adopted a protective and proprietary attitude toward Jerry, screening him from both the teacher and his parents. She became a black hole into which vital information disappeared. Home and school remained disconnected in Jerry's ecosystem. In the task the therapists assigned family and school, the counselor was restored as a channel of communication between parents and school.

The Social Context

Jerry has his personality, his family, and his school, but also lives in a sociocultural-political context to which all in the session also belonged. In this case, the social-cultural context was highly relevant to Jerry's school problem and to what took place in the interview. Jerry was part of a second-generation, Italian family that lives in an old, close-knit, working-class neighborhood. That social context certainly helped shape the gender roles his parents held in their family. These gender roles played a part in the control each had with the boys, which was an important dynamic in Jerry's troubles with his brothers. The mother could not control them; only the father could. Yet, the parents did not expect the father to take a more active role with the children at home even though he was home all the time. His health was a factor; however, had the mother had the heart condition she would likely still have been the one responsible for the children.

All of Jerry's teachers were women. One can only speculate about how Jerry's home conditioning about the roles of men and women influenced his attitudes toward his teachers. Would he have tested the limits so forcefully in his homeroom had the teacher been male? Would he have slung racial slurs at a black homeroom teacher who was male? The therapists needed to consider these factors. They looked to activate the father not only to monitor Jerry at home, but also to represent the school in handling the school assignments with Jerry.

Sociocultural considerations were also highly relevant to Jerry's aggression toward his homeroom teacher, which took the form of racial slurs. America's emotionally charged black-white racial division was the spirit of hate that lurked in the shadows of the family-school drama. A racial insult to this African American teacher had a special meaning in the context of America's history. That history was inside her. It carried a legacy of pain and degradation for her that that boy could not have understood. However, all the adults in that room knew it in some way. One could look at what the boy said as the product of an emotional problem. Unwittingly, he drew the weapon from a social context of conflict and hatred. That social meaning of the boy's remarks inflamed the encounter at the school. Something needed to happen to address the issue without letting it overwhelm everything else that was happening.

That Jerry's words came from the streets was likely. Whether they also came from home, no one could know. What was evident at the time was that the parents were in great pain when they apologized to the teacher. They addressed her with a directness and simplicity that appeared sincere. They came in with their own heritage—Italian and probably Catholic. There was an old world respectfulness about them. They had a humility that seemed natural and even becoming—humility that came from an old society that understood authority and the respect that was its due. Jerry brought two worlds into a painful encounter. The parents spoke what they felt. The teacher was left with what she felt.

Everyone in the room was hyper-aware of the tension related to race when the homeroom teacher passed around the note with Jerry's words. If the other two teachers with whom Jerry got along had not also been African American, it would have been difficult to get past the racial issue. They spoke comfortably about Jerry. They helped refocus on Jerry as an angry and anxious acting-out boy who happened to have picked up a weapon of hate that was at hand in a racially conflicted environment.

THE PROCESS AND GOALS OF
THE INTERVIEW

The therapists worked with the systems through the decisions they made in engaging with the parties in search of solutions. At the beginning of the family-school session, the therapists took the initiative of organizing the seating in the room, not only to facilitate talking among all those present but also to help establish their leadership in the process. Once that was done, the principal launched into listing Jerry's offenses. As soon as the therapists realized what was happening, they asked the principal if they could first give the family a chance to introduce themselves and say something about Jerry at home. Had the principal controlled the initial transactions and fixed the focus on Jerry's bad behavior, the session could well have been about a delinquent boy, instead of about a troubled boy. Much of the therapists' efforts would have been absorbed in trying to dig out of a negative hole. Instead, it began with a rather caring and warm family talking about their troubles and how hard they were trying to do the right thing. As part of that family, Jerry began to look like just a youngster with some understandable problems.

One therapist then moved to connect with Jerry. He wanted the boy to feel some safety in the room so that he could both tell his story and be open to hearing everyone else. He hoped the boy's anxiety at the moment would subside enough so that he could drop his sullen mask and allow his vulnerability to appear. The therapist also hoped others would soften enough toward Jerry to be more open to understanding and helping him.

The therapists also gave the parents a chance to show both that they were holding Jerry accountable and that they felt horror about the hurt he had caused the teacher. The school personnel did not have to criticize or pressure them to do right by the offended teacher. The parents, indeed, demonstrated themselves to be without any defensiveness about what had happened. They genuinely wanted to repair the wrong.

This freed the homeroom teacher to return to her classroom knowing she had been justified by all. The other school personnel did not have to come to her defense. The therapists were free to engage with the school staff to concentrate on fixing Jerry's problem. The staff moved toward making changes in the school and accepting the parents' cooperation. Jerry was getting in place an ecosystem that could help him.

The family and school contracted in that very first session to follow a course of action that began during the session and lasted several months. The basic goals of the first session were to gain a consensus among all parties about the formulation of the problem, the specific goals of the joint effort, and who and how to approach a solution in a coordinated and cooperative fashion. The joint family-school interview gave all the work that followed a powerful starting boost. Jerry, his family, and the school eventually achieved all their major objectives.

6. "Too Many Bosses"

Any family therapy model based on systems thinking that intends to integrate the community into its approach must include the community with the family in its field of intervention. This field includes parts of the community that proximately contribute to a family's problems and that are, immediately, potential resources in solving a family's problems. The terms "proximate" and "immediate" refer to the direct influence on a family's daily life that a community agency, organization, or even individual professional may have on a family. Less proximate and immediate community influences may, indeed, be social conditions that create a context for a problem, but they do not directly generate the specific issue.

A FAMILY IN TREATMENT WITH ITS COMMUNITY

The preceding chapter described a session with a family in a school with all the main players from the school: the principal, the teachers, and the school counselor. Here I present segments of two sessions with a family in a mental health center with representatives from two agencies, the state's child protective services and a local shelter for youth. Because these institutions were vitally

Theresa Romeo-Aponte contributed invaluable editorial assistance on this paper.

This interview was originally presented in an edited videotaped version with commentary entitled "Too Many Bosses," which was developed at the University of Medicine and Dentistry of New Jersey with the assistance of Monica McGoldrick.

involved, any effort to resolve the family's predicament had to include them. The work with the agencies in this example turned out to be more of a challenge for the consultant than the family.

Let us look at the plight of a woman, whom we will call Doris Daniels, who is at the heart of her family's turbulence and in the middle of a labyrinth of social institutions. She is African American, in her early thirties, working, and in her second marriage. She has a three-year-old daughter by her current marriage and two children by a prior union, Stanley, nine, and Nadine, 13. Nadine is her main source of worry.

Nadine has been running away from home. Otherwise, she is a good kid. She is cooperative at home and attends school regularly, even when she takes off from home. However, at this point she has elected to be in a youth shelter rather than return home. No one can understand why. When the court agreed to Nadine's placement in the shelter, it referred the family to a community mental health center for counseling.

A consultant was called in by the mental health center to meet with the family. He requested that all family members be invited along with any social agencies that were involved with Nadine's problem. I will present excerpts from the consultant's two sessions with the family and agencies. Therapeutically, the clinician worked both strategically and supportively. More than that, at the heart of his approach with the family was his commitment to their freedom and their power to choose their own destiny.

The family members who attended the first interview were Doris, her children, Stanley and Nadine, along with Doris' mother, who is an outpatient at the center, and Shirley, Doris' 17-year-old sister, who is living with Doris by court order. Doris' husband, Howard, who is Stanley's and Nadine's stepfather, would not come and kept their three-year-old daughter home with him. The representatives of the agencies who attended were a social worker from the state's child protective services, who is supervising Shirley's placement with Doris, and a counselor from the youth shelter where Nadine lives by court order. In the second session of the consultation, a therapist from the community mental health center, who was to continue with the family, also joined the consultant, along with Doris, Nadine, and the counselor from the shelter.

The center's therapist had seen the family between consulting sessions. The proceedings from that session are not reported here.

Why the Crowd?

Doris does not operate alone. Her care of the children involves a lot of other people, who now claim a share of Doris' life. Her husband, Howard, has a say in all her disciplining of the children at home. Because Doris also has her sister, Shirley, with her, their mother, who is at war with Nadine, regularly advises Doris on Shirley's care. Moreover, because Shirley is with Doris by court order, the child protective worker and, through her, the courts, also oversee Doris' care of Shirley. Finally, because Nadine is in a shelter, the staff from the shelter is in the middle of Doris' relationship with Nadine. Indeed, Doris' world is a complex one, not unlike that of many other low-income parents who depend upon public agencies.

The inclusion in our sessions of Doris' family, along with the social agencies, gave us a chance to see most of the people who were active players in Doris' life. Having them participate allowed us to influence their roles in the drama. In the segments of the sessions reported here, we demonstrate a simple clinical strategy to empower a woman in her family and social context.

The First Session

The session began with Doris introducing her family to the consultant. The social worker from protective services and the counselor from the shelter introduced themselves.

Doris' mother started the session aggressively accusing Shirley of being a "troublemaker." Shirley became defensive. It became evident why Shirley was living away from her mother. They could negotiate nothing between them. The session stalled and the consultant turned to Doris, looking for somewhere to go.

DORIS Okay. Well, I don't really know where to start. I don't know whether to start with my sister and I don't know whether to start with my daughter, but first we'll get on my daughter

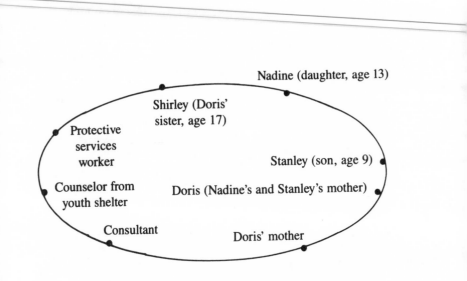

Figure 6.1.
Seating in Stage One of the First Session

because she keeps running away from home. Okay. Last Sunday she ran away from home. . . . She left home because she had a disagreement with her stepfather saying that she couldn't go skating.

. . .

And I guess she didn't like what he told her about not going. So, she left the house. She didn't call home. I didn't know where she was. . . . And then the next morning I decided to call the school to see if she was there, and she was in school. . . . She talked to the vice principal by herself and said she didn't like my husband, something like that, and I asked her, you know, like, well, before we got down to the Youth Office [of the police department], I asked her if she wanted to come home, and she told me, ''No.'' She didn't want to come back to the house. She didn't really give any stable reason why. She didn't want to come back. He asked her what she wanted to do. Well, he couldn't just release her . . .

CONSULTANT Right.

DORIS And so he gave her a choice. He said, ''Well, you could go to the youth shelter or you could go home with your mother,'' and she said she wanted to go to the youth shelter . . . so we went to court on Wednesday, and she still refused to come home. So that's where she is now, in the youth shelter. And I want to know what's her problem.

. . .

CONSULTANT Why don't you ask your daughter why she doesn't want to live with you?

DORIS Why don't you want to live with me?

NADINE I don't know.

DORIS You have to have a good reason. You just can't keep taking off and doing what you feel like doing.

NADINE I don't have a reason.

. . .

DORIS There has to be a reason Nadine. What is it?

NADINE Nothing.

DORIS (*To the consultant*) We could go on like this for hours. We're still not getting anything out of her.

CONSULTANT Nadine, is there anybody at home that you do talk to? You're not friends with your brother here?

NADINE We always fight.

. . .

CONSULTANT What about Shirley?

. . .

NADINE I talk to her, but I don't talk about no problems.

CONSULTANT (*To Shirley*) Are you two friends?

. . .

SHIRLEY Uh huh.

. . .

CONSULTANT (*To Shirley*) . . . you don't look happy.

DORIS She's not happy.

CONSULTANT Now, you didn't want to come here today, right? I assume that's part of the reason why you're not happy, but is there any other reason why you're not happy?

SHIRLEY Uh huh. I don't believe in coming to see no psychiatrist. There ain't nothing wrong with me.

CONSULTANT Living in her [Doris's] house. Is that all right with you? You like it there? . . . What is not going well at home?

SHIRLEY Arguing.

CONSULTANT Who's arguing?

SHIRLEY Me and my mother. . . . My sister's mean . . . 'cause she got my mother talking to her on the phone and that's why. And she be talking about stupid stuff.

. . .

CONSULTANT But what does your sister pick on you about?

SHIRLEY Cause the things she [Mother] be calling her [Doris] up and telling her.

CONSULTANT But, then your sister says the same things your mother does.

SHIRLEY Yeah, 'cause she [Mother] goin' keep calling her. Keep telling her this and that. Now why do [she] want to hear all that?

. . .

CONSULTANT All right. Because when you said somebody was mean you were talking about your sister. Right? . . . is that the reason why Nadine doesn't want to be in the house?

SHIRLEY Is that right Nadine?

NADINE I don't know.

SHIRLEY You know that. Cause you even said that yourself.

. . .

CONSULTANT [Nadine said] "My mother's mean," and she doesn't like Howard?

SHIRLEY Uh huh.

CONSULTANT So then we do know why she doesn't want to be in

the house. . . . You just don't want to say it. . . . (*To Nadine*)
Your mother's mean, and you don't like Howard. Is that right?

NADINE I guess so.

. . .

CONSULTANT But, now the court's got you.

Nadine would not talk, but we had the advantage of having
her 17-year-old aunt, Shirley, in whom she confided. Shirley
spoke for herself and Nadine. She described how her mother was
putting pressure on Doris about Shirley. Doris, reacting to their
mother in turn pressured Shirley. She was becoming "mean."
Howard was also playing a role in making Doris "mean"—how
becomes clearer later.

The consultant then engages the two agency representatives.

CONSULTANT (*To both*) Who represents the court? Do either of
you? . . .

PROTECTIVE SERVICE Well, I was present at the time when Mrs. Daniels was given temporary custody, but I don't actually represent the court. I'm aware of what went on.

CONSULTANT But you're here in reference to Shirley. Aren't you?

PROTECTIVE SERVICE Right.

CONSULTANT Then what's your relationship to Shirley?

PROTECTIVE SERVICE I'm Shirley's social worker . . . from Youth
and Family Services.

CONSULTANT Has the court then said to Youth and Family Services,
you are to provide these services for Shirley? And do you report back to the court?

PROTECTIVE SERVICE Right.

CONSULTANT So, you tell on her in court.

PROTECTIVE SERVICE Okay.

CONSULTANT (*To the shelter's counselor*) And you're in the same
position with regard to Nadine?

COUNSELOR Not in such a—she's like her case worker. I just work
at the shelter where Nadine is.

CONSULTANT Right. But still, Nadine—the court knows that Nadine
     is at the shelter.

COUNSELOR Right. They put her there.

CONSULTANT Okay. So then the shelter represents in some way the
     court.

COUNSELOR I guess you could say so.

PROTECTIVE SERVICE I guess you could say we are connected some-
     what, but we don't—well, I don't like to say that I represent
     the court, you know, directly.

CONSULTANT But, you kind of have the court behind you.

PROTECTIVE SERVICE Well, I have to do what the court orders. Let's
     put it that way.

CONSULTANT Right.

The two agency representatives were there to help Shirley and
Nadine. While they were reluctant to be identified with the courts,
the consultant drew out that they operated with the power of the
courts behind them. They represented agencies that were not just
"helpers" to this family. Their word to the courts could decide the
family's future. The courts lent a coercive influence to the relationship these agencies had with Doris. It becomes evident that, inadvertently, the power of these agencies vis-à-vis Doris's parental
role contributed to disabling Doris.

In the second stage of the interview, the consultant asked everyone to leave the room except Shirley and Nadine. They blamed
Doris for their problems. The consultant employed a paradoxical
approach (a strategic intervention) with the girls of heaping more
blame on Doris to get the girls to push back and defend her.

CONSULTANT What are you two ladies going to do? You're really
     living in a place [where] you don't want to live—you know—
     in her house. What are . . . you going to do to get out of there?

SHIRLEY Stay with somebody else.

CONSULTANT Shirley, why do you stay with your sister?

SHIRLEY Because I can't get along with my mother.

CONSULTANT But, you don't like your sister.

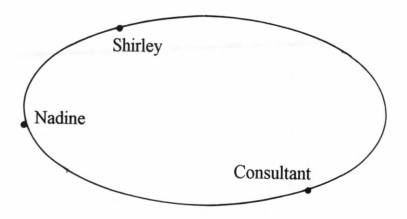

Figure 6.2.
Seating in Stage Two of the First Session

SHIRLEY My sister, she's all right.

CONSULTANT You don't really like being there. And neither does
    Nadine. (*To Nadine*) You know, your brother says he doesn't
    like it. He says your mother is mean. Has he said that to you?
    (*Stanley had earlier in the session also criticized Doris.*)

NADINE Uh huh.

CONSULTANT What is she like, that nobody wants to stay with her?

NADINE Some time she in a good mood, some time she just—I don't
    know.

CONSULTANT Is she in a bad mood a lot?

NADINE Most of the time, yeah.

CONSULTANT Your brother said it right to her face. He said what you wouldn't say.

NADINE What?

CONSULTANT Well, he said that she was very mean and he said that—he didn't run away because he didn't know where to go.

NADINE He ran away before.

CONSULTANT What?

. . .

NADINE Yeah, to my grandmother's house.

CONSULTANT Maybe your brother should be in this room, too—I mean, your mother seems to be trying, but your mother seems to be failing with you. . . . Nobody likes your mother. What is it about her that she gets in bad moods? I don't understand.

NADINE That's because her husband be there. . . .

CONSULTANT What does her husband have to do with it?

NADINE Cause he mean—and the things [he] be doing. He gets after her and he don't like the things and all.

CONSULTANT He doesn't like what?

NADINE He just don't. Mostly he don't like—say, if we sitting down and she sitting down and the house ain't cleaned up, he'll say, "Can't anybody clean up in here?" and he don't do nothing in there.

. . .

CONSULTANT . . . You mean he talks to her in a way that gets her to get down on everybody else? That right?

NADINE Yeah.

. . .

SHIRLEY Nadine and [Stanley] ain't got the same father and that's their stepfather, and he treats Nadine different from the way he treat his little girl.

. . .

CONSULTANT Yeah, but still, you know, it's her own mother who is not treating her right.

SHIRLEY Yeah, 'cause of him. . . . They wouldn't get along, like, you know, 'cause when he be there and, everything, like he tells Nadine and them to do stuff, and you have to listen and everything, and then he told them to clean the basement and things don't even need to be cleaned up.

CONSULTANT What did you say about their getting along?

SHIRLEY Oh, they don't, 'cause her and Howard—like he gots another girlfriend and everything, and Doris is trying to make her marriage work and everything, trying to keep their house together because, you know. . . .

. . .

CONSULTANT So, she has to get along with him, and to get along with him, she's got to be mean with you?

. . .

SHIRLEY Yeah, 'cause she listen to everything Howard say.

CONSULTANT (*To Nadine*) Is that true?

NADINE They get in arguments. And he tell her to shut up, and she say, "You ain't my father telling me what to do," and when she tell him to shut up, he like get mad and stuff like that. He don't like nobody tell him what to do, so he tells her what to do instead.

CONSULTANT Do you think your mother would be different if Howard were not there?

NADINE Uh huh.

By this point, the lineup is complete. Not only are Doris' mother, the courts, and the agencies converging to supervise Doris, but also her husband, Howard, is watching her every move. Under scrutiny from all sides, Doris is more pressured than helped. She is even being criticized by her own children and her sister, who are targeting her in their rebellion. Trying to satisfy everyone, she succeeds only in becoming prey to their control. The consultant needs to *support* Doris's position of authority in the family against the incursions of power from everyone around her.

The consultant now invites Doris to join him and the girls. As a *strategy* he paints Doris as a person made to fail, hopefully a sympathetic figure to Shirley and Nadine. He wants Doris to let go of responsibility for what she cannot control. Her efforts to help where she is in reality helpless just bring her stress, blame, and disappointment. He wants to free her to reconnect with her sister and daughter with her love for them and not a fruitless power struggle. He works to bring her in from the cold.

CONSULTANT *(To Doris)* When you were away, I ended up feeling sorry for you because it sounded to me like you are not leading a very happy life now. Your mother is putting a lot on you to help her, and that's a really bad pressure on you. Shirley doesn't want to be with you. Your daughter doesn't want to be with you. Stanley doesn't want to be with you. And from

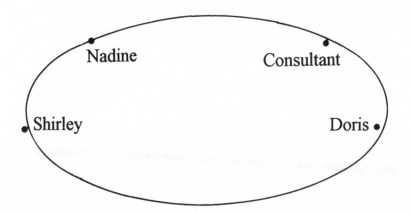

Figure 6.3.
Seating in Stage Three of the First Interview

what they told me, your marriage isn't very great. Is that right? (*Pause*) Nadine says that you've been crying? Right? In some ways it sounds to me like you are suffering and nobody is realizing how tough your life really is. Everybody's turning to you to save them, and the fact is that everything is working out wrong for you. Because I was asking, who's worrying about Doris? Doesn't seem like anybody's worrying about Doris. Everybody thinks Doris is going to fix everything up. Doris can't fix herself up. . . . You're trying to act like the one who is going to take care of everybody, including your mother.

DORIS It's always been like that.

The consultant now attempts to force Doris from the seat of overresponsibility by calling her a "failure," a strong word for a woman who is already discouraged. While in literal isolation the word appears to be critical, in the context of the relationship it communicates caring, someone who sees just how bad things are for her. Her reaction is the relief of tears.

CONSULTANT Doris, you've failed. And your life is falling apart right now. So, why fake it? Why keep acting like you can do something that you really can't do? You have too many people's problems on your shoulders, and it's not working out—
        Is your marriage going to make it?

DORIS I doubt it.

CONSULTANT You doubt it.

DORIS I don't think I'm going to make it sometimes.

CONSULTANT What do you mean by that?

DORIS I'm just tired.

CONSULTANT I can understand that . . .

Doris cries quietly for a long while. No one speaks. Shirley is seen wiping tears away from her eyes. Nadine is looking down sadly. The consultant hands Doris a tissue. Doris goes on to tell about the despair of her childhood. The consultant speaks to the loneliness of today.

CONSULTANT Who do you tell when you get like this?

DORIS There's nobody to talk to, really. Sometimes I talk to my friends, but, you know, it's not like I express how I really feel inside.

CONSULTANT (*The consultant worries about suicide.*) Have you ever thought of killing yourself?

DORIS Not as yet. I just get away from everything. I just be by myself. Because the more I try to help, the more worser it gets.

. . .

I never had that many friends. I was, you know, basically by myself . . . when I got married to [Nadine's] father it got worse because he wasn't ready . . . we separated and I went back home and home got worse. I moved out . . . with her by myself and I couldn't make it. . . . I really wanted to be married with somebody that was stable and her father wasn't stable— he just wanted to—go and wanted no responsibility. After that I started going to church and then I met my present husband. . . . He seemed like . . . somebody that was going to work and be responsible . . . but, you know, we argued and fussed . . . the marriage became sort of shaky because we couldn't have a relationship. . . . I just tried to bear it and then my mother came with her problems and was always back and forth— back and forth—back and forth. I tried to help her and things weren't working out right. Everything's been shaky. . . .

CONSULTANT (*To Shirley*) Your sister's life doesn't sound very different from yours in some way. You don't have any place, really, where you feel happy and Nadine is going the same route. She doesn't have any place she feels happy either. All three of you are going through—have gone through—feeling more unhappiness. Actually, Doris is going through it right now. Her life isn't settled.

. . .

Doris, you love your sister. That doesn't mean you can take care of her. I think she loves you. As you were talking about how really bad things were, she was crying for you. Okay, but if you two have any basis for getting along, it's because you care for each other, not because you're going to be her mother.

You two have to sit down as sisters, not as mother and daughter, and if you two want to have any kind of closeness, you two have to sit down and talk about that. . . . Maybe you can be a place that Shirley can stay for a little while before she decides to go off on her own—she's going to go off on her own.

DORIS I know that.

CONSULTANT But, the only way she can stay with you is because your mother is not a part of it. Your mother has to stay out of it.

DORIS That's easier said than done.

CONSULTANT You can't pass on your mother's messages. If your mother's got a problem with Shirley, your mother's got to deal with Shirley herself, and Shirley's going to have to battle her mother herself, and you've got to stay out of the middle. . . . With Nadine, it's not different, unfortunately. The sadness here is that Nadine is your daughter. But, if you can't handle it with Nadine, you can't handle it with her. You cannot force her. She's too old now. If Nadine doesn't want to be with you, she doesn't want to be with you.

DORIS Then who does she want to be with, then?

CONSULTANT That's up to her. You know, you have something to offer Nadine that nobody else in the world can give her, that's your love of her. Everybody in the world can discipline her. She can go to the detention center and they can discipline her. She can go to a foster home and they will discipline her. Okay. The court will discipline her. Nobody can give her the love that you have for her. Hold on to that. Let Nadine decide whether she wants to be with you. . . .

Doris, this has been a consultation. . . . I'm going to be working with some of the people at the [mental health] center that you go to. Maybe I can have you come back. I don't know if you want to come back to try to help you get a little control of your life . . . so instead of being responsible for your whole family, you're responsible for yourself. Okay? If anybody wants to be close to you that's up to them. . . .

The consultant shifted the focus of the interview from the troublesome girls to the troubled Doris. Her life is full of loneliness and disappointment, but she is conscientious and tries to do it all. She is overwhelmed.

The consultant creates a connection between Doris and the girls by talking about the love between them and getting away from words of coercion that would come from the courts, Doris's mother, and Howard. He wants Doris and the girls to identify with one another and feel the affection between them. He wants them to feel free to move toward one another, so they can choose the closeness and intimacy of their relationships if they so wish. This is a *supportive* intervention.

The consultant then tries to gain the cooperation of the agencies with his strategy. He meets with them alone in stage four of the session.

CONSULTANT . . . The reason why I told Nadine and Shirley to start thinking about going is to relieve them of the expectation that they *have* to be in Mrs. Daniels' home. If they want to be there, it's up to them. . . . It's sad—very sad—but you can't force them.

PROTECTIVE SERVICE I understand where you're coming from. The unrealistic part of this is where it's going.

CONSULTANT I have no illusions about that. I know what that's like, but I mean, if we try to force them together, it just makes it worse. . . . I offered that we would try to be of some help to Mrs. Daniels. She said she wants it. . . . And I said if Nadine wants to come in and if Shirley wants to come in and be part of that, it's up to them. . . .

PROTECTIVE SERVICE Okay. Did she explain to you what went on in the courts that day? I think she just felt like being the party that should have taken responsibility for her sister that particular day. Otherwise, she probably would have gone into detention or possibly a foster home, should we have been able to find one for her. But, Mrs. Daniels felt, "Okay, what am I supposed to do? I'm the older sister and I'll take her rather than send her to the detention home."

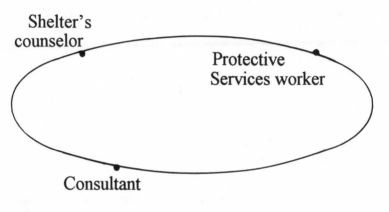

Figure 6.4.
Seating in Stage Four of the First Session

CONSULTANT I'll tell you what I would suggest at this point. . . . You talk seriously, each of you, with Nadine and Shirley about what alternatives they [have]. If they want to go back with Mrs. Daniels, then I think they need to talk . . . with her privately about why they want to be there and how they would work it out. . . . I think something can be done to help them—it can't be done without you because this is a situation where these young people without you have nobody [outside the family]. I don't know where they'd go and they need somebody to help them make decisions. . . . That's all I see this as, a period of decision. . . . They'll need some support. . . . There were no other resources. . . .

PROTECTIVE SERVICE Like I said, I'm here. . . .

The strategy was to change the girls' perception of Doris from someone who controls them to someone who loves them. By freeing Doris of having to compel them to stay with her, they may see her as someone with whom they *want* to be. This strategy would not be practical unless the agencies offered alternative living arrangements to the girls. The protective services worker and the shelter's counselor agreed to the plan with misgivings about what alternatives they could offer to Doris' home. Doris left the session knowing she had been trying to do the impossible, and that she needed to listen to her own counsel.

The mental health center's staff, who witnessed the session from behind an observation mirror, agreed to the consultant's plan. The center assigned a therapist to the family.

The Second Session

Things did not go as planned. Within a week of the session, the shelter, which had a policy limiting how long they kept youngsters, informed the mental health center's therapist that they could no longer keep Nadine. They insisted that Nadine be returned home. The therapist and Doris, believing that they had no choice, acceded. They, with the shelter, acted out of a sense of powerlessness in the face of bureaucratic policy. The needs of the family were lost in the process. Predictably, within days, Nadine again ran away from home and was back in the shelter.

Two weeks after the consultant's initial session with the family and agencies, he was invited by the therapist to meet with her, Doris, Nadine, and the counselor from the shelter. There was a remarkable change in Doris. She was obviously not depressed. She was energetic, assertive, and attractively groomed. Even Nadine appeared more relaxed and open.

What was different was that Doris no longer felt responsible for Nadine's choices, and so she could hold Nadine and the shelter accountable for their decisions. She was free to take a position that was her own in the face of whatever everyone else wanted to do. You could feel a weight had lifted from her shoulders.

We enter the session as the consultant is concluding a discussion with Nadine about arranging to see her mother regularly if

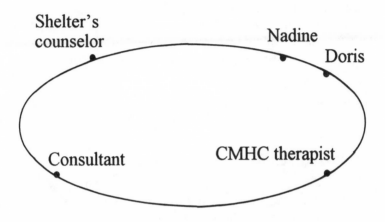

Figure 6.5.
Seating for Second Session

and when she decides to go to a foster home. The consultant was *strategically* offering her the option of living away from her mother while nurturing the bond with her mother. He then spotlights for Doris her *free choice* to hold onto her power to decide about what to do with Nadine when confronted by the power of the system's pressure.

CONSULTANT (*To Nadine*) Okay. That's clear. When you go to the foster home, would you like to visit this lady [her mother] or have her visit you once in a while? . . . Would you like to be friendly with her?

NADINE Uh huh.

. . .

CONSULTANT (*To Doris*) I've done your job for you.

DORIS Thank you.

CONSULTANT I have only one question of you at this point. . . . Is the case worker going to be able to talk you into forcing Nadine back into your home?

DORIS No. Not if she don't want to be there. No. Uh uh. I'm not taking the chance that she's going to run away from home. I know the judge on Wednesday said that she had nine months probation.

CONSULTANT (*To Nadine*) You're going to run away again, right?— if you go home.

NADINE I don't know.

CONSULTANT Oh, come on. Sure you do. You'll run away again because nothing's changed [at home].

. . .

(*To Doris*) She [Nadine] loves you, and she'd like to be connected with you. So, there's a part of her that's going to want to give in and go along with that [urge to return home] with this little unrealistic hope that things are going to be different. They're not [yet]. Can you refuse the case worker and say, "No. I won't accept her home"?

DORIS Uh huh!

CONSULTANT Do you feel convinced?

DORIS Very convinced. . . . Since the last time I've been here, I feel good. Now, since I talked about it last night, if she doesn't want to come home, you know, I'm not going to force her to come home.

CONSULTANT By the way, her not coming home doesn't mean she doesn't love you.

DORIS I understand that.

CONSULTANT Good. So that means then that she can be at the shelter, or she can be at a foster home, care about you . . . and not have to fight with you and you not have to fight with her. Then maybe you two can become closer than you have ever been. . . . So, if she goes into a foster home, you can visit together, talk together. . . . She doesn't want to be cut off from you. You are free.

The Agency's Problem
or the Family's?

The consultant then turns to the counselor from the shelter to ask whether she sees merit in giving Nadine the option of finding another place to live.

CONSULTANT Does any of this make sense?

COUNSELOR . . . Unrealistic, but it makes sense, I guess. It's unrealistic.

CONSULTANT What's unrealistic?

COUNSELOR Just 'cause the whole plan—I mean it sounds nice for you to sit there and say you can't go home and so on and so forth, but when it comes down to actually putting Nadine someplace else. . . . It's like there aren't any foster homes, but that's just an old story. So, it's unrealistic, but we'll see what happens.

CONSULTANT Well, I'll tell you. The unrealistic part of it is going to be Nadine's problem with the [shelter].

COUNSELOR Right.

CONSULTANT (*The consultant becomes an advocate.*) It will not be Doris' problem to figure that one out. That's going to be somebody else's to figure out how to deal with this. . . . I know how difficult it is, but it is as unrealistic for Nadine to go back, more unrealistic for her to try to go back home where she's not going to stay, than for other arrangements to be made for her. And that is the reality that has to be faced. . . .

DORIS That's true because you know I tried, and she came right back home and ran again. . . . I mean, the next time she might run I might lose my temper and then they may have me for child abuse, and I'm serious about that. Very serious.

CONSULTANT See, 'cause you are . . . pushed to act in violent ways you don't want to act in when other people coerce you to do things that you know you can't handle.

DORIS I've tried.

CONSULTANT And they put you with your back up against the wall and everybody says to you they can't change—you must make the impossible work. That's when you don't do well.

DORIS What if I die today or tomorrow? . . .

CMHC THERAPIST What you're saying is that they'll have the responsibility then and there's no reason. . . .

DORIS Yeah, the responsibility then. . . . If she's not happy, I can't force her to stay home with me, and I'm not going to try.

CMHC THERAPIST It's a good point. Say that to the worker.

DORIS No, I am—I pay taxes. I'm working every day, you know. Somebody's got to do something. They do it for everybody else. I don't see why they can't do it for my house. . . .

CONSULTANT I think you're very clear.

DORIS I am very clear.

Doris had changed markedly since the first consultation two weeks before. She had set limits on how much interference she would take from her mother and her husband about her care of Shirley and Nadine. Even in the face of opposition from the shelter, she assumed a firm attitude about what help she expected from the agency. Doris got out of her powerless position in relation to the agencies. Also, while obviously caring about Nadine, she took a well defined position with her about her running away. She reported doing the same at home with Shirley about her behavior. In the midst of all the pressures and involvement from family and agencies, Doris set definite boundaries around her supervision of the children and assumed control of her own life. She could now begin to solve some of the other problems she shared with the rest of the family.

Spirit

Doris brought to the work a deep sense of responsibility toward her family. It worked against her when it seemed that everyone saw her as responsible for solving all the family's problems and the limitations confronting the agencies trying to help. The convergence of her disposition to take on responsibility and others' tendencies to place responsibility on her just crushed her. The consultant helped her distinguish between her responsibilities and those of her daughter and the agencies. That freed her to do what she thought right for herself and Nadine, and put her in a position to hold the agencies accountable for their job.

Love was also a key element in this effort. Behind the fighting there was much caring among Doris, Shirley, and Nadine. Once the therapist tapped into their affection and commitment to one another, their love became a powerful source of trust and motivation in their transactions with each other. In the end it allowed them to differentiate from one another without feeling that they were losing one another. Doris's moves to separate her responsibilities from everyone else's and her growing security about the love between her and Nadine and Shirley empowered her in her dealings with the agencies.

Bread

The shelter faced the difficult reality of limited resources—in this case, foster homes for adolescents. The shelter staff did not believe they could find an alternative to returning Nadine home. Consequently, the shelter unintentionally shifted the burden of the problem onto the client. In this case, Doris and Nadine would have been defeated had Nadine been again prematurely discharged to her home. She was not.

Would the consultant have fully appreciated what Doris faced from family and agency had they not all been present in the sessions? Would the two professionals have gone as far as they did toward agreeing to the plan if they had not observed Doris's distress and determination and shared in planning a solution? Would Doris have taken a strong stand with the agencies had she not experienced the consultant's and therapist's support? With the help of these interventions, Doris rebounded and insisted on her rights with the agencies. Subsequently, with the backing of the community mental health center and the conflicted cooperation of the agencies, Doris prevailed and followed through with the agencies and her family.

CONCLUSION

To carry out his strategy for Doris and her family the consultant needed to meet with both the family members and the agencies' representatives in the same room. The solution to Nadine and Doris's problem nested in the family and in the family's relationship with the community agencies. The heart of the work revolved around a recognition of Doris's spirit of commitment to herself and her family. It was nourished by the mental health center's active support and advocacy for Doris and her family. The spirit of this family held it together against all odds. The bread of activism moved a difficult system to provide what it did not think it could.

The example cited here of dealing with the community as integral to the treatment of a family represents a way to look at therapy with a community perspective. Such a model calls for a reorganization of the service delivery systems as radical as family therapy's challenge to individual therapy. Agencies relate to the social, economic, and political environment of the community they serve, as well as to the case by case relationship of community to families in treatment. Clinicians make assessments not just on the basis of the internal organization of families but also on the interface between family and community. The administrative organization of clinics and their funding need to support this work, which is incompatible with the 50-minute hour. Teams of clinicians, community specialists, and agency administrative leaders need to organize flexibly to contend with the complex family and social circumstances faced by families today. We speak here of a model that radically reorients therapy for everyone and is not just limited to the treatment of the poor.

Our future as therapists lies in being able to understand the relationship of today's society to family life and in being able to intervene effectively in the relationship between the two.

Don't Get Simple, I Cry"

On rare occasions, an encounter with a family becomes a beacon to a career. So it was with a family I call the Hannons, which demonstrated not only classic struggles, but also the spirit and courage to overcome both the family's own limitations and the obstacles of poverty and race. A single consultation crystallized my understanding, empathy, and hope for the Hannons of this world.

The Hannon family is poor, African American, and headed by a single parent. The Hannons live in an urban ghetto. They are a classically underorganized family lacking the constant, coherent, and elaborated internal structure necessary to meet adequately the personal needs of its members and the demands of the world outside. They live with constant stress.

Social service agencies and mental health clinics find it difficult to work with the Hannons of this world. Its members present a myriad of personal, familial, and social problems. They live from one crisis to another. In therapy they appear chaotic, but hidden behind the apparent confusion is anxiety, depression, and fear. Such a family can be a source of discouragement for therapists who do not see and connect with the pain, struggle, and potential of its members.

THE SESSION

The opening moments of the initial session with the Hannon family were disconcerting, but as the session evolved the family revealed itself with piercing clarity.

Theresa Romeo-Aponte co-authored this chapter.

For its first session at the clinic, the Hannon family came with nine of its members from three generations: Mrs. Hannon, 47, her children, Vera, 22, Toby (a.k.a. Marie), 18, Joan, 17, Jack, 16, Mark, 12, and Earl, 11, and Vera's two children, Rita, 3, and Curt, 1½. The identified patient was Joan, who reportedly was having problems in school. She is a heavyset young woman with a cherubic face and intense manner that ranged from manic to sweet, quiet seriousness. Her mother had made the appointment.

The session begins with the family walking into an interview room equipped with an observation mirror, microphones, and TV cameras. One of the youngsters is loudly playing a portable radio as family members walk about examining and commenting about the strange environment. The therapist is standing, observing and trying to settle them into their seats.

JACK You see the camera over there?

JOAN (*Looking at the microphones hanging from the ceiling*) They just want to know how crazy we are.

(*In her first statement, she tells us she and her family are troubled.*)

THERAPIST I don't want anybody in the corner over there. (*Pointing to blind corner where the TV cameras are located*)

JOAN Get out of the corner, Vera.

(*Her second statement allies her with the therapist to direct the family.*)

THERAPIST Come on and join us somehow. Pull the chair over. Yes. Right.

Most of the children are talking loudly, over each other and over the radio music. The therapist is drowning in noise, but persists in trying to seat the family. Mrs. Hannon, the mother, is quiet, watching. In the whirl of noise and movement, Joan is acting like a manic ring master. She is hyperalert, anxiously overseeing all that is happening and talking compulsively. She tries to respond to the therapist and manage her siblings, who are milling about like a class without the teacher. She rather sadly ridicules herself, saying, "I ain't got no sense, no way," and then, "I told you I was crazy." Joan even invites her siblings to tell the therapist how "crazy" she is. She will later characterize this behavior of hers as "simple." The pain behind the words stings.

A pattern emerges early in the session. The mother withdraws from the confusion while Joan attempts to tame it. To the therapist, Joan is taking on too much responsibility for organizing her family. She is trying alone. Working on this hypothesis, the therapist initially chooses to avoid reinforcing this role for Joan and directs most of his remarks to the other siblings. He uses what is happening to connect with the youngsters. He defers calling upon the mother, who looks but volunteers nothing.

The therapist then tries to involve some of the other older siblings, Vera, Toby, and Jack, in managing the commotion. He tests whether with some encouragement they can take over from Joan—to no avail. They seem unaffected by the confusion, which strengthens the therapist's impression that Joan has assumed a special role in the family. The worried pressure with which she describes how she, along with her siblings, are driving their mother "crazy" hints at a function that her centrality is serving— the protection of her mother.

The therapist then tries to engage Mrs. Hannon but is unable to keep her center stage for long.

THERAPIST Mrs. Hannon, everybody else looks pretty happy except you.

JOAN She ain't got no sleep that's why.

VERA AND MARK (*Speaking simultaneously—inaudible*)

JOAN She just got home from work.

THERAPIST Did you really just get home from work? (*Walks across the room and sits next to Mrs. Hannon*)

MRS. HANNON Uh huh.

JOAN Tired as a (*inaudible because Vera talks simultaneously and Curt yells at Earl*).

EARL I bet she is gonna go to sleep as soon as she go home.

. . .

THERAPIST What do you work at?

MRS. HANNON Cleaning offices, eleven to seven.

THERAPIST Eleven to seven every night?

MRS. HANNON Uh huh.

THERAPIST And you have all these kids to take care of by yourself?

(*The children are teasing Curt, who suddenly yells as the noise escalates.*)

VERA We all take care of each other.

THERAPIST (*To Mrs. Hannon*) Are you just tired or are you really as unhappy as you look?

MRS. HANNON No, I'm just tired.

VERA She's not unhappy.

JOAN (*Curt yelling persistently as Joan talks.*) Yes, she is unhappy. She just don't want to tell nobody. I'll tell you why she is unhappy. She is sick and tired of us. She wants me to go to school and get graduated, but I don't like school. She wants her [Toby] to stop acting like a fool. She wants him [Jack] to mind his business and stop messing around. She wants her [Vera] to get a house and get her kids and get together. She wants him [Earl] to get straightened out and go to school. And she don't worry about him [Mark], 'cause he ain't home. And me, I got nerves. Boy, I got some nerves on me.

EARL (*Pushing Curt who is wandering about*) Get out of here.

JACK I don't cause no problem for you all.

THERAPIST No?

JOAN (*Overlapping*) Ever since I can remember I had bad nerves. I shake, shake, shake. (*Gesturing*)

The therapist learns from Joan exactly how Mrs. Hannon is burdened. She works all night and takes care of her family during the day. Joan details how each of the children is a problem to Mrs. Hannon. One need only consider the overlaps—the way the siblings interrupted one another and spoke simultaneously—to appreciate how, except for Joan's, their roles in the family are indistinct. The therapist then tries to get a reading on the mother's position on the family.

Her Gorilla Suit

THERAPIST *(To Mrs. Hannon)* How do you handle all this?

JOAN She don't. She don't.

THERAPIST *(To Joan)* No, wait a minute. *(To Mrs. Hannon)* I can't even talk to you 'cause everybody is talking for you. How do you handle all of this?

MRS. HANNON Put on my gorilla suit. That's all.

JOAN That's what she do. She can get very violent when she gets ready. Boy! *(Excited laughter and chatter among the children)*

VERA Everybody running in all directions to get away—"Don't run way from me!"

JOAN *(Overlapping)* She gets violent!

THERAPIST *(Ignoring Vera and Joan, and addressing Mrs. Hannon)* I imagine you have to get violent to keep things under control.

MRS. HANNON I'd better. If I don't get violent, they'll put me out of my own house.

THERAPIST But if you—tell me something—if you work all night, how do you rest in the daytime?

JOAN She don't most of the time.

THERAPIST *(To Mrs. Hannon)* See. I can't talk to you 'cause they talk for you.

MRS. HANNON I really don't.

THERAPIST You don't rest.

MRS. HANNON I get about two or three hours of sleep.

THERAPIST That's why you're so tired.

MRS. HANNON Uh huh. right.

THERAPIST How long have you been at this job?

MRS. HANNON Since March.

THERAPIST I mean, there must be something you can do in the daytime.

MRS. HANNON I prefer night. See, I have my father with me.

THERAPIST You have your father to take care of also?

MRS. HANNON Yeah, he's 77 and senile. So what else you going to do?

JOAN That's why we're here.

THERAPIST (*Ignoring Joan*) Man! No! You really—you can't get more than two or three hours of sleep if you're taking care of your father, all these kids. What did you do before March?

MRS. HANNON I didn't do anything. I was on DPA.

THERAPIST Why did you go to work?

MRS. HANNON Because I wanted to. I make more money.

THERAPIST Yeah, you make more money, but you must have gotten some rest that way.

MRS. HANNON Well, sure you get rest. You ain't got nothing else to do but stay home.

THERAPIST Do you like being out of the house to work?

MRS. HANNON No. I'd rather be home, but finances is finances.

THERAPIST You need the money.

MRS. HANNON That's right.

Mrs. Hannon is a poor, African American, single parent taking care of six children, two grandchildren, and her sickly father. She appears depressed, withdrawn, and overwhelmed by it all; however, she has a spirit, an inner strength, that does not let her quit. In the end she will be there for all of them and they know it.

THERAPIST (*Following a hunch*) How's your health?

MRS. HANNON Fine.

THERAPIST It's holding up?

MRS. HANNON Yeah.

JOAN Except for one thing.

THERAPIST Except for what?

JOAN Her nerves.

MRS. HANNON My nerves.

(*Confirmation!*)

THERAPIST Well, I'm not surprised. What is wrong with your nerves?

EARL (*Overlapping as he points to Curt who is standing on a chair while Mark teases him*) Get down from there. (*Curt yells in protest as Mark tries to pull him down.*)

MRS. HANNON They're tired that's all.

THERAPIST Were they like that before you went to work?

MARK (*Overlapping to Curt, who is yelling persistently*) Sit down!

MRS. HANNON Uh huh. Right. (*Children laugh at Curt.*)

THERAPIST Is anyone helping you with your nerves?

MRS. HANNON Like what?

THERAPIST Are you seeing a doctor?

MRS. HANNON Uh huh. Yeah, I have a doctor.

THERAPIST You have a doctor? Did he give you some pills?

MRS. HANNON Uh huh.

THERAPIST Do they help?

MRS. HANNON Right.

MARK (*To Curt, who is standing on a chair and still yelling*) You had better sit.

CURT No! (*Mrs. Hannon and the therapist stop talking as all watch the struggle between Mark and Curt.*)

THERAPIST (*Too distracted to continue talking to Mrs. Hannon*) (*To Curt*) You're a tough guy, aren't you.
(*To Vera, Curt's mother*) How old is he?

VERA A year.

THERAPIST Boy! You'd never know he was only a year old. (*Mark tries to pull Curt down and Curt yells and kicks him.*)
(*To Vera*) Let me see. Do you think they could take care of him downstairs or would he not stay downstairs with the baby-sitter?

VERA No, I don't think he'll stay.

THERAPIST You don't think he'll stay.

(*The therapist is stymied by Curt, and Vera offers no help, but Mrs. Hannon reads what is happening and comes to the rescue.*)

MRS. HANNON (*To Mark*) Just ignore him. (*To Curt*) Sit down boy. Hey! Sit down! Down!

JOAN (*Overlapping*) Sit down, man.

MRS. HANNON Leave him alone, Mark. (*To Curt*) Hey! Sit down! Sit down! I'll bet I'll bash you if you don't sit down. (*Children guffaw.*)

JACK (*Overlapping*) Sit your behind down, boy. You better sit down.

JOAN That is why he is so super mean. 'Cause he don't like nobody to tell him what to do.

(*Mrs. Hannon walks over with a rolled-up newspaper and strikes Curt lightly on the legs.*)

MRS. HANNON Sit down! (*Excited comment and laughter from the children as Mrs. Hannon physically takes Curt off the chair and Curt whimpers and sits down quietly*)

MRS. HANNON You better shut it up.

(*Vera, Curt's mother, laughs like one of the children.*)

MRS. HANNON (*To everybody*) Now, leave him alone. It's not funny.

THERAPIST (*To Vera*) Would he listen to you the way he listens to her?

VERA Nope.

JOAN (*Overlapping*) No. He won't listen to nobody.

THERAPIST (*To Mrs. Hannon*) So you're kind of a mother to everybody.

MRS. HANNON I'm the mother of all of them.

This last scene epitomized for the therapist the dominant structural problem in the family—its underorganization. While Mrs. Hannon, stressed and overwhelmed, seeks refuge in withdrawal from the cacophony, Joan in her own way tries to take over for her. However, Joan has no authority over the other children. She is only able to draw the family's distress to herself and away from her mother through sheer manic energy. When the family needs someone to exercise authority, the mother is alone.

When Curt's screaming takes control of the session, no one can do anything with him except Mrs. Hannon. She spontaneously takes over when she sees the therapist's helplessness after Curt's mother, Vera, admits she can do nothing with Curt. Mrs. Hannon rescues the therapist as she does the family at home. She acts swiftly and firmly to quiet Curt by putting on her "gorilla suit." She carries the weight of executive authority totally on her shoulders. When the responsibility goes over her threshold, she withdraws and leaves the family in chaos. Joan then does her best to give her mother a respite, and offers herself as the emotional lightning rod for the stress and anxiety in the family. For this she pays a high price.

The therapist has become convinced that mother needs to get out of this isolated responsibility. However, Joan is not the solution. Joan is being crushed. Mrs. Hannon needs to be back in charge, but with help from everyone in the family.

THERAPIST You know. They said that Joan here was the one with the problem. I feel more for you than I feel for anybody else in this family. (*Mrs. Hannon laughs.*) I'm not kidding you. Don't you have any sisters or anybody else who can help out?

MRS. HANNON Sure I have sisters, but they're busy with their own problems.

THERAPIST They got their own problems. Okay. Tell me what was the problem with Joan.

When the therapist asks Mrs. Hannon about her family network, she replies as women in these circumstances are wont to answer—that their relatives are as overwhelmed as they. Each has to fend for herself. Yet we will later see that a sister does help. Right now, the therapist expands the exploration for resources into the Hannon family's community.

The Schools

MRS. HANNON Listen. I don't know what Joan's problem was. Joan didn't want to go to school. She came and told me she didn't belong.

JOAN I don't.

THERAPIST You don't?

JOAN Nope.

THERAPIST What do you mean you don't belong in school?

JOAN 'Cause people make me so mad. Boy! Like I go to school and they gave me the same thing over that I already had, and if I sit there and don't write it down on paper, boy!—they get so mad! And it's right.

THERAPIST Yeah?

JOAN And they give me a test. I don't even bring them home or study them or nothing, and I get a test. They say, "You didn't study." But I say, "I got it right." They think I cheat.

THERAPIST Yeah?

JOAN So, I ignore them.

VERA Rerun. Rerun. Rerun.

JOAN I just ignore them and I don't come.

VERA The stuff you get in elementary school you get in high school, and get the same thing, and you get tired of it and bored with it, and you don't want to do it, and they get all—

JOAN Like when I go to my geometry class—

THERAPIST Yeah?

JOAN And like say, I ain't been in about three weeks, and I go in there, and they have a test, and I do it right, my teacher swears I done cheated on somebody, cheated on somebody's paper. I just ignore her, tear it up, throw it in the trash, don't come the next day.

THERAPIST And you didn't cheat?

JOAN Uh uh!

VERA She had it already.

TOBY The same thing she had in elementary school and junior high school, that's all. Like the math—

MRS. HANNON Joan has repeated tenth grade three times.

VERA But they're giving her stuff that she already knows. Like she wants stuff higher that she can learn, so when she gets out of school and has kids and everything that she'll know what it's all about.

dramatic difference in this part of the session after
takes charge and focuses the family on Joan's school
re is no talking over one another, no competing; Vera
upportively validate Joan's experience. Their perception is that school does not teach, does not challenge, and, in fact,
does not expect them to learn. For these young people the world
outside the walls of their house is not only unhelpful but also inval-
idating and dangerous.

Feeling Scared

VERA 'Cause like she [mother] said, she was going to take me down
to get a job.

THERAPIST Yeah?

VERA She's still willing to help me and everything, and I'm still
willing to get out [of the house] with my husband or without
him. Like I want to get out on my own. Like my husband
don't decide to come or whether he do.

THERAPIST You don't know whether he's going to stay with you or
not?

VERA No. Like I want somebody in that house with me, because I
am afraid.

THERAPIST What do you mean you're afraid?

VERA I am afraid to be in the house by myself. Like if it ain't
nobody home but us kids, and I know they are all there, I will
sit up all night long and watch the door, the cellar, everything,
because I'm scared to be in there by myself.

THERAPIST Are you scared even though they're home?

VERA Even though they're all there because if he's [Jack] sleeping
and I go up there, "Jack, Jack, wake up!" (*Mimics him struggling to wake up*) Somebody walked in the house, looked upstairs. She [Joan] was in the kitchen washing dishes. My
brother was on the couch. He [the stranger] comes walking up
there. I look up there. I said, "Hey, who's that?" He goes
flying out the door, and all of us was in there, and her [Joan's]
boyfriend was upstairs in the bed sleeping. He was in the back
room sleeping.

. . .

THERAPIST Toby, are you afraid also?

TOBY Yes.

JOAN (*Overlapping*) You should—

THERAPIST (*Interrupting Joan*) Wait. Wait. (*To Toby*) Why are you afraid?

TOBY You feel like you're in a room by yourself, and everybody is closing in, and I can't be in a room by myself.

THERAPIST I mean, you're afraid when you're home, Toby?

TOBY Yeah.

THERAPIST Even when the family's there?

VERA If my mother's there, I'm not afraid.

TOBY If my mother's there, it's all right.

THERAPIST If your mother's there, it's all right.

TOBY Yeah, it's okay. Like when I get off from work, she's [Vera's] up waiting for me.

VERA I let them go to sleep, and she don't know I'm scared, but I sit downstairs watching television. I even watch television when there ain't nothing on there.

TOBY And like, when I come in there at two-thirty, she's up.

VERA And like when my mother do come in, when it does come daylight, then I fall asleep. I'll be so sleepy the next day that I don't want to be doing anything, long as they all sleep.

THERAPIST Yeah, but you stay up so that they'll feel better when they get home after they're out or what?

VERA No. While they're sleeping, I stay awake.

THERAPIST But why do you stay up? To watch them?

VERA 'Cause I'm scared to go to sleep. 'Cause something might happen and I might not wake up. Somebody breaks in or something might happen. And then, when I'm downstairs awake and they're upstairs sleeping, I go upstairs to check on all their rooms to make sure everybody's all right.

TOBY This is why we can't move out. 'Cause we're both scared.

THERAPIST This is why you can't move out. 'Cause you're both so scared?

VERA Right. See. Like to tell the truth, like I would of been gone a long time ago, but the situation was I knew I had to get out, right? Sooner or later. And I know my husband is not there too, right?

THERAPIST I understand. I understand.

This is a remarkably clear statement about the fear with which these young women live and which prevents them from moving out on their own. This underorganized family has not nurtured differentiated, strong individuals. The family members have no extended family support. Their neighborhood is dangerous. They cannot count on their community, as evidenced by the schools. In short, their world is too hard for them, and they are not internally prepared as individuals or a family to contend with it. Their mother stands as the lone knight protecting them against these dragons. But she is alone, and she gets tired.

The young women at times huddle to reassure one another, but do not see strength in themselves. The young men do not see themselves having any role at home. There was no male model for them at home. They are vulnerable in their own way. Doubtless, these boys' position outside in the community is also amorphous, unless they have gangs to give them some sense of belonging and power. They are all vulnerable.

THERAPIST And you're Mark, right? And who are you living with, Mark?

MARK My aunt.

THERAPIST (*To Mrs. Hannon*) That's your sister?

MRS. HANNON Yeah.

THERAPIST (*To Mark*) How did you get to—how come you're living with her?

MARK To go to school.

THERAPIST I don't understand. Why are you living with her to go to school?

MARK It's closer where my aunt lives.

MRS. HANNON Because he didn't want to go to one junior high school.

THERAPIST Yeah? Which one was that?

MRS. HANNON Washington.

MARK Yeah, Washington Junior High School.

THERAPIST (*Looking at Mrs. Hannon*) Yeah? He was afraid?

MRS. HANNON I was afraid myself [for him].

THERAPIST You were afraid? All right.

MRS. HANNON So I got him to transfer to Eighteenth and High Street, but in order for him to go to Bavok Junior High School, he had to live in my sister's house.

THERAPIST Is that a better school?

MRS. HANNON Well to him, he thinks so.

Fear of violence in a school has forced Mark to leave home at age 12 in search of a safer school. One of Mrs. Hannon's sisters furnishes Mark an official haven. Because the school near home could not provide for his safety, he lives out his teen years away from his mother and siblings. Add this to the girls' complaint about not learning! And to their fears about violence at home!

When Joan Can't Cope Any Longer

As the youngsters tell their stories, it is apparent that they are all good-hearted, but unable to take care of themselves and one another. There is little help from the children for Mrs. Hannon. The therapist asks all to leave but Mrs. Hannon and Joan. The therapist chooses to see the mother and Joan alone without the distraction of the others to search for a solution to the mother's biggest concern at the moment, Joan.

THERAPIST Mrs. Hannon, I don't know how you do it.

MRS. HANNON Uh huh.

THERAPIST You know, you really have more than one problem at home. You know that?

MRS. HANNON The whole batch is a problem!

(*She speaks with a full, confident voice for the first time.*)

THERAPIST That's right. Why did you pick Joan to ask for some help for her?

MRS. HANNON This is supposed to be my sensible one.

THERAPIST Yeah?

MRS. HANNON When she starts goofing off, I know the whole house is crazy.

THERAPIST She helps hold things together?

MRS. HANNON Right. And when she's blowing her stack and falling apart, it's time to find out what's the problem.

THERAPIST Okay. You need her to help you. . . .

MRS. HANNON I can always depend on her, you know.

. . .

But, when she starts falling apart, well, shucks—(*Shaking her head*)

JOAN That's why I fell apart.

THERAPIST That's why you fell apart. Because she depends on you?

. . .

JOAN Because when she wants me to do something and I can't do it.

(*She buries her face in her hands and starts to cry quietly.*)

THERAPIST (*To Mrs. Hannon*) She's upset.

MRS. HANNON (*Nodding*)

(*Long pause as Joan cries*)

JOAN (*Wiping tears away*) I got tears. (*Giggles through tears*)

THERAPIST That's all right.

JOAN I don't like to cry. (*Moves closer to Mother and gets tissues*)

THERAPIST That's all right. That's okay.

JOAN No, no. That's all! (*Sits up straight*) No more! I get mad at myself when I cry.

THERAPIST You don't have to.

JOAN I do. (*Dabbing eyes and recomposing herself*) Now let's talk.

THERAPIST Okay.

JOAN (*Pause*) If I get simple, then I can tell you what's wrong with my mind. If I don't get simple, I cry.

With this statement, Joan explains
"simple" to a serious and sensitive y
youngsters leave, she no longer needs
can let go. She cries. Her mother and
point of tears. But then she recovers, de
together. She is not accustomed to giving voice to
need.

THERAPIST All right. Okay. What's wrong with your mind then?

JOAN Boy, I worry too much. She [Mother] going off to work; she have an accident. (*Laughs tearfully as she relates her fears, imaginary but too close to reality in her world*)

THERAPIST Go ahead. Go ahead.

JOAN Jack gets shot walking down the street; Earl having a train accident.

THERAPIST Yeah?

JOAN Rita and Curt choke to death. Vera gets shot by her husband, and me—I'm going crazy.

THERAPIST Yeah, but you haven't always been this upset. Why are you getting upset? Why have you been upset lately?

JOAN 'Cause they don't do what I say, and I know I'm right.

THERAPIST How long has it been? How long have you been getting so upset? Since everything's been getting so bad?

JOAN Since June I guess.

THERAPIST Since June? What happened? What happened then?

JOAN A whole lot. I can't stand it. Well, not so much, except they just get on my nerves.

THERAPIST No, no. Something happened. Something has changed at home since June. Why is it worse since then?

JOAN Let's see. They don't listen to what I say.

THERAPIST (*To Mrs. Hannon*) Do you know what happened?

MRS. HANNON Think I do.

THERAPIST What?

MRS. HANNON Charles and Vera. They's been fighting, right?

. . .

(Interrupting) I told my sister—

THERAPIST *(To Joan)* Wait. Wait. *(To Mrs. Hannon)* Go ahead.

MRS. HANNON And like, she feels as if they should have been gone because I have gave them a set date in June to have themselves a place before they got married. I said, "Find yourself a place." And instead of it getting better, it just gets worse.

JOAN I told my sister, "Don't get married. If you get married you're going to be sorry," and that's what she is, sorry.

THERAPIST Why?

JOAN 'Cause it wasn't going to work out. 'Cause they wasn't even getting along before they got married. I told her, "Don't get married."

THERAPIST Why has that made a difference at home [for you]?

JOAN I don't know.

MRS. HANNON It just seems to me that since then, there just hasn't been no getting along.

THERAPIST Do you know why? *(Pause)* I don't really understand how Vera's situation made it so much worse.

JOAN Because she always tells me all her problems and then I try to figure them out, and when I tell her what I think, she don't want to listen, but she always wants me to figure them out.

THERAPIST So Vera tells you her problems. Who else do you have to worry about?

JOAN I don't know. I just worry for no reason I guess.

THERAPIST No, but you're supposed to worry about other people in the family. *(To Mrs. Hannon)* She's really been like part of you.

MRS. HANNON Uh huh.

THERAPIST To take care of things and hold them together because you can't possibly do this by yourself, and she's been the only one you could really depend on to handle things.

MRS. HANNON Uh huh. Right.

THERAPIST You know, when I talk to you, when you first came in here you looked very tired. You looked out of it. The kids have all left, and I can really see you now, and your eyes are very clear, and I think they're very clear because you see a lot, and

I think maybe your nerves are as bad as they are because you
see too much and there's nothing you can do about it.

MRS. HANNON (*Softly*) I'll go along with that.

THERAPIST And she [Joan] is trying to carry this burden with you.
(*Mrs. Hannon nods.*)

(*Pause*)

I can understand why she can't worry about school; she's got
the worries of any woman, not a 17-year-old kid. (*Mrs. Hannon nods.*) She couldn't have more worries if she had ten kids
of her own.

(*Pause*)

You don't really have any help from the outside.

MRS. HANNON No, they don't even care.

The therapist sees a world of problems facing Mrs. Hannon.
He helps her by (1) helping her take charge of the solutions, (2)
giving her external supports, and (3) prioritizing issues in a way
she can manage them. He starts by focusing on Joan's distress,
which is also the mother's prime worry. He also addresses how
Mrs. Hannon feels alone with all of the family's problems. He
reaches for some palpable and practical solutions in this first session. He wants her going home with hope.

Solving One Big Problem

THERAPIST Okay. Vera doesn't talk like she's going to leave.

MRS. HANNON Right! Now you understand. Right! Right! Right!

JOAN Anyhow, if I stay home and watch all those kids and make
her go out and get a job. . . . Like two days ago, I woke her up
and said, "Come on, Vera, you're going to get a job," took her
out and she went and got lost. She just didn't even want to go.
She didn't get lost.

MRS. HANNON I feel like this. If Vera was to find a place and get a
job, take her children—I don't know what Toby's going to
do—and just leave the household to my five dependent children, four dependent children, which I do have, I think things
would be better. I really do.

)u may be right.

Uh huh. I told them. I said, ''Look, you got your
ns. I have mine. Pack your problems up and go ahead
for yourself and leave me with my four dependents. That's all
I ask.''

JOAN (*She is still trying to help her mother.*) She won't have to live
alone. She could get an apartment. There'll be people downstairs. She could make friends with them, and then go out, and
all she have to do is go downstairs or upstairs and get them.
She only needs two bedrooms and an apartment got two bedrooms.

THERAPIST (*Avoids reinforcing Joan's feeling of responsibility for
her mother, and addresses only Mrs. Hannon*) You don't have
any family that she [Vera] could go live with, have you?

MRS. HANNON Nope, just two sisters, that's all. One has a small
apartment, the other has a small house.

THERAPIST I interrupted you, Joan. You were going to tell me
something. You said, ''And there's another thing—''

JOAN I just forgot. Oh yeah, I do that a lot, too, I make myself
forget stuff.

THERAPIST Joan, you have so much on your mind that I think you
need to forget a few things. You can't keep all those things in
your head at once or you'll go crazy.

JOAN I know I'm crazy. That makes me mad (*laughing*) 'cause I
can't do nothing about it.

THERAPIST Yeah. This kind of thing would drive anybody crazy.
You're crazy because you have too much to deal with. (*To
Mrs. Hannon*) I guess, in a way, that what we really should
be concentrating on first is Vera and her kids. If we can get
something done for her and her kids—

MRS. HANNON Right. Right.

THERAPIST I think the other problems will fall right into place and
everything will be all right.

. . .

(*To Joan*) Do you agree with your mother about Vera? (*Tests
whether Mrs. Hannon can expect any opposition to her solution from Joan*)

JOAN Well, this is what I think. I think all the
hop off and get away. I think that my m
another place for my grandfather . . . 'cau
along.

THERAPIST Who doesn't get along?

JOAN Me and my grandfather.

THERAPIST Yeah?

JOAN Boy. He—for one thing, he throws them riddles at me (*the
talk of a "senile" man*) and I don't know what the heck he's
talking about, and by the time I figure out what he said, he
done changed his mind. Like he said—

THERAPIST (*To Joan*) Wait a minute. (*to Mrs. Hannon*) She wants
your father out, too.

MRS. HANNON (*To Joan*) And where am I going to put him?

JOAN I don't know. Somewhere. Find somewhere. But I know she
can't find no place that's safe, 'cause that's why he got put out
of the nursing home. . . . they had to get the people out. And
they only had one accident. If there was a fire, they all would
have got burned up.

THERAPIST (*To Mrs. Hannon*) We already had something like that
happen in Philadelphia.

(*Only a couple of weeks before, there had been a fire in a nursing
home occupied by mostly poor, black residents. There were some
fatalities. Again, a failure of the system.*)

JOAN Right. So she took him out.

THERAPIST (*To Mrs. Hannon*) And you don't want to have something like that happen with your father there?

JOAN Right.

. . .

THERAPIST (*To Mrs. Hannon*) You know, the life in the city isn't
helping you any, either.

JOAN She wants to move to Jersey.

THERAPIST (*To Mrs. Hannon*) Well, there's a lot of things working
against you. You shouldn't be poor. Nobody should be poor.
That would solve a lot of our problems.

MRS. HANNON (*Laughs*) You can't have everything.

The social circumstances the family confronts at every turn magnify each family problem. They could not even find a safe nursing home for Mrs. Hannon's ailing, "senile" father. Their poverty limits their options, but Mrs. Hannon does not expect to "have everything." She will confront life if she can find the strength and solutions she can manage within her resources, such as they are. She takes aim at her first concern.

Taking Care of Joan

JOAN And you know, I think things won't ever go my way.

THERAPIST Why do you say that Joan?

JOAN I don't know—'cause they don't.

THERAPIST Joan, you know, right now you can't live for yourself. You're living for a lot of other people. At this point in your life, you're not thinking about what you're going to do for yourself or where you want to go tomorrow.

JOAN Nope.

THERAPIST You're thinking about what you're going to do for all of these other people in your house.

MRS. HANNON (*To Joan*) And that will make you sicker than anything in the drug store. It will, because you can't solve everybody's problems. This you can't do. We just have to make arrangements with them and if they can't solve the problem, I can see if I can help them solve the problem and get them off your back, and maybe you can solve some of your own problems.

(*She spontaneously takes over for Joan, ousting her from the job of worrying for the rest of the family.*)

THERAPIST (*To Mrs. Hannon*) I'm listening. I'm with you a thousand percent.

JOAN I think I need to find me—learn how to do something so I can get me a job.

THERAPIST . . . you're not going to be able to worry about a job, or school, or anything until we solve some of these other problems.

MRS. HANNON Right.

THERAPIST Vera and—

MRS. HANNON Right.

THERAPIST And your grandfather.

JOAN But I don't want to stay home and do nothing.

THERAPIST No, no, no, really—you're too smart for that. (*To Mrs. Hannon*) She really is too smart for that. . . . Nobody should be doing nothing. But if you have these worries, you can't do a lot of things.

MRS. HANNON (*To Joan*) You can't. You can't sleep or think. You can't really remember what is one and one.

THERAPIST (*To Mrs. Hannon*) And you can't help her if you're overwhelmed, because I know you would help her. See, right now, you're calm, and think very clearly about what she needs, but when they were all here, you know, you were out of it.

MRS. HANNON Right.

THERAPIST I would have been out of it too, because I would have said, you know, what can I do? I was having a hell of a time myself keeping everything straight in my head. Worrying about Vera and worrying about her kids, and worrying about Toby and watching Mark, not Mark—

MRS. HANNON Earl.

THERAPIST Earl causing some trouble. Everything was just—(*With a hand clap, the therapist changes direction.*) Okay. Look. I think you laid it down absolutely right, and I want to see what I can do to help you. And I think first things first, and that is to try and get some help for Vera to plan her life. She needs somebody to really work with her to plan her life. Okay?

MRS. HANNON True.

THERAPIST Then I want to see what I can do about getting some help for you to see if anything really can be done about your father. (*Mrs. Hannon nods.*) Okay? We have medical people here. I can get other contacts, I can get a number of people working together with you. If we can take care of those two things, get some progress on them—then we will get on this, this problem with Joan.

MRS. HANNON Right.

The therapist was part of a child guidance clinic associated with a pediatric hospital. With an underorganized family in difficult social circumstances, he expected the family to present a variety of closely related problems at once. It would call for team work—workers who have special skills with families, individuals, and with practical social needs. He knew if he tried to solve the problems alone, he would soon find himself where Mrs. Hannon and Joan were.

THERAPIST We'll try to move fast because I don't want Joan to miss too much school.

JOAN That's okay. I already know everything they got . . .

THERAPIST Okay, girl, but you know, there's not but just one school in the city. It could be that the school is not handling things right for you, you see. If we could get your life in order a little bit, we might be able to help you get to the right grade in the right school so that you can do something with your head.

MRS. HANNON Oh, that would be beautiful!

THERAPIST (*To Mrs. Hannon*) All right, but I don't see where we're going to succeed if we can't begin to do something about the other problems.

MRS. HANNON Right. We got to eliminate the biggest problem. Then, I think, if you get to the biggest problem, I think the rest of it will fall in place.

THERAPIST Right. We start taking care of this, taking care of your father, helping Joan out. And then if we can think of anything more that you need—you may not need anything more.

MRS. HANNON No, I'll have peace of mind when I get rid of the biggest problem.

JOAN Toby, don't forget her.

THERAPIST Okay, I won't forget her. I'm just trying to get some order.

JOAN I can't stand that girl.

THERAPIST All right. Okay. I think we did a lot of work. I think things are clear (*Mrs. Hannon nods*) and I'm going to get other people in to help with this 'cause I, I can't do it alone.

MRS. HANNON I know it.

JOAN You want to know a little secret?

THERAPIST Yeah, what?

JOAN When I was coming up here, I was singing a song: "When the nuts come marching in, oh, when the nuts come marching in, all the psychs gonna jump out the window, when the nuts—"

THERAPIST (*Smiling*) Okay. Nobody's going to jump out the window. What's going to happen is that you're going to get more people connected with your family, and we're going to try to get things in order. All right?

MRS. HANNON Uh huh.

THERAPIST Okay, let's stop here.

MRS. HANNON Come on, Joanie.

THERAPIST Mrs. Hannon, it's been nice meeting you. (*Shaking hands with her*)

MRS. HANNON It's a pleasure to talk to you. You ready, Joan?

JOAN Okay.

MRS. HANNON Okay. (*All leave.*)

Epilogue

The last report on Mrs. Hannon and her family was that her father had died at home. Vera had reunited with her husband, who joined the Air Force, and they moved to the West Coast. Joan did not return to school, but earned her high school diploma by passing the GED examination. And it was rumored that Mrs. Hannon had entered the ministry!

SOME COMMENTS

The Hannons offer an eloquent example of the relationship of social ecology to a family's problems. The ecostructural approach grew out of work with poor families like the Hannons, and is meant to address family problems rooted in their social context. However, today it is not only the poor who are facing stress from social circumstances. We all are. Moreover, family underorganization, of which the Hannons are a classic example, is also not limited to the poor. A society with a disarray of values and ambiguous social structures weakens the structure of the interpersonal contract in all relationships. Today, quality of organization becomes for all families an issue that, distinguished from family conflict, needs attention from family therapists.

The Hannon family illustrates more than what society can do to families and its members. At a personal level, this family showed us nobility and strength, as well as caring and sacrifice in the deepest poverty. It was this spirit that fueled its members' lives. In therapy we do not supply a family's spirit. However, we can participate in it, and perhaps even enkindle new energy and determination if we join our own spirit to theirs. Therapy calls for us to recognize a family's spirit, draw it out, and fly with it. It is our own spirit that allows us to see and speak to a family's spirit.

8. Training of the Person of the Therapist for Work with the Poor and Minorities

Therapy with the poor in America means working with cultural, ethnic, and racial minorities who fill the ranks of low-income America. Some of these poor bring poverty with them when they immigrate from underdeveloped countries. Others bear the burden of America's legacies of ethnic chauvinism—slavery and land confiscation with forced internment in reservations. African Americans and Native Americans saw their cultural and economic lives crushed. Puerto Ricans suffered colonization. Poor whites who were isolated in relatively impoverished sections of America also experienced the strangulation of cultural life.

Common to all these groups are the effects of radical damage to the cultural roots of their communities. Many in these groups have known poverty for generations. Many suffer deficiencies in education. Some lack the socialization to navigate society successfully. They lost their ancestral cultural and spiritual roots, and have not absorbed the dominant society's values. An impoverishment of spirit lends a devastating quality to their economic poverty.

Therapists who counsel individuals and families from these groups have to deal with much beyond economic privation. Their clients' emotional struggles intertwine with low self-esteem, anger, and suspiciousness. Their going it alone in life shows the effects of fractured family and community life. In the face of the deprivation of life's material necessities, they have little else to sustain and motivate them. Spiritually, they have little reason to try their hardest, to endure the sacrifice of discipline, and to trust themselves to enduring, committed love.

I believe therapists need special, personal training as part of their preparation to treat these families, who live with legacies of social, cultural, and spiritual deprivation. This training needs to go beyond the emotional realm of the therapist's experience. It must also reach into the economic, class, cultural, ethnic, racial, and spiritual contexts of society.

DIVERSITY

In the personal and social dimensions of the therapeutic relationship, therapist and client identify with and differentiate from one another. As in any relationship, they look to see and feel themselves in one another while maintaining their separateness. Out of the identification will spring vulnerability and openness to one another. The differentiation (Kerr, 1981) will allow them to be separate, to decide freely, and to act independently within the relationship. The polarities of identification and differentiation also generate forces of new identities and differences. These differences produce new divisions and complementarities within and among people. The powerful electromagnetic forces of these polarities produce the potentially destructive and creative tensions of the dialectical (thesis, antithesis, and synthesis) process of diversity.

Diversity is dynamic. It is not a static mosaic with no possibility of change. This dialectical process is true both for the individual and for groups. Conceptually the process begins with the uniqueness of one's cultural, racial, and ethnic experience. Then, diverse forces from within and without contend with one another to stimulate the evolution of new forms and shapes of identity. These forces, which may appear inimical to one another, also provide each person with challenges to learn from the other through identification and differentiation. These forces act across identities of culture, nationality, and race between groups, between individuals, and between the individual and the group. At the levels of socio-cultural role and adaptation, the same is true of gender difference. The successful dialectics of evolution bring together differences and push to new levels of identity and complementarity.

No race or culture can be both static and flourishing. No individual matures without new discoveries about self. Sameness becomes stale without diversity. Diversity is chaotic without sameness. Oneness implodes without separateness. Separateness scatters without oneness. People need a core of family tradition together with cultural and racial identity. They also need the uniqueness of their existential selves, which goes beyond group labels. The tension of diversity is partner to the harmony of unity. These complex dialectics of diversity are the axes of therapists' perspectives on people's personal and social identities.

Diversity in Therapy

Because the boundaries of therapy encompass the entire process between therapist and client, these dialectical dynamics converge in the therapeutic process. In deciding what to do with these forces, the therapist is guided by therapeutic objectives, assessment schemas, and intervention strategies. The client pursues the personal goals of the contract—personal solutions to personal problems.

The dialectics of diversity are an issue for both therapist and client. Clients struggle to open themselves to the outsider, the therapist. They hear a beckoning to share control of their lives for a while. At the same time, they hear that they are responsible for their own destinies. The decisions are theirs. Therapists, on the other hand, strive to maintain a sense of self, personal and professional, as they enter clients' most personal life experiences. They reach into their clients' experiences of life to understand and connect, yet must be true to their personal and professional selves in the relationship. Somehow, out of this encounter something new and beneficial must evolve for the client, something that is also good for the therapist.

THE BASICS OF THE
THERAPEUTIC RELATIONSHIP

In the intimate process of therapy, clinicians work with and through complex connections with their clients. Figure 8.1 pictures the therapist-client relationship with both therapist and client. There is a personal component of the relationship into which they both bring their histories, values, and emotions. There is also the professional component at the core of their relationship, through which they funnel all their efforts.

Therapists discover their clients both through a personal, *internal* experience and through social transactions. How profound the "inner" experience of the client will be for the therapist depends on how open the therapist is to the client. Therapists take in what clients relate of their stories and observe what they enact of their issues in therapists' presence. When clients come in with their families, therapists have special entrée to a vital portion of their clients' reality in the family enactment. As such, therapists have the opportunity to live the client's experience from outside, without direct interaction with the client. Therapists can see themselves in their clients' lives or can vicariously share in their clients' lives by projecting themselves into the clients' experiences. These are essentially internal psychological processes. For therapists, these inner experiences of themselves in relation to their clients' experiences serve as sources of insight into the client and the basis for empathy.

Therapists can also know their clients by directly sharing life with them as they connect and struggle in the odyssey that is therapy. In this case, therapists know their clients through what they directly see, hear, and feel of them within the interaction. When therapists actively transact with clients, how they relate to clients is in itself both a means of assessment and an intervention. In that meeting therapists encounter themselves as well as their clients. Therapists experience themselves personally, through their reactions, and professionally through the effectiveness of their work. If therapists understand their participation in the transaction, they will understand their clients' participation, which will give them access into their clients.

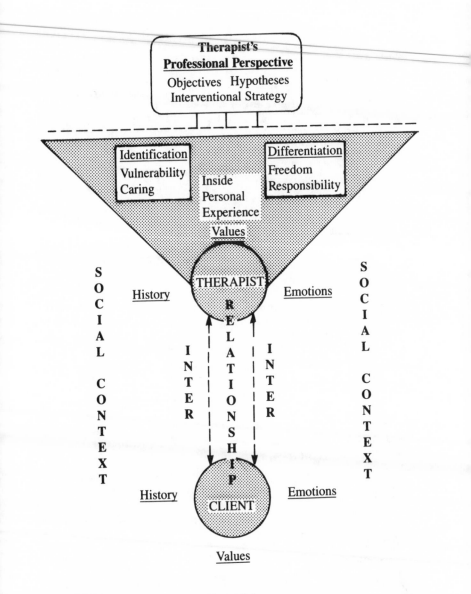

Figure 8.1.
The Therapeutic Relationship

From these experiences of themselves within their "inner" and "inter" experiences of their clients come insight into their clients and the bases for therapeutic relationships. Training the person of the therapist focuses on the "inner" and "inter" experiences therapists have of themselves in relation to their clients.

Consider, then, the complex levels of connection therapy demands of a therapist. Consider what clarity of vision a therapist must have to see truly from outside and from within a relationship, and from both vantage points of identification and differentiation! What mastery of the *personal self* the therapist needs to intervene with sensitivity, power, and intensity through distance and closeness in relationships! However, these therapist insights through the inner self and the self that engages with the client take on meaning not only through the personal intimacy of the therapist-client engagement but also through the political and social dramas of society that frame that connection.

The Social Factor in the Therapeutic Relationship

The personal intimacy of the human relationship in the therapeutic relationship affixes to the intimacy of the personal material treated in therapy. Add to this double intimacy the dynamics of race, ethnicity, culture, socioeconomic status, gender, and religion of both therapist and client! The process between therapist and client now has that many more motifs. In therapy these themes build into a complex drama. Moreover, the therapeutic drama does not exist as a purely private chamber play. These are not just issues between therapists and client. The drama plays out on the stage of a society that is itself struggling with a myriad of issues. Society's travails live in the relationship and transactions of therapist and client. As the social context of the therapy, they shape the therapy and affect its outcome.

The key to working with these social factors in therapy is the same one that works with personal emotions and human needs in the therapeutic relationship. Therapists can treat the social, as well as the personal, dynamics as forces in the dialectical process of the therapeutic relationship. They work with sameness and difference as forces that belong together in an enriching process. They approach these opposite forces as potentially leading to new levels of experience. The dialectical process in social diversity passes through tension, and often pain and conflict, to resolution and growth or division and destruction. Therapists can work with social identification and differentiation to unite, separate, and complement. How they work with these similarities and dissimilarities will affect the relationship, assessment, and intervention.

Sameness and difference between therapist and client linked to sociocultural factors will color therapists' vision. For example, affinity in personal and social moral values can spawn intuitive understanding, while strong differences can distort mutual understanding. However, differences in moral perspective can also expand and enrich the visions of therapists and clients in their shared work. Also, shared and disparate social experiences can affect therapist and client definitions of therapeutic issues. They also offer the possibility of expanding the options for solving a problem. Finally, between therapist and client, gender can be just as powerful a defining factor as culture, race, and socioeconomic status. The therapist uses social ingredients to separate, unite, and complement the experience of therapy.

The Challenge of the Therapeutic Relationship

The process, itself, of a therapeutic relationship and all the anxiety, conflict, and pain associated with a client's issue will present personal and social difficulties to therapist and client. Overtly or covertly, within the therapeutic process, both therapist and client will have to contend with their own issues and those of the other. They engage in an encounter that touches the most vulnerable aspects of human experience in order to explore the risky territory of change. How do therapists prepare to deal with the therapeutic process at this profound level in a way that will be beneficial to the client and true to the therapist?

THE PERSON OF
THE THERAPIST

Therapy has long recognized the need for training of therapists to manage their personal issues in the context of therapy in ways that are not harmful to clients. Freud made the initial call because of his concern with how analysts' reactions to their patients' transferential material could affect their objectivity. He encouraged therapists to analyze their *countertransference* (Freud, 1937) throughout their professional careers.

Classical psychoanalysis called for a detached and passive stance in therapy, with analysts keeping their feelings private. This minimized analyst interaction with a patient. In contrast, today's active therapists involve themselves much more personally with clients. Their responses are less private and less insulated from the dynamics of therapist-patient interactions. Lynn Hoffman (1990, p. 5), for example, speaks of how "A second-order view would mean that therapists include themselves as part of what must change; they do not stand outside." Moreover, work with low-income families by its very nature calls for an even more active approach. Therapists put more of themselves into the work to repair the effects of social deprivation and damage to the psyche and family.

The underorganization in many poor families calls out for therapists to offer palpable help with organization and communication. The urgency of family crises precipitated by social problems also compels therapists to actively pursue tangible solutions. Moreover, families' social needs will draw therapists into negotiating between families and their community's institutions. From any and every perspective, therapy with the poor is an active, involved affair for therapists. Therapists state opinions, give advice, and become activists with both families and community. Many who have experience working with the poor urge some special personal training for therapists wanting to help low-income families, training analogous to what Freud wanted for his followers.

The Call for Person Training

In order to pay "careful attention to the human element . . . [in] the essential relationship between the therapist and the fam-

ily," says Nancy Boyd-Franklin (1989, p. 95,
plore ourselves as people, as men and women,
pists." Poor families whose personal boundaries
confusing need therapists who are going to be ac
with them *and* anchored in their own personal live,
having considerable clarity about their own social and cu...
views will help therapists contend with the social issues intrinsic
to the problems of poor minorities.

Speaking to the need for therapists to look at themselves, Pinderhughes says, "It is not possible to assist clients to examine issues
concerning cultural identity and self-esteem if helpers have not
done this work for themselves" (1989, p. 19). The extent to which
therapists understand and have resolved their own stories will determine how sensitive they are to their clients' stories. Their ability
to deal with pain associated with their own ethnicity, race, and
economic struggles dictates their ability to work with the personal
meanings and emotions associated with similar issues in their clients' lives.

Certainly, having the "correct" attitudes about race and socioeconomic status will not be enough. Who is to say what is the right
outlook? Training should not be cultural brainwashing, as has
sometimes happened in our pursuit of the "politically correct."
Forcing a prescribed way of thinking and feeling will only stifle
what is natural in the therapist. Moving therapists away from what
is genuine and spontaneous in themselves will only further distance them from their clients' truth. The challenge is not to think
"correctly" about the client but to feel *with* the client who is so
different that one fights with oneself to get close and touch.

If therapists are able to see and feel the pain of their own
experiences and to accept the contradictions and inconsistencies of
their attitudes toward others, that will help them deal with similar
feelings in their clients. Dividing the world between oppressed and
oppressors will only distance therapists from their clients. This division calls for judgments about the good guys and bad guys.
When we put ourselves in that position, we look to assign blame.
Who then is free of blame? Ourselves? Our clients? We create anxiety about being wrong because it distances us from the wrong
doer—separating them from us and us from them. It makes it im-

ossible for us to be honest with ourselves or for our clients to be honest with us.

Yes, we will have and need to have opinions about right and wrong. There are public forums where we can take our political battles. But our clients need for us to care for them personally—to touch their wounds, even those that are dangerous. We live with our own dirty wounds. Therapists can understand their own hurts through awareness of their ethnic, racial, and socioeconomic heritages. They need to see how their own experiences are like and unlike those of their clients. They need to know how their experiences help and hurt them in order to understand their clients' lives. The purpose of person training on the social facets of our lives is not to be correct, but to understand, empathize, and care.

Person Training to Work with the Poor and Minorities

Technically, therapy with the poor brings together individual psychology, family dynamics, and social reality. Person training of therapists serving the poor should mirror this complex of perspectives, which must then be funneled through the relationship between worker and client. Training on the person of the therapist needs to run in conjunction with clinical training. To this end I will describe a person training model tailored for work with the poor. It is a *personal-social* approach that incorporates the personal, cultural, and political realities of a therapist's life into a clinical framework.

First, I wish to cite two training approaches that exemplify the components of a personal-social training experience. They are Elaine Pinderhughes' "experiential group model" (1989) and the Aponte and Winter "person-practice model" (1987).

Pinderhughes pursues personal understanding in the therapist, "by exploring within a group format the participants' own feelings, perceptions, and experiences vis-à-vis ethnicity, race, and power" (p. 211). The model emphasizes the "in vivo" experience in the group. It deals not only with attitudes, but also with interaction across cultural difference. It looks at values "on both personal and societal levels" (p. 212). This sharing in the group context around the interpersonal dynamics within the group extends through *discussion* to practitioners' clinical work (p. 240).

The Aponte/Winter person-practice model complements Pinderhughes' approach. As with the "experiential group model," the primary setting for training therapists in the person-practice model is the trainee group. The person-practice program works with therapists' life issues, including their values, but does not have Pinderhughes' primary focus on ethnic differences. Its emphasis is on therapists' personal family issues; moreover, it places a high premium on the practical, clinical formation of trainees. Person-practice training includes supervising the clinical application of therapists' personal work. The model uses live supervision as the ultimate, integrative experience.

This emphasis on clinical application coincides well with the principle that therapy with the poor be grounded in practical life experience. Therapists in person training should be seeing the kinds of families with which they wish to learn to do therapy. Clinical practice will give their personal training real-life reference points and offer them a practical arena in which to test their learning.

PERSONAL-SOCIAL CLINICAL TRAINING MODEL

Presented here is an outline for a personal-social training program organized for therapists wanting to work with low-income and minority families.

Composition of group:

- Number: Ten participants with terminal degrees in mental health or counseling.
- Mix: Ideally, trainees from a variety of racial, cultural, and socioeconomic backgrounds, reflecting the make-up of the clientele.

Frequency and length:

- Two-year program (first year stressing personal issues and social background of the trainees and second year focusing on the clinical application).

- Two-day sessions convene monthly for 10 months (creating an intensive group experience with trainees during the two days).
- After seven hours of work, trainees eat meals and socialize jointly.
- The two-day session begins and ends with a one-hour group discussion.
- Throughout the two days, trainees rotate giving presentations, individual one-hour talks discussing personal or clinical issues, with the option of using audio or videotape (50 minutes talking with the leaders and 10 minutes interacting with the group about the presentation).
- Live, supervised two-hour clinical sessions, including a one-hour interview and another hour split for discussion before and after the session.
- Each trainee presents for 10 hours per year, e.g., four individual one-hour presentations and three two-hour live supervised sessions.

Leadership:

- Ideally, male and female co-leaders with ethnic and socio-economic backgrounds reflecting trainees' and the clientele's backgrounds or with experience working with families like trainees' cases.

Setting:

- Training center outside trainees' settings, protecting trainees' privacy within their work environment.
- Commitment to confidentiality by all participants.
- Training center to have video and observation rooms.
- Trainees' agencies agree to center's supervising trainees live with agency clients and having contact with the communities of the families.

Goals of the Model

The personal-social model has several basic goals for trainees, namely to:

1. Understand and conceptualize issues from their lives by:

   a. Identifying and interpreting personal and social themes in their lives and their successes and failures in dealing with them;

   b. Accessing emotions, attitudes, and values from their own personal life and clinical experiences, past and present;

   c. Making explicit personal and professional values and philosophy that drive their lives and affect their therapy.

2. Gain mastery over their personal and clinical issues through:

   a. Taking into personal therapy unresolved issues, especially those experienced in the professional context;

   b. Learning to think about, feel, and live with resolved and unresolved issues to facilitate working with them in therapy;

   c. Pursuing further understanding, resolution, and management of their personal-social issues through their clinical practice.

3. Learn to use themselves in therapy by:

   a. Developing the capacity for personal intimacy, mutuality, and commitment with clients within professional boundaries;

   b. Developing the skill to work with the connections between their own and clients' values, personal life experience, and socioeconomic backgrounds;

   c. Integrating their personal work with a professional model of therapy to achieve theoretical and practical congruity of self with therapy.

In summary:

1. Therapists develop the capacity to assess their personal emotions, memories, and attitudes when in the therapeutic transaction.

2. They learn how to interpret what they access about them-

selves in relation to their clients' lives and the therapeutic
process.

3. Finally, clinicians learn how to forge interventions that
take into account their own and their clients' personal
and social issues.

As an example, all of this training can come together in a training module, the existential experience of the therapist-client encounter. Figure 8.2 depicts the frame of the therapeutic process.
Within it a therapist can develop the ability to focus self on the
client in the session. The therapist can take this image of the client
into the therapist's internal experience of the moment. The internal experience is like the membrane of a drum, which reverberates
to the percussion of the incoming stimulus of the client's image.
The reverberations are the emotions and memories of the therapist
that are aroused, as well as the ethnic, cultural, and spiritual con-
notations of the experience. While locked into this focus on self
with the client, the therapist further expands awareness to allow
the professional self to assess, hypothesize, and consider interventions. The therapist then acts out of that existential encounter. The
ability to imbue the perceptions of the client with all these rich
personal associations depends upon the therapist's having accessible that full experience of the self in the present. The ability simultaneously to monitor and act therapeutically from this personal
experience comes from having integrated the experience of self
with one's therapeutic persona.

Training the person of the therapist opens therapists up not
only to themselves, but to the existential boundaries between their
own and clients' personal lives and social contexts. Therapy beck-
ons therapists to gain mastery of themselves in their relationships
with their clients' personal selves, their family lives, and their social contexts.

A Special Emphasis on
Values and Society

Within the framework of the personal-social training model,
trainees give special attention to personal and social values. How-

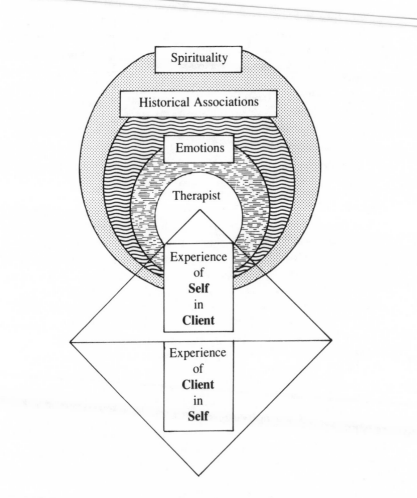

Figure 8.2.
The Existential Experience in the Therapeutic Encounter

ever, just as the training program is not a place for personal therapy, it is not per se the place for trainees to find new values or social attitudes. Just as trainees looking for therapy need to go outside for a therapist, those looking for new approaches to their values will need to look into the world outside training for their answers. However, out of their own process, trainees may arrive at some new thinking while in training. Training is the context for looking at self, understanding others, and putting it all together in therapy. It does offer the opportunity for seeing and thinking; it does not provide the doctrine.

Value Training

Therapists may or may not be settled about the history of the evolution of their values. These values have their origins in their ethnic and racial roots, in their families and communities, and in their religious and spiritual experiences. Therapists will want to look at the evolution of those values and how they were shaped by life experiences related to family, community, and church, as well as the connections between their principles and their relationships to people and society. They need to consider how their values link to relationships that are important to them today, how adhering to or rejecting their historical principles have furthered or endangered those relationships. This opens up the question of what work they want to do today with their families, communities, or religious affiliations to resolve value issues.

Therapists' clinical work should also serve to help them see where they are currently wrestling with values. The questions raised by clients' issues or relationships with clients can challenge therapists' attitudes. The clinical experience provides another context—in fact, a very relevant real-life context—for therapists to confront their value issues.

The Group

One must also highlight the use of the group in this training. The group is a social context in its own right, with all the caring, support, insights, perspectives, prejudices, and divisiveness of any heterogeneous social gathering. It offers a mix of people's psychology, life experiences, ethnicity, and socioeconomic backgrounds. Within the training program, the group creates another opportunity for trainees to learn about how their own values affect their relationships with others. With other therapists trainees can directly address personal and social issues that they cannot talk about with clients. The commitment the trainees share motivates them to help one another with these difficult and risky issues. The leadership helps them to do so in safety.

The Development of Personal-Social Trainers

Of course, of paramount importance are the leaders who will guide the trainees through the labyrinths of their personal and social histories. Just as therapists need to know where they are in their personal lives when helping clients, person trainers need to have done some serious work on themselves. Considering the complexity that a personal, social, and clinical experience presents, it helps for trainers to have worked on their personal and social issues in relation to low-income and minority families. They also need expertise in a method of integrating personal and professional insights in the personal-clinical training of others.

Let me say one more thing about a basic challenge for the leaders of person training, especially when the training deals specifically with social issues. Therapists who gravitate toward social issues often have strong political convictions. They tend to stand aggressively behind their beliefs, a position that often carries over into their teaching. Our professional associations are taking ever more public positions about political, social, and moral issues, which leave the membership with implicit messages about what their professional positions on these issues *should* be. These official positions are then incorporated into what we teach in our professional schools. By the time it gets down to the level of clinical practice, clinicians have so assimilated these political, social, and moral positions that they may not be aware they have assumed viewpoints that are not shared by their clients. It may not even occur to them that their clients have a legitimate right to adhere to different values *and* that their client's convictions may be valid. Moreover, new professionals may even come to believe that the solutions to their clients' problems lie in their adopting the values the workers have learned in school. NOT

While our professional ethics preach restraint in pushing our personal and social values on clients, they do little to protect trainees from trainers' and supervisors' personal crusades. Regarding the influence of leaders in person training programs, trainees are vulnerable. I believe that trainees deserve the same safeguards accorded to clients. There is no easy solution to the question about the relationship of our political and social convictions to our clinical work. The debate is divisive within the field, with much heated debate about how "to make the links between social issues and clinical practice even more explicit" (DeMuth, 1990, p. 13). The question of the social values of trainers in training should be treated as seriously as therapist values vis-à-vis clients in treatment.

THE STORY OF A TRAINEE

Len is a social worker, a young African American with considerable professional skills and personal presence. He was one of two black trainees in the training group. The other was a woman. Because of his obvious personal attractiveness and air of competence, he commanded respect and drew people to him. He was friendly and gracious, but acknowledged that he hid much inside, emotionally distancing himself from people.

Len did three particularly important presentations in his first year in the program. In the first, he presented his genogram, and with it his life story. In his second presentation, he conducted a clinical session, with his colleagues role-playing family members. In the third, he conducted a live session with a family.

Len is the third of six children. He described his mother as "warm, nurturing [and] accepting." His father was a tough man who "demonstrated [his strength] by [his] ability to experience hardship without a display of emotions." However, his father confused him because he was also "fond of having philosophical talks with [him] about education, money and life in general." Len revealed that he lived with conflict and shame that during his childhood his parents had become emotionally estranged. His mother had been an alcoholic and his father a philanderer. His mother's death during Len's youth left her in a special and painful place in his heart. Len had grown up feeling protective of his mother and angry with his father.

Len also took on the burden of the "responsible" son. He became the "hope" of his family, the one who would achieve. He left home for a better education in military school. He was to be mostly among whites. He knew the pressure to perform in the face of a tough life and troubling emotions.

As he told his story, the tension between his loyalty to his roots and his wish to fulfill his family's aspirations for him in the outside world emerged. He felt driven to compensate for his personal shame with achievement and the mask of competence. He was to live out the boyhood role of helper to others who hid his own pain from family and neighbors. This same boy also learned to cover up his self-doubts and fears in that outside, often white, society, which like his family grew to expect much of him. He developed into a man who avoided intimacy in relationships for fear of exposing his needs and vulnerability. He knew this was affecting his relationships with women and guessed it was impairing his therapy, although he was not clear how. Through the exploration of his genogram he committed himself, in his words, to do something about his "vulnerability as it relate[d] to [my] role as therapist."

The genogram work served to set the theme for his training. There followed a clinically oriented presentation that helped him get further into the work. In a simulated family session, he played therapist and several trainees played the family members. The trainers used the experience to interrupt the process at several points, asking the "family" members to feed back to Len how they were experiencing him. It was apparent that Len was feeling pressured to perform and was becoming uptight in his fear of failing. His colleagues in the simulated family were able to tell him how unconnected they felt to him, how cool and rational he had become. These were his friends talking. It was a powerful and disturbing confrontation for Len.

In having to perform with the simulated family, he was dealing at some level with his family of origin, and at another with that outside world of school that was testing him. He had to struggle with the issue of his ability to relate to a woman and to white and black in a white context. He resorted to competence and withdrew emotionally. The discussion in the group about how he had changed with them when playing therapist and how they cared about him personally gave him welcomed feedback. They could talk frankly with him. He wanted to trust his colleagues. He talked it out with them, and asked for their emotional support in the training. He would try not to go it alone in the training. Len also chose to enter personal therapy outside the training group, a decision commonly made by trainees in the program.

In his next clinical presentation, Len brought in a family for supervision. He saw the family live with the leaders and group behind an observation mirror. Len brought in a white family. He felt he had a good relationship with the family members, but knew he needed to push hard on some issues that would be threatening to the mother in this single-parent family. He needed to help her stop being overprotective of her troubled and immature son. However, when confronted by Len in the session, she became defensive. Len just as quickly reacted defensively. Again, he faced another test before his peers.

The training leader called him out of the session and got him talking about what was behind the woman's defensiveness—her fear of his criticism and rejection. The trainer helped him talk about his own fear of failure and embarrassment at that moment. Len and the trainer eventually agreed on the trainer's joining the session. The trainer encouraged Len and the mother to talk about the history of their relationship and the good work they had done together. They relaxed. The trainer left.

Len was feeling safer, with less need to hide his vulnerability. He was able to engage with the mother and allow himself to take in how much she trusted him, even in her anxiety. He conveyed his acceptance of her and his understanding of her struggles with her son. She felt safer with him and heard his therapeutic message. Even in the face of his client's being a woman and white and of having to perform before his colleagues, Len had personally engaged with the woman. He discovered that even as a professional he could relate through the person he really was—with the full reality of his emotions, gender, and race.

In his second year, Len continued, within the context of his clinical training to work on his family of origin. He needed to get beyond his shame about his parents and, with that, of his roots. He presented several times on his parents. That led him to look at both the good in his parents and their very human vulnerabilities. He wanted to reach a place where his memories and emotions about his personal life would not overwhelm him with painful shame, but would, instead, serve as a resource for understanding, feeling with, and relating to his clients.

His mother had been an exceptionally loving person, loved and appreciated by those who knew her in spite of her drinking problem in later years. His father had been a rock, taking care of his family, and also the spur of Len's professional aspirations. Len's mother had died years before, but his father was still living. Len was coached to talk with him over a series of visits. To his amazement, once his father sensed safety in his son's genuine interest in talking with him, he showed himself eager for a relationship with his son. When Len asked, this tough, independent man opened up about his own fears and vulnerabilities. He released Len from the old image of his father as the "hard-face." Father and son also talked about their respective views of Len's mother. Both had loved and respected her; both had suffered about her.

With a more complete picture of the good and the bad in his family, Len could accept his family and himself. He also experienced his colleagues' acceptance of this more complete depiction of himself. Consequently, Len was able to offer more of himself to his colleagues and to the families he treated. He entered a doctoral program upon graduating from the training program, but he did so sharing his fears, asking for support and continued contact.

9. The Negotiation of Values in Therapy

In the study of the therapeutic process, much attention has been given to the inevitable emotional connections between therapist and patient. Relatively little attention has been given, however, to the interaction between the *values* of the therapist and the family. This chapter focuses on the influence of values in therapy. It speaks to how therapists can consciously use the interactions of their own values with the values of clients to benefit treatment.

Values, as an issue between therapist and client, is of special relevance to work with low-income and minority families because:

1. Underorganized families also tend to be underorganized about their values, lacking a strong sense of identity, self-worth, and life purpose;
2. Families with underdeveloped value systems are vulnerable to the imposition of values by agency workers who have legal authority and may control access to society's resources, such as hospitals, schools, and public welfare agencies;
3. The ability of these clients to assume direction of their lives and solve their problems depends on their having a value system that supports the autonomy and power of their self, family, and community.

EMPOWERMENT

We can talk all we want about empowering poor and minority families, but unless we strengthen their values, culture, and transcendent purpose in life, they will not know their own power. They will know neither personal autonomy nor the ability to decide for themselves.

For one reason or another underorganized families have suffered damage to their cultural and religious value systems. Lacking their own internalized and developed value systems, they will not be able to take charge of their lives. Personal and cultural values give them independence of spirit and freedom in the face of daunting social pressures and privation of economic and political power. Within a dependent therapeutic or counseling relationship, a family's freedom and ownership of self are critical to the survival of the human spirit and to the family's ability to make decisions and help itself.

Poor families, accustomed to being dependent upon social agencies and medical authorities, are often conditioned to giving up control over their lives. They learn to respond to the expectations of those who have power to give them money, housing, medical care, and education. They frequently lack confidence in their ability to self-direct their lives, a self-doubt often fed by the authorities. Some submit and fail because they do not believe in themselves. Some quit the system to do it their way and fail because they realistically lack the necessary resources. Families need the system to nurture their power, which means their ability to judge, choose, and do for themselves. The core of that freedom comes from their claiming, cherishing, and exercising their personal, cultural, and spiritual values.

VALUES IN THE THERAPIST-CLIENT RELATIONSHIP

When therapist and family engage in therapy, they embark upon a personal relationship framed by professional parameters. This is particularly true in the more worker-active therapies, such as family therapy. Clinicians are more likely to give opinions, share judgments, make suggestions, and assume overt relational positions vis-à-vis family members when trying to influence them. Clinicians put themselves into the work, along with their world views, philosophies, spiritual perspectives, and cultural biases—not to mention their emotional baggage and family history. The more active the therapy, the less able they are to separate their personal selves from their professional selves.

Therapists draw upon both their professional training and their personal life experiences and values to understand and intervene with families. Professional and client, sharing the same society, are influenced by the same social trends, stresses, and controversies. The personal problems that families present also have elements in common with the issues therapists have had and are currently dealing with in their own lives. On top of the social and personal influences therapists bring into therapy, their professions add philosophies, biases, and prejudices.

Values frame the entire process of therapy. Values are the social standards by which therapists define reality, identify problems, formalize evaluations, select interventions, and determine therapeutic goals. All transactions between therapists and clients involve negotiations about the respective value systems that each party brings into the therapeutic process.

VALUES IN THE
THERAPEUTIC PROCESS

Like therapists, clients must deal with their values in therapy. Values conveyed by the therapist confront the individual's and family's own values in the therapeutic process. Depending upon their school of therapy, many therapists speak of their work as "technical," "scientific," or perhaps even "aesthetic," but in any case, free of moral and social value biases. This is not only patently untrue but impossible. At the other end of the continuum are therapists who proclaim their political and social values to be the healing elements of their therapies. These therapists' positions become problematic for clients who differ when the therapists press or insinuate their views about social roles and personal morality as the *therapeutically* correct standards for healthy functioning. I believe that, in all cases, the values of therapists become an essential part of how they conduct therapy.

Consider some quotations. First, from an individually oriented, psychoanalytic therapist: "This concept of good [for a patient] must derive from what I want for myself together with an identification with the human community . . . [while] the therapist . . . functions not only as 'good parent,' but also as a representative of the community" (Graham, 1980, p. 371). One family therapist states that "if . . . there is an inequitability of give and take . . . interactions become ethically stagnant or pathological" (Boszormenyi-Nagy & Ulrich, 1981, p. 167). Another family therapist approaches the family problems of some children by assuming that if "the hierarchy in the family is in confusion . . . the therapist should side with the parents against the problem young person, even if this seems to be depriving him or her of individual choices and rights" (Haley, 1980, p. 45). Finally, from a Bowenian point of view, another therapist sees emotion as impeding intellect, saying, "as the intellectual system gains more separateness from emotional influence, it is freer to define principles and beliefs based on objective assessments of available knowledge" (Kerr, 1981, p. 238). This differentiation becomes the basis of the therapeutic work.

CIRCULARITY: A THEORY

Since relatively few therapists explicitly acknowledge and identify the values underpinning their theories and methods, it is difficult to compare systematically their implicit values on the same continuum. The preceding quotations offer glimpses and clues about the variety of values represented by therapists. Their values are inherent in their theory as well as in clinical application.

To further illustrate the pervasiveness of values in therapy, even at an abstract theoretical level, take the concept of "circularity," an idea drawn by family therapists from the work of Gregory Bateson. The circular model contrasts with the linear. In the circular view, transactions have no beginning or end, cause or effect in the loop of social interaction. In the linear perspective, people interact in the direct sequence of cause and effect.

In recognizing the systemic nature of human relationships, the circular model emphasizes interdependence in social interactions. Consider one interpretation of the implications of circularity in social systems:

The therapist can no longer be seen as "impacting" on the client or family. . . . The therapist is not an agent and the client is not a subject. Both are part of a larger field in which therapist, family, and any number of other elements act and react upon each other in unpredictable ways. (Hoffman, 1981, p. 8)

Circularity would appear to stand as a principle free of social bias, but this interpretation of the concept also seems to negate personal responsibility. If cause and effect cannot be assigned in a transaction, then how can one assign responsibility? Take away responsibility and one loses independent choice. Without that there is no free will. In that light, what does personal power mean? If poor families need to be in charge of their lives, to be empowered, where does such an interpretation of circularity leave them? As I see it, personal identity and self-worth are essentially bonded to the notion of having power and the freedom to use it well or badly. Choosing good or bad, right or wrong, is about values. Tradition, religion, and spirituality are all rooted in the social ligatures of culture. In the case of minorities that has to do with culture, ethnicity, and race.

CLINICAL APPLICATION

At the level of clinical application, values are a relevant issue, even in such an elemental matter as the selection of the object of therapy. For example, theorists and practitioners in the field of family therapy consider the object of therapy, the family, to be many different things. A therapist's decision about what "parents" to include in the therapy—whether a biological parent, a stepparent, or a live-in partner—may have socially sanctioned or disqualifying implications, whatever the therapist's rationale or intentions.

Take, for instance, the value perspectives inherent in Keith and Whitaker's discussion in the "Divorce Labyrinth" about their work with Ed. Ed had separated from his wife, Molly, and was living with Linda while trying to decide about divorcing Molly. In a session with Molly and Ed, the therapists included Linda and, apparently, Ed's children from his marriage.

> Molly and Linda noted with amusement how they would sometimes pair to mother Ed. The children steered clear of Linda. They orbited mainly around Ed and Molly. The two women, however, were the best weekend parent set for the boys. (1977, p. 125)

The therapy seems to accept the two women, in the extramarital triangular arrangement, as a de facto parenting pair. Whether intended or not, the therapists send a message that legitimizes the arrangement, even if temporarily. Consider a parallel scenario: What would be the therapeutic implications of approving an underorganized single mother's allowing her occasional lovers to assume the role of sometime parents to her children?

The therapist's value system also determines the definition of the client's problems. The issue exemplifies Elkaim's thesis (1979) that when the problems of an individual or family are the result of society's failures, society must assume responsibility for changing along with the client. In his work with disadvantaged families he treats society as part of the problem and helps families organize to confront their communities. For him the problems of the poor include not just families, but also their communities. His expansion of the playing field for therapeutic intervention conveys his social values.

Again, values are also central to assessment and evaluation in therapy. One cannot evaluate without standards. Evaluative standards are drawn from society's, the professions', and individual therapists' ideas about what is functional and appropriate. Culture, ethnicity, race, and even socioeconomic status have influenced diagnoses. Lawson speaks to the effect on African Americans of racially colored diagnoses:

> In mental health, blacks are more likely to receive the least desirable, least optimistic diagnoses. In the past, blacks were more likely to be diagnosed as schizophrenic and recent research suggests that many of these patients had an affective disorder that was misdiagnosed. (1985, p. 96)

Therapists are often unconscious of their biases, but nevertheless operate through them in therapy.

Values are also a factor in the therapeutic approaches assumed by therapists, sometimes matching and sometimes not matching the cultural needs of families. In talking about poor Puerto Rican families, Garcia-Preto asserts that "the therapist's influence in the system [the Puerto Rican family] will automatically increase if the family is able to relate to him or her as they would do to a comadre or compadre" (1982, p. 179). Her statement reflects the value that Puerto Ricans traditionally place on personalizing relationships. She further states that "the therapist's willingness to meet the family's request for concrete services and to act as their advocate is an important vehicle for establishing a trusting relationship" (p. 180). She recommends structural family therapy because the "emphasis that the approach places on engaging the family in such a [personal and trusting] relationship is a reason for its success with Puerto Ricans" (p. 183). Whatever one's opinion of the writer's conclusions, they demonstrate the kinds of cultural values that influence her choice of a model of intervention with a particular kind of family.

Regarding values in the determination of therapeutic goals, we see this issue arising in the practical, day-to-day ideals that therapists communicate to families. For example, the role of women in families is one of the most commonly debated issues in the field. Hare-Mustin summarizes a feminist perspective that views the traditional role of women as pathological when she says that:

> A feminist-oriented family therapist can intervene in many ways to change the oppressive consequences of stereotyped roles and expectations in the family. (1978, p. 192)

Goldner offers a specific application when she advises therapists against trying to keep families together when that may not be in the woman's best interests. She warns against assuming that the concept of family is a "moral good" (1985, p. 23) and offers a feminist perspective that family is a "social arrangement" (p. 23) that does "not benefit men and women equally" (p. 22). She is, therefore, more readily prepared to work for the woman to escape the "arrangement" than someone who holds marriage to be a "moral good." It is evident that these strongly held perspectives on gender, family, and marriage affect therapeutic goal-setting.

My contention here is that value biases are pervasive in all aspects of therapy. The question is not one of *whether* the therapist's values will come face to face with the family's values in the crucible of therapy, but *how*. How can therapists work with their professional and personal values to benefit the families they treat? Negotiating the values that form the basis of problem definition, assessment, therapeutic interventions, and goal-setting becomes central to the therapeutic process.

THE NATURE OF THE NEGOTIATIONS

Negotiating values is more vital to therapy in today's society than ever before. Less is accepted on the strength of tradition and precedent; more is debated and discussed. There are reasons for this transformation. The speed of technological and social changes is greater today than during any previous period in human history. People have more choices, more options, and fewer rules to guide them.

The explosion in the amount and quality of information available through the media, telephones, computers, and easier travel accelerates social change. Quickening feedback loops open the entire ecostructure of society to rapid and pervasive change. Walls collapse and options multiply. Traditions, customs, and roles within social relationships transform. They resist, accommodate, mutate, or vanish within this swirl of social movement.

With the loosening of social structure, people gain greater personal flexibility in their own lives—separating their destinies, and thus their paths, from the rest of society. In America, society has sanctioned such personal latitude through legislative and judicial decisions formalizing the separate, widening, and competing rights of all segments of society. Children divorce their parents. Women choose pregnancy through contractual liaisons or anonymous donors. People obtain "marital" benefits through duration of association. People have more individual possibilities, but also more personal stress, as they find themselves progressively more on their own to work out their own destinies. In today's world, therapy has taken on the task of assisting people navigate this social evolution. The problem is that therapy and therapists themselves are immersed in this same tangle of divergent paths.

STRUCTURE, VALUES, AND FUNCTION

This evolutionary process depends upon continually negotiating relationships. Today, this also means negotiating the very societal, philosophical, and moral premises upon which the structure of people's relationships rest—their roles, alignments, and power. People find themselves negotiating the values that intrinsically mediate structure and function in their interactions. As people decide *how* to relate to one another *(structure of relationships)*, they are not just motivated by the expedience of the *outcome (function)* they seek. They are also searching for the values, principles, and ideals around which to build their relationships. Values are a variable to be negotiated in the relationship between the structure and function in their social relations.

For therapists, values have become an overarching factor in their work. When they meet with families to help solve specific problems, they do not just look to "achieving outcomes." The task of helping has become more than healing psychopathology or fixing social dysfunction. It also contends with the most fundamental assumptions about the meaning and purposes underlying their lives. For example, therapists do not now assume a "standard" contract undergirding family life. Society is questioning formerly accepted family roles, moral obligations, and functions. Society's questions, doubts, and ambiguities are chipping away at the institutions that supposedly ground people's lives. Families are affected, but so are therapists and their therapy. Today, therapists struggle to find the attitudes, behaviors, and relationships that will serve as appropriate solutions to people's problems. That makes it a daunting task for therapists to work even with families that are still together and living in relatively stable, culturally defined communities.

With underorganized poor families coming from depleted communities and beleaguered minority groups, therapists face even greater challenges. Here even the most fundamental questions of structure, values, and function cry out for an answer. With underorganized families, therapists encounter exceptions to all aspects of family life. They are forced to struggle with fundamental questions about who is in and who is out of the family today. They face questions about the roles of people connected to the family—what roles they *should* have when they live in or out, or are just passing through. For example, is the mother or grandmother the executive parent? What parental role *should* the absent father have versus the mother's current live-in lover?

Moreover, these families have relationships with their communities that call for negotiations. For poor families, their communities represent the bread of the agencies that provide the basic sustenance of income, housing, and educational and medical services. Their communities are also the spirit of extended family, neighbors, and church that give love and a sense of belonging. For disadvantaged families with few personal resources, these ties to community mean survival. However, in today's world the rules by which they relate to community require divining, negotiating, and renegotiating. People are having to figure out the rules for entry; once in they have to struggle to maintain their own identities and power. They have to do so in a world where the rules keep changing, as parties, interest groups, and ideologies vie for influence over government and its resources. For example, their churches may or may not agree with their public schools about sexual morality for their children. Their personal values about family roles may or may not coincide with their public welfare worker's.

Families that have racial and cultural identities distinct from the dominant society have the added challenge of contending with bias and chauvinism. Moreover, in America the question is even further complicated by the common mixture of ethnic and racial identities in families. These families and their members are in a continual state of negotiating values, rules, and roles. Professionals approach them with their own stereotypes and confusion, further complicating the family's relationship to the services. For example, in what kind of foster family (race, economic status, and religion) will a minority child, especially a mixed race child, be placed temporarily during a family crisis? At the heart of the relationship of poor, minority families to society and its services will be questions about personal morality, family loyalty, and social conformity in the context of race, ethnicity, and culture.

CLINICIANS CONFRONTING VALUES IN THERAPY

Not only clients face this challenge to values; therapists do as well. They, too, are part of a society that is undergoing an uncertain, unsettled, and conflicted evolution in social values. On a daily basis therapists find the constancy and clarity of their values challenged ever more profoundly. Therapists face the call to help families resolve their personal problems with the related value issues. In the process, they must confront their own issues with values—about culture, race, morals, and spirituality. Viewed in this way, the negotiation of values in therapy is a vitally dynamic process. It requires that therapists secure clarity and competence in dealing not only with their clients' values but also with their own.

The Challenge

This challenge to competence about values is ultimately a challenge to be an effective and ethical therapist. The therapist's negotiation around values with a client is further complicated by the reality that the therapist is in a special position of power. Such leverage raises certain clinical and ethical concerns: when to communicate values to a client and when not to; what values to communicate and how? The therapist's job is to further therapeutic goals, but within personal and social moral frameworks.

Managing Negotiations in Therapy

In practice, therapists who do not attend to the transactions over values between themselves and their clients are not fully in charge of their therapy. They are not taking responsibility for one of the fundamental forces shaping the therapeutic process.

These negotiations over values are held at a variety of levels of abstraction. They range from "parents should love their children" (general principle) to "this parent should love her child" (particular implication) to "in these circumstances this parent should demonstrate her love for her son in this particular way" (operational application).

The more abstract the value level, the more likely the agreement between therapist and client. Naturally, the odds in favor of agreement also improve insofar as the parties involved share similar personal backgrounds. The closer one gets to the operational applications of a value or the greater the social differences between therapist and family, the more likely the gap between them will be an issue.

The model of therapy, the characteristics of the clientele and their problems, and the personal styles and social attitudes of the therapist will all influence the extent and nature of the therapist's involvement in a client's values. Problem-solving approaches to therapy, such as the structural, use practical action to achieve therapeutic results. Consequently, they tend to involve therapists in judgments and decisions about the operational applications of value principles. Some therapists are also just oriented toward *doing*, and naturally tend to push their agendas in concrete ways. Some have attitudes that incline them to patronize and, therefore, operate from an assumption that they have a special wisdom that their less educated, poorer, troubled clients lack. Some just have strong convictions about their values, whether moral or social, and will want to "correct" their clients.

Client issues themselves pull therapists into the arena of value negotiations. Some problems that clients present have value issues by implication, such as disciplining children, which involves both family structure and standards of behavior. Values can also be the source of conflict within individual clients or between family members. Clients' struggles with moral questions, for example, can affect their emotional life and family relationships. However, conflict over values can also become a mask behind which to hide other pathology. People can externalize a conflict and blame their culture or church for what is essentially their own reluctance to hold themselves accountable.

When determining how to approach values in therapy, therapists need to understand their clients and the clinical issues, and to
have a handle on their clients' values and their own value issues.
The challenge can be particularly difficult when:

1. There are differences between therapists and clients that
   have powerful emotional, moral, or social charges for
   each;
2. Therapists are uncomfortable getting into values because
   of their own discomfort with certain racial, cultural, gender, or moral issues;
3. Therapists are simply unsophisticated about values as a
   factor in psychology and personal relationships and find
   themselves shocked, anxious, and defensive with their
   clients in this arena.

In the current atmosphere of heightened sensitivity to diversity,
incompetence about values can seriously handicap therapists.

Whether therapists care about values or not, the poor are
likely to draw them into dealing with values as an issue in therapy.
Because their life issues tend to be practical and concrete, the poor
are likely to seek answers to their problems at the level of the
operational applications of values. Underorganized families, for example, are likely to have issues that involve basic and compelling
questions about family roles and rules. In effect, where there is
poverty, minority status, and underorganization, there is greater
likelihood that workers will contend with personal and family
issues that touch on values.

In general, therapists also need a sensitivity to how people's
values are embedded in their life experience. This means being
able to perceive what values people profess, how conflicted or
unformed they are about their value system, and how they are
actually applying their values to their everyday life. Therapists can
observe these various facets of values in life through people's relationships with themselves, their families, and communities. Ultimately, therapists anchor all they see about clients' values in the
problems people present for therapy. Let us briefly look at a thera-

pist confronted with cultural values as an underlying issue in his work with a family.

THE TOLEDO FAMILY

The father is 40 years old and from Spain. The mother is 35 and from Puerto Rico. They have two daughters, 18 and 15. The 15-year-old, Gloria, is the parents' worry. She wants to go out on weekends and stay out as late as her friends, at least until midnight. During the week she wants to spend time, standard American adolescent time, on the telephone. She hangs out in mixed company and is much interested in boys. She shows little interest in school, although she has ability.

Her father objects to virtually all of the above. He is vocal in telling Gloria what he thinks, which he sees as part of exercising proper parental authority. When Gloria has answered him back disrespectfully, he has slapped her. She reported him to Child Protective Services. The mother tries to mediate between the two. She feels her husband is unreasonable and her daughter stubborn. She has both her husband and daughter angry at her much of the time for what each perceives is her loyalty to the other. Nevertheless, it is she who keeps the situation from exploding.

The mother is quite Americanized, but the father is from a rural, traditional Spanish family. Moreover, as a boy he felt that his father favored his brothers over him. For that reason he left home and country and eventually landed in the U.S. He spent much of his life wanting to prove himself to his father. Unfortunately, a few years ago, he was in an automobile accident and suffered moderate brain damage, which has left him permanently disabled. He has much trouble with short-term memory, is irritable and short-tempered. He also suffers from depression and has been drinking, feeling that he is no longer much of a man. All this further adds to his need to feel like a functional husband and father in his cultural tradition. When his daughter challenges his authority, his pain is acute. Privately he talks of feeling worthless.

The situation has escalated until the mother has asked for therapy for the family. Gloria is feeling more and more alone at home. She is talking about hurting herself and her father. She has times of some emotional intimacy with her mother, but then becomes angry and withdrawn again whenever her mother does not side with her against her father. The mother has a good grasp of what Gloria is experiencing, but finds herself between a rock and a hard place. She loves them both.

Once therapy begins, the therapist finds himself in a position analogous to the mother's. With the father, he has the advantage of being a Latino male, albeit an American-born Puerto Rican. Because the therapist is Latino and male, the father looks to him to side with him against the women. However, the father is also emotionally vulnerable to the therapist, who is an authority, male and older—a perfect stand-in for the man's father. The therapist's siding with the mother or the daughter could further risk the father's losing face at home. On the other hand, the therapist is as Americanized a Puerto Rican as the mother and, with his wife, is raising his adolescent daughter with much of the same flexibility of structure that the father eschews. Within him lives the tension between traditional Latino values and Anglo-American culture. Aware of his own internal dialogue, its contradictions and discomfort, he can identify with the parents' respective differences.

The therapist learns to play both sides of the net and manages with difficulty to win everyone's trust. Each party needs to believe the therapist understands both the social values and emotional issues involved. More than that, it becomes a matter of convincing all parties that he cares even when he disagrees. He has to supply the trust to glue the various parties together in times of conflict and hurt.

When matters between Gloria and the father reach a crisis point, Gloria becomes more provocative and father feels more frustrated and helpless; his drinking escalates. The therapist confronts them with the growing risk that father or daughter could spin out of control. He convinces Gloria to seek refuge in her mother. He challenges the father to find competence as a father and a man in new ways. He will need to trust his wife and the therapist. The therapist suggests to the father that he loosen up his efforts to help his daughter through his paternal authority, the cornerstone of his old world view of fatherhood. The question is how to do it and not diminish the man.

The therapist decides to approach the man through their identification with one another. The father feels vulnerable. The therapist has to be personal but also professional with him, genuine but strategic.

The therapist can identify with the father's plight. As the father of a teenage daughter, he has learned the wisdom of depending upon the mother. The therapist offers this father a model that gives more centrality to Mrs. Toledo with their daughter, in which the father exercises his role more as support than authority.

Strategically, the therapist is able to approach the father as another Latino father who has found himself up against it in America where authority must be exercised within a more reciprocal relationship. He is able to tease the father as one man to another about his doomed efforts to stay the old course. The therapist understands the challenge of making the change. He appreciates the father's fear that he will lose the ability to guide and protect his daughter, but also knows that paradoxically he will gain both respect and leverage with her. The father is able to hear it. The mother is glad to accept the job she has been trying to take on all along. However, she cannot help but needle the father about his not accepting advice she had already offered and his receiving it now only from another man. Gloria softens when the father's pressure lessens and when she sees mother and father together.

Discussion

Values are a dynamic variable in therapy, not a staid monument to culture, race, or religion. Clients' values are a fundamental resource for living life, and an essential resource in therapy. Negotiating a modification of values is relevant to therapy when a therapist judges that some change is necessary to the solution of a client's problem, as with Mr. Toledo. Where that contingency between values and a client's problem does not exist, therapists are out of bounds if they seek to influence clients' values.

In this case, the therapist deemed that a change in values about family structure was necessary to solve the problem the family wanted solved. These are tough calls—it is a question of judgment, but whose judgment? With the Toledos, could a father who was not brain-damaged and who was better connected emotionally to his daughter have successfully maintained a traditional Spanish father role even in today's America? Why not, particularly if they were in a Spanish immigrant community that would have supported the family in its traditions? We will never know. For the Toledos our solution worked.

NEGOTIATING PRINCIPLES

There is a spectrum of active influence a therapist may exercise when dealing with clients about values. At the minimum, therapists can offer clients technical help in evaluating and adjusting their own values in relation to the life problems they want solved. This means assisting with the formal aspects of the negotiating process, such as identifying the values for discussion, how they relate to the issues, and how members of a family can most profitably go about deliberating together. At the other end of the continuum, therapists can make a conscious effort to influence clients' values, as they do when they tell parents what the law prohibits when it comes to physically disciplining children. Somewhere in the middle, therapists may insinuate other perspectives to enrich the repertoire of viewpoints people are considering. I believe there are legitimate reasons for therapists to follow any of the above courses so long as they adhere to some fundamental principles.

The basic principles I suggest for therapists to follow in their attitudes toward client values are that therapists:

1. Attempt to exercise no more influence over clients' values than is required to address clients' problems.
2. Where ethical and functional, work within their clients' value frameworks.
3. Where it is not possible to stay within clients' systems, suggest values that allow clients:
    a. to know that these values come from the therapist;
    b. to discern whether it is the therapist's personal or professional opinion; and
    c. to have the freedom to accept or not these views.

When in the third instance therapists negotiate values between themselves and clients, clients will feel free to disagree only if therapists treat them as having the right and the power to differ without losing the relationship with the therapist. This implies that therapists will communicate the same respect and concern for them whether the clients agree or disagree. Moreover, therapists can be respectful and care about their clients even if they must exercise legal authority, such as reporting illegal actions. They must however, be sensitive to whether their influence is a legitimate professional effort or an insidious personal manipulation.

Nevertheless, situations in which therapists disagree with clients on purely ethical grounds are very difficult. Generally, therapists can disassociate themselves from the moral decisions made by clients. However, there will be times when therapists, because of their own moral principles, cannot allow themselves even a remote association with clients' moral decisions. Just like their clients, therapists must be free to stay within their own value system. They need to have the option of discontinuing therapy with clients and referring them elsewhere. No professional organization can expect therapists to work with clients on the basis of moral principles that are incompatible with therapists' values.

10. About Forgiving

Therapists strive to understand and relate to their clients. This calls for an emotional intimacy. To touch clients emotionally is to relate to them within a professionally bounded range of intimate sharing—visiting their life story as we engage with them in the therapeutic relationship. We also fuse with them within our own psyches, emotionally and intellectually identifying with them—thinking, feeling, and sensing their inner experience of life. Abstractly, all this may sound noble. In practice it involves opening ourselves to ourselves and to others—a vulnerability that may be painful, arduous, and conflict-laden.

Connecting with others is not just about sharing emotional experiences. It also means contending with values in ourselves and others that are part of all human encounters. Values can be as powerful as any force in joining or separating people. As therapists, we have our own cultural identities, family legacies, and personal values. We cannot and should not lose them in these therapeutic encounters. Yet, doing therapy calls for therapists to reach across differences in life perspectives in the most personal circumstances of clients' lives.

The question becomes: To what extent are we able and willing to join others in their current experience in order to accompany them into a new experience of life? In today's adversarial world of gender versus gender, race versus race, moral philosophy versus moral philosophy, it is hard to be intellectually open and emotionally vulnerable to others, especially if they are different. Sometimes it seems that difference in values has become a greater obstacle to trust and intimacy than difference in race. Because in contrast to race we can choose where to draw the line on values, that choice defines more personally our relationships with one another. Moreover, our philosophical viewpoint will define the meaning of race in our lives and relationships.

Relating to clients' lives involves a series of profoundly personal choices for therapists. Because we are all different, no matter how similar we appear, we face choices about how far to stretch to be empathic with others, knowing we will always fall short in some way. This empathy is a form of love, as it involves vulnerability to another, sharing in another's experience, and caring about another.

Relating from a distance can be easy, because it costs us little in terms of vulnerability to make some room for the other in the privacy of our psyches. However, this distance also allows us to hide our emotions and convictions while counterfeiting a personal connection. Looking concerned, we do not have to feel the other and absorb much of the other's soul.

On the other hand, therapist and client jointly participate in shaping a relationship. They choose how vulnerable to be to one another to achieve understanding, trust, and commitment in therapy. Therapists can reach deeply into their own life experience to understand their clients. They can stretch beyond the familiarity of their own experience (with the accompanying emotions and values) and open themselves to the experiences and perspectives of their clients. Clients themselves help therapists make empathic connections with them when they accept the risk of opening up their lives. They can make it awkward, stressful, and even dangerous to get close. They can also work with therapists to create a joint journey of risk with trust. Caring and empathy may call for heroic efforts from both therapist and client.

THERAPIST CHOICES

As they intervene, therapists are always making decisions about how to relate to clients; at one level they are deciding how to intervene, and at another they are choosing how to relate. The relationship decisions are the foundation of the entire therapeutic process.

As therapists, we decide what effort to invest, risk to take, commitment to make to the client. Everything follows these decisions. If we choose to care, then we take on both ourselves and our clients. We challenge ourselves and them to overcome the barriers that stand between us in order to make possible the work toward change. These decisions are continually renewed with every transaction. Therapists decide whether to commit and extend self, while clients decide whether to trust and join the effort. For therapists, consciousness of the choices they face puts them in touch with their own internal doings in the therapeutic relationship. Their knowledgeability and freedom to navigate within themselves are the foundation of their ability to choose wisely and effectively.

In this chapter, I speak to the nature of these choices, focusing on gaps around the differences that face therapist and client in the therapeutic relationship. An account of a clinical encounter follows to illustrate a therapist's personal struggles in a session and their implications for the technical strategy.

DIFFERENCE

The gap between therapist and client can lie in difference about values, identity, and background, that is, economic conditions, gender, race, culture, religion, political leanings, etc. The gap can also be around life decisions—the choices people make in particular life circumstances, decisions based on their beliefs and backgrounds. Differences in belief, being, and background are more about who people are than about what they do. Differences about life decisions have to do with the paths they have chosen in life. Whether the differences between therapist and client lie in who they are or in what they choose to do, the differences can be either stumbling blocks or stepping-stones. The therapist is in the position to decide whether and how to build a wall or a bridge with those stones.

THE CHOICES FOR
THE THERAPIST

In facing difference therapists choose between two paths:

1. *Reaching out to understand:* Therapists inform themselves about their clients at the levels of clients' emotional

makeup, relationships, values, identity and background, and life decisions;

2. *Reaching within to understand:* Therapists work with their own attitudes, beliefs, and life experiences to open themselves up to what is different and difficult for them about their clients.

The first path assumes that the gap between therapists and clients can be narrowed by exposing therapists to the life experience of their clients. This essentially says that we can grow to respect difference in others either by understanding the common elements of the human condition or by learning to appreciate what is special about them. Intellectual and emotional understanding creates the potential for caring.

However, understanding only accesses for us the other's experience. We still have to decide whether, how, and to what extent we want to empathize with what we see and understand. We must know that we have those choices. Person training (see Chapter 8) helps us grasp the nature of what is going on within ourselves when we react to what we experience with another person. Were person training to presuppose agreement with and emotional acceptance of another's values and personal decisions, the program would not be respectful of difference in the trainee. We must be free to choose a stance.

We may find our client compatible, and find it easy to identify with and care about the other. It is like caring about ourselves. However, we may disagree, be repelled, and choose to disassociate ourselves from something we see in a client—and still decide to look for a way to care and connect. To care for someone with whom we strongly disagree or of whose choices we disapprove, we may need something from the client that will free us to care, such as some human vulnerability or remorse for a past action. Whatever the case, trainees will also need help to understand the therapeutic implications of their decisions to agree, accept, and care—or not—relative to their clients' issues.

The second path to facing difference is uniquely personal—our own path based on our values and life experience, as well as our emotions. Our own life history, whether in our families or in society, can make opening up to another a serious challenge. As therapists we can choose to consider whether our thinking or emotional responses are distorted or faulty. We all have our own vulnerabilities. We hide from our own pain. We may not want to open ourselves up to the experiences of others that will unearth our own experiences. We may also have our own prejudices and narrowness. Out of identification with our families, ethnic groups, or political clans, we may close ourselves to others. Anger growing out of past social hurts may color our own attitudes towards others. Depending on the source of the ailment, we can choose to pursue remedies that fit the sickness.

Yet again, we may feel secure about how our thinking and life experience have shaped our attitudes about certain differences in others. We may have worked hard to get to where we are in our beliefs, and hold them dearly. Our life experience, whether personal crises we have confronted or our family legacies or culture, may rightly be important to us. In those cases, to ignore or deny where we are for the sake of our clients may be to betray ourselves.

WHAT TO DO WITH
THOSE CHOICES

This leaves us with some options:

1. If we believe our thinking and emotional responses are uninformed and/or distorted, we can work to clarify the beliefs and resolve the personal issues standing in our way.

   a. This means choosing to let in some light about our clients' lives, with the assumptions that understanding does not necessarily mean agreeing, and that not agreeing does not necessarily translate into not caring about the people themselves.

   b. This also means something about ourselves, e.g., that we may need to rethink our attitudes about others, or heal wounds from our personal lives that make it hard to be open to what is difficult for us in our clients.

2. However, where we believe that our thinking and emotional responses are as we want them to be, we can choose from various other paths:

   a. We will not work with people who represent certain differences in beliefs, identity, or background, or in life decisions.*

   b. We will try within ourselves to see past the differences we cannot accept and work with those clients' issues around which we can join.

   c. We will challenge the relationship and engage clients to see whether with their cooperation we can find a way of working together across our differences.

In circumstance 2b, therapists seclude themselves from aspects of their clients' lives to which they do not choose to relate. They relate to the aspects of their clients' lives they feel free to join in, and stay within those fences. In circumstance 2c, therapists, with the help of the client, look for how they can connect in order to do the therapy. Therapists and clients may or may not modify what they stand for or how they emotionally respond to each other in order to join around the common goal of solving the client's problem.

Therapists may not directly address the values or behavior

---

*This is a difficult one. I make a distinction. I will support people who have moral, ethical, or religious principles that do not permit them to even appear to condone certain choices or lifestyles in their clients. I believe they deserve our respect and that we should not penalize them for their convictions. However, that does not mean that a sectarian agency, for example, should be compelled to allow them to practice on the basis of principles that are contrary to those of the agency. On the other hand, I cannot in any way personally support people who make choices about clients because of their prejudices against certain groups based on ethnic, racial, or nationalist exclusiveness. I do not believe society has any obligation to cooperate with them by, for example, permitting them to practice their prejudices through institutions that represent those biases. Moreover, people may hold to certain moral principles that violate the general moral principles of our society and that society, as well as our professional organizations, may want to outrightly condemn. In our pluralistic society none of this is simple, but it does need to be confronted at the level of society and at the level of our own personal consciences.

to which they object if they believe their silence does not imply concordance. However, they may feel compelled to voice their opposition to the values or behavior of a client to free themselves to connect with the person. In that case, it is clear for all concerned that working together does not imply the therapists' endorsement of all that person represents. It also frees therapists emotionally to relate with all of themselves, that is, all that agrees and all that disagrees.

Therapists will have to come to their own solutions. These solutions will shape what kind people they will be as therapists. They may set a goal for themselves of accepting and caring about every one of their clients. Trying to understand and care about someone despite disagreement and incompatibility means reaching deeper into self and into the other person. Insofar as the other person or family can join in the effort of creating a therapeutic relationship, they are also reaching more deeply into themselves. This very personal, shared effort may translate into all parties' being more personally accessible and vulnerable within the therapeutic relationship without having to betray themselves. The safety of the therapist's personal commitment and honest position allows the client greater freedom to take in the therapist in the therapeutic experience. Clients can then choose to open themselves to the relationship and to change—or not.

A DIFFICULT SESSION

The following session was with a family seen as part of a workshop consultation. We have no information about what happened with the family after the session.

The session was difficult for the consultant-therapist, beginning with the preparations. The information given the therapist before starting was that the stepfather, John, had had incestuous relations with both stepdaughters, Barbara, aged 22, and Bernice, aged 16. He also almost certainly had violated an older stepdaughter, Lucy, who would not be present. The stepfather was an alcoholic who had stopped drinking in the past year and was now working regularly. He had been convicted of sexually abusing his stepdaughters and now faced sentencing. The therapist was also told that the mother of the girls, Mary, had witnessed and abetted the violation of her daughters. She, too, would participate in the session.

The stepfather was a Native American; the mother, caucasian. Family members had been in a variety of counseling situations separately, but not as a family. Bernice was still living at home and Barbara was visiting regularly, although she would have little to do with her stepfather. Against everyone else's wishes, Barbara was, in fact, actively lobbying with the presentence investigator to have her stepfather imprisoned.

For the therapist the session presented several personally difficult issues. The therapist was himself the father of a daughter. The stepfather's violation of his daughters emotionally alienated him from the stepfather. However, the therapist felt even more troubled about a mother who reportedly had actively facilitated the violation of her own daughters. This felt like the most fundamental kind of parental betrayal.

On top of that, another source of conflict for the therapist was that the stepfather was a Native American, with which the therapist instinctively identified, counting among his ancestors Puerto Rico's Taino natives. The therapist was vulnerable emotionally to a whole range of feelings toward the father, ranging from shame and anger to the impulse to rescue and rehabilitate the man. There were moral, cultural, and emotional issues here that permeated the therapeutic relationship and clinical thinking of the therapist.

Initially, the therapist invited the family to set the agenda. They talked about the problems Bernice was having in school. This early part of the session allowed the therapist to make some connection with each member of the family. However, for the therapist, the discussion of Bernice's school issue failed to generate anything viscerally significant. He decided to plunge ahead into the topic of the incest, which they had not even mentioned up to that point.

Once into the topic of the incest, the emotional tone of the session became intense and deliberate, punctuated by silences. The pace was set by the therapist, who was struggling to make room within himself for each of the various family members. He related readily to some, and to others with difficulty. The members were coming as a family, but they were also divided. For the therapist, the stepfather was the bad guy and not as much a part of the family as those related by blood. Barbara, the one trying to get the stepfather incarcerated, was the good guy. The therapist felt pulled by some members to split the family and by others to unite them. He had his own questions about what family configuration to support.

In the Interviewing Room

The therapist sits with the family in a semi-circle. The stepfather is a man about 50. He has thinning hair and a face that looks weather-beaten. His expression never changes. He is intense, nervous, and smokes nonstop. His head has a tremor that is exaggerated by tension. The mother is a heavy-set woman with sad eyes in an impassive face. Barbara is medium built, tense, and also a heavy smoker. Her dark eyes are alert and full of feeling. Bernice is a little heavy. There is a blandness about her at the surface, with the hint of a deeply hidden wound.

Dialogue

THERAPIST You're talking now like a family that has the problems that we all have, and you talk like a family that's moving ahead. Now, the incest was a big part of your lives for how long? For how many years? . . .

JOHN . . . Barb?

BARBARA I was wondering if he was going to ask me. To me it's since I was seven. So how long is that? Years and years and years. Too long.

. . .

THERAPIST But it started 16 years ago and maybe ended last year [with Bernice]?

JOHN Yes, last year.

THERAPIST Okay, so it was a very long time. It was a big part of your lives. You don't go through something like that for that many years and just walk away from it.

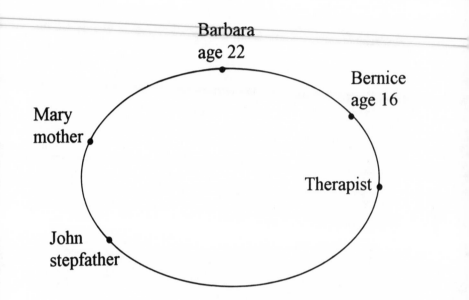

Figure 10.1. The Family Session

JOHN No, you don't.

THERAPIST 'Cause you can't look at each other without remem-
   bering.

JOHN True. It burns in me every day, every night. Every day, every night it's on my mind. I can see it on Barb's face. I can see
   it in her eyes when I look at her. Not only right now, but when
   she comes over to the house to eat dinner or when we go out
   to eat dinner. It's tearing me up on the inside. It has been for
   some time. I think it will tear me up till I go to my grave.
   It's something you don't forget. There's such things as being
   forgiven, but there are also things that can't be forgotten.

John raises the issue of forgiveness. He implies he would like
forgiveness, but does not ask for it. He talks graphically about his
pain and guilt. The issue resonates in the therapist, who has his

own issue with John. He is struggling to empathize with John's pain, which would be a kind of "forgiveness" for therapist. The therapist latches onto the question of forgiveness.

THERAPIST　Have you been forgiven? . . .

JOHN　No. It has never been voiced.

THERAPIST　Have you ever asked for forgiveness?

JOHN　No. Why? I'm afraid of a refusal. That would even hurt worse. (*Long silence*) I'm hoping in due time that the girls will see fit to forgive me, but to forget it—they can't forget it, no more than I can forget it. . . . My biggest ambition right now . . . I want to be the kind of dad that they can look at and say, "Hey, that's my dad" with pride.

THERAPIST　John, until you—

JOHN　That's gonna take time.

THERAPIST　It's going to take more than time. Until you ask for forgiveness and you receive the forgiveness, you will not be able to be the father you say you would like to be.

JOHN　Well, what about a rejection, a refusal?

THERAPIST　It won't change it. If they haven't forgiven you now, whether they say it or not, you will not be able to be their father.

JOHN　Barb, can you forgive me?

BARBARA　No!

JOHN　Bernice?

BERNICE　Yep.

THERAPIST　Do you believe Bernice's forgiveness?

JOHN　I believe in what she says.

THERAPIST　Barb, do you believe Bernice has really forgiven your dad? I'm afraid she just may be trying to be good to him, be kind to him, and to say that even though she hasn't really forgiven him.

BARBARA　I really don't know. I use to get angry at her for still being able to call him "dad" and I don't. It used to make me angry when she would even want to associate with him or have anything to do with him. So I don't know. I now see us both as individuals. She can do and feel about things the way she wants to, and me too. So I don't know. All the things she used to do would make me angry. I use to think, "Why can't she get mad at him, why is she still calling him dad, why is she still talking good about him?" and I used to get mad at Mother for staying married to him and for saying, "Oh, John's stopped drinking and John's doing this and John's doing that," and I didn't want to hear that. I didn't want to hear if he was doing good, bad, or otherwise. I didn't really want to know and the whole family just made me really angry because they were all together and I was against it.

THERAPIST So, you still haven't forgiven Bernice?

. . .

BARBARA I don't understand it. No, but I accept it. I accept it.

THERAPIST Did you ever ask her why?

BARBARA Why?

THERAPIST Yes.

BARBARA "Cause he's the only dad I know," and he is for her. I do know another one. I do know that I have a father that has my blood and didn't do those things to me. So you know, John is not my father, somebody else is.

. . .

THERAPIST Your natural father, have you ever met him?

BARBARA Yeah, I remember him. I remember him a little.

THERAPIST Do you ever see him?

BARBARA Not for many years, but I did when I was younger.

THERAPIST How come you haven't seen him?

BARBARA Because Mother got married to John and we left the state and my real father got divorced from Mother and got remarried . . .

MARY He had to marry her. . . .

. . .

He filed for divorce simply because he got this other woman pregnant and the parents of this other girl said that if he didn't

marry her, they were going to press charges on him for statu-
tory rape, I believe it was.

THERAPIST How old was she?

MOTHER She was about 18—17—somewhere around there. She
was young.

. . .

THERAPIST (*To Barbara*) How come you never went back to look
for your father?

BARBARA Oh, I don't know. Sometimes I think about it, but I don't
know.

THERAPIST How do you feel about him?

BARBARA I don't know that either. I wonder how he feels about
me (*tearful*).

THERAPIST Are you afraid to find out?

BARBARA Sort of. Because I wonder if he would have been an
abuser. . . . I was feeling like, well, he's probably like that too.
So I guess that's it.

MOTHER Well, in a way he was an abuser, maybe not in an incest
way, but in beating ways, yes he was.

BARBARA I remember when we ran away.

MOTHER Yes, I took her and we ran away, because he was going to
beat on her and I wouldn't allow it. And I took her and I left.
So, in some ways he was an abuser if beating is as much as
abusing, too.

. . .

But, incestways, no, not that I know of, nothing like that ever
happened.

THERAPIST (*To Barbara*) You don't have a father.

BARBARA That's all right, it's all right with me.

THERAPIST It's not all right.

BARBARA Yes, it is.

THERAPIST I wish it were.

BARBARA But it is.

THERAPIST Okay. (*Long silence*)

Barbara has cut off her stepfather. She wistfully talks about having had a "real" father who did not do "those things" to her. Yet, when it comes down to it, she does not trust her real father either. She tries to deny that is a problem for her. The therapist will not accept that. Together with the question of forgiveness is a companion issue, that of the loneliness around cut-offs. The abuse—beatings and incest—have made trust and intimacy hard to come by in this family. Barbara gives voice to it. The therapist is feeling some of her pain and imagining others in her family feeling that loss of intimacy. What are the stories of Bernice, Mary, and even John?

THERAPIST (*To Mary about John*) Have you forgiven him?

MOTHER Well, yes. There for a while, no, I didn't. I realized there, too, that I was putting all the blame onto him, but actually part of that was on me, too, for not hearing the girls, for not hearing them when they told me what he had done. I just didn't want to hear it. I just turned it off. But yes, I've forgiven him because I've seen a good change in him.

Mary had not witnessed the abuse as was originally reported, but she knew and had not stopped it. She now confesses her guilt to her family. However, no one responds directly to her, and she goes on to finish talking about forgiving her husband. The therapist is aware within himself of his own feelings about her failure to protect her daughters. He is touched by her remorse more than by the stepfather's. He can feel the openness and painful vulnerability in her confession. The therapist wants her family, particularly her daughters, to hear her. She needs to confess. Are the daughters trying to protect her? She has protected herself from the pain of reality in the past. She seems ready to face it now. The therapist is not going to let her moment pass. He goes straight to her pain.

THERAPIST Have you forgiven yourself?

MOTHER No, I'm still tossing that around. . . . I think about it now more than I ever have.

THERAPIST Have the girls forgiven you?

MOTHER Well, I don't know about Barbara, but Bernice said she has. But I don't know about Barbara.

THERAPIST Have you asked her?

MOTHER No, I haven't. (*To Barbara*) Have you forgiven me?

BARBARA I don't know. I don't know.

(*Silence*)

THERAPIST Barbara breaks my heart because she not only does not have a father, but she doesn't have a mother.

(*Silence*)

JOHN And, have I forgiven myself? No, I haven't.

THERAPIST Would you like to talk about it?

JOHN Not really, I've got to prove something. I've got to prove this to myself, that I am the kind of a husband or dad that's expected of me before I can prove to others.

Internally, the therapist reacts with irritation to John's intrusion into Mary's moment. Emotionally, he is still with Mary and Barbara. John cuts in to talk only about himself, apparently insensitive to what they are going through with each other at that moment. The therapist associates to what self-absorption must have allowed John to abuse the girls. The therapist is having trouble being open to John. He takes this visceral reaction and converts it into an effort to give John an opportunity to do something for Mary. It could be good for him and good for her.

THERAPIST Do you realize that Mary carries this burden with you?

JOHN I know she does.

THERAPIST She was part of it.

JOHN I know it. And that's why right now I've got a point that I've got to prove. I've got to prove it to this guy sitting right here.

THERAPIST Have you forgiven her?

JOHN Yes. I've forgiven her.

THERAPIST You don't hold it against her that she just let this thing go on, and let you go on doing what you were doing?

JOHN No.

THERAPIST She could have stopped you, you know.

JOHN Yes, if she had knew, yes.

THERAPIST She knew.

JOHN I said, "*if* she knew."

THERAPIST She did know!

MARY Yes, I did know.

BARBARA She knew.

JOHN (*To Mary*) I assumed you didn't.

BARBARA How could she not know when Lucy gets married at a very young age and you both sign for her to marry this older man, twenty years older than her, and you both agree to do that with Lucy. You run out of state and leave me. You know she knew. You know she was helping to protect you and cover up everything. You know she knew. . . . You know she knew. All the signs are there—mother knowing—most definitely.

MARY (*To John*) You ought to remember, too, that I did ask you and told you what the girls did say to me one time, and of course, you denied it, which I expected that, but I just didn't want to deal with it. Really, I'll admit. I didn't want to deal with it. I didn't want no part of it. I didn't want to deal with it at that time.

JOHN I guess so.

MARY It's no guess. It's for sure. I know and I'm feeling every bit of it, too. (*Crying*)

JOHN So am I.

(*Long silence*)

THERAPIST Do you love her, John?

JOHN More than anything in the world.

THERAPIST Could you hold her hand now?

JOHN Sure.

THERAPIST She needs you. She just told you something that was very hard for her to say.

JOHN Yes, I know. (*He reaches for her hand and holds it.*)

THERAPIST Okay.

(*Silence*)

JOHN What comes up on the twelfth, come what may I ain't gonna change my mind about my feelings or how I feel about my family.

THERAPIST When you go to court, there is a chance you might get put away?

JOHN There's a possibility. That's what quite a few people are hoping for.

THERAPIST Barb?

JOHN For one.

THERAPIST Anybody else?

JOHN Presentence investigator.

THERAPIST Well, John, you did something that deserves for you to be punished.

JOHN I don't deny it.

THERAPIST Okay.

JOHN I did deny it for quite a while . . . but not anymore.

THERAPIST If you do get sent away, Mary will have helped send you away, too, you know. It will be on her, too. She will be feeling that, and feeling responsible.

JOHN I don't like her to feel that way.

THERAPIST John, you can't take away her responsibility for what she did. You can understand it.

JOHN I can understand it, but I can't take away her responsibility. . . .

THERAPIST That's right.

THERAPIST She will need your understanding. What just happened now was very important.

JOHN It's very important.

THERAPIST She told you and you finally heard her. Okay. Because everything that goes on now that hurts you, that hurts these two girls, Mary is going to be living with that. It's a very heavy burden. One can say you are their stepfather. She is not their stepmother. (*Pause*) You two need to talk about this. You two

need to get together privately at home and sit down and look
at each other and talk about it.

JOHN   I take responsibility for not doing that. There has been times
where she wanted to sit down and talk to me. I just don't want
to discuss it. I just don't want to talk about it. I can't forget it. I
just want to try to block it.

THERAPIST   John, you've got to stop being selfish. This woman is
suffering too much for you to act like it's just your burden.

JOHN   That's true.

THERAPIST   . . . That means . . . you have to face her and let her tell
you where she's at.

JOHN   That's true.

THERAPIST   Nobody else in this world can do for her right now what
you can. She needs to talk with you about it.

JOHN   We'll talk tomorrow.

Mary finally confesses, and is heard. Not only does John acknowledge her, but Barbara has an opportunity to say forcefully
that she knew her mother knew and did nothing to stop him.
For the therapist the wall between him and Mary has dissolved.
However, he is still struggling with his own feelings about John's
admission of guilt.

The therapist continues to be reactive to John's preoccupation
with his own needs and feelings. His lack of sensitivity to his wife
and daughters in the session keeps reminding the therapist about
the man's past manipulation and betrayal of Mary and his exploitation of the girls. In order to connect to the man, the therapist
needs to be genuine with him. The therapist needs to be able to
relate to John about what is going on in him, but in a way that is
therapeutic for the man and the family. He speaks directly to John
about his "selfishness" and about how he "deserves" punishment. The therapist is able to get out what he needs to say for
himself in a way that gives John a chance to own what he has
done and to give something back to Mary. While the therapist still
has trouble emotionally empathizing with John, he gives John a
chance to give back to the women in the family through Mary. It

does not come easily to John, but he responds. The therapist still has unfinished business with Barbara.

THERAPIST (*To Barbara*) I worry about you.

BARBARA Why?

THERAPIST Oh, come on, Barbara—

BARBARA What makes you think I should be worried about?

THERAPIST I didn't say you should be worried. I said I'm worried about you.

BARBARA That's what I said, I said—maybe I didn't say it right. Why?

THERAPIST You've been hurt all your life and you're still being hurt, and that bothers me. It's like, it's not over for you.

BARBARA I don't see it that way. I don't. It still hurts, but—

THERAPIST Barb, you can't even talk to your mother. There's now a wall between you and your mother.

BARBARA I can talk to my mother.

THERAPIST About her? What she did?

BARBARA No!

THERAPIST Okay. Okay.

MARY (*To Barbara*) That's what he's saying. (*To the therapist*) I understand what you're saying. No, we've talked, but not for what my part was.

BARBARA You've always—

MARY I've shied away.

BARBARA It's, "I don't want these groups, I don't want—you know, I have written this clarification letter for you and I tell you it's hard, you know and I—" Well don't write it then. I don't really want it then. It's all right. I don't really need it.

(*Silence*)

MOTHER Would you like to talk about it?

BARBARA Sometimes I would, and sometimes I wouldn't.

MOTHER Whenever you feel you're ready, let me know.

BARBARA And you'll just be ready?

MOTHER I'll be ready.

BARBARA You're sure?

MARY I'm very sure.

BARBARA For some reason, I don't know—I just—

MARY It's okay.

BARBARA It's hard for me to believe that—

MARY I understand that, but I am ready. I'm here. Whatever you have to say, or talk about my part of the incest.

(*Silence*)

BARBARA Okay.

MARY (*To the therapist*) I want to talk about it, at her convenience. (*To Barbara*) I'm not just going to plant it right on you. I want you to be ready as well as me.

BARBARA And I've been waiting for you to say, "Okay Barb, I can talk now, I can handle it"—and you haven't said that, so I've been just kind of in limbo.

MARY Well, I'm saying it now.

BARBARA Okay.

MARY It hasn't sunk in though—

BARBARA I don't know if I believe that.

MOTHER You own it. It's your feeling.

(*Silence*)

THERAPIST I believe you, Mary.

MARY Oh, I'm serious.

THERAPIST I know you are. You couldn't be anything but serious about something like this. (*To all*) We're finished. I wish you all well.

JOHN Thank you.

THERAPIST It won't be easy.

JOHN No, it's not going to be easy.

THERAPIST But that doesn't mean it can't be better.

The circle is completed between Mary and Barbara. This still leaves Bernice who has been absorbed in what has taken place between her mother and her sister. She seems shocked by mother's admission. She is holding much down. She does not have ready access to it. She has much work to do yet with her mother and sister, as well as with the man she wants to hold onto as her father. However, she needs to get in touch with what was down inside her first.

John seems to be looking at himself and trying to be honest. There is still something missing in him, in his ability to concern himself about others. Yet he appears ready to work. One suspects that all he has in the world is his family. He is holding onto it, such as it is. He wants to redeem himself.

FORGIVENESS

The theme of this interview was forgiveness. The stepfather raised the issue. It was his only issue, a question of redemption. Yet, he was the person who would find it most difficult to find redemption in the eyes of others. His crime of incest was naturally reprehensible and repulsive. Moreover, he had a character trait behind his transgression, an absorption in himself, that made it difficult to empathize with him and to trust him. Barbara, a stepdaughter whom he had violated and scarred, not only refused him forgiveness, but wanted him punished. She also happened to be the one who was the most articulate and sympathetic figure in his family. The daughter who was most ready to forgive was the most repressed emotionally, the most difficult one with whom to empathize. The mother, who also wanted to forgive, had not redeemed herself with her daughters, and consequently her forgiveness of him could come across as protecting her own complicity. It did not further the stepfather's cause.

What right did the therapist have to judge this stepfather? None. However, the therapist was human. He could have denied his personal reactions. To have done so would have meant distancing himself from himself. In so doing, he would have distanced himself from the family's drama. The stepfather was seeking to redeem himself in his own eyes and those of the family. The family was divided over whether to forgive him. At stake was the intactness of the family.

The therapist was able to take the question to the point of helping them all articulate it for themselves. The stepfather could acknowledge his guilt and his deserving punishment to the extent that his restricted emotions allowed expression. The mother and daughters could speak their hearts. Forgiveness and condemnation were clearly not just matters of yes or no. They were human emotions with deep roots—family relationships to be healed or broken, social justice to be meted out, and pain and anger to be faced.

For the family, the encounter with the therapist was one more step in a very complicated and human drama. Hopefully, it was a step that would free the family members to deal with their lives. The healing of souls and relationships depended upon it. The therapist took a step that seemed to expand the issue for all of them, by including Mary in the question of forgiveness. He drew the stepfather away from himself into helping Mary with her pain. Barbara could finally have the satisfaction of honestly confronting her mother. Bernice's denial was shaken. The emotional logjam in the family loosened. The members of the family could now deal with themselves and with one another with a greater degree of freedom.

The Therapist

It is evident that the question of forgiveness was an issue for the family. However, one must also ask why this therapist responded to it so readily. Another therapist might have picked up on something else the family raised. The answer would seem to be that there was a convergence between what was capturing the therapist's and the family's emotional attention. The therapist was struggling with his own conflict between feeling closed toward these abusive parents and wanting, as a therapist, to reach out to them. It was a question of the kind of commitment he could make to work with the parents in this family. Committing to them would mean identifying with them, engaging with them—touching them emotionally. To help the young women he would need to engage with their parents. Moreover, he felt an obligation to offer what he could to these parents. These people, whatever they had done, needed a chance to right their own lives for the girls, each other, and themselves.

He would have to "forgive" them in some sense of the word, but in what sense? He would have to get beyond their abuse and betrayal of these young women to care about the people themselves. The therapist could not just wish away the obstacles to connecting with the parents. However, given the nature of his job, he knew that understanding, relating to, and helping this family depended on how successfully he wrestled with and worked through these obstacles.

It would be a matter of finding ways to overcome the obstacles in himself and between him and them to making this connection. It was no surprise to discover in the process that each family member in his or her own way was struggling with feelings similar to his own. In working on his own issues he would work on theirs, and when dealing with theirs he would be dealing with his own. His issue with them and theirs with one another converged.

The therapist had to go through a rather complicated process. First, he needed to connect with the young women and know that he was taking care of their needs. Early in the interview he tried with Bernice, but was not able to empathize with her position of wanting to forgive the stepfather. Her anger and pain around the incest were so barely accessible that the forgiveness felt shallow. He could, however, feel with her need to be back home with her parents, even if it meant not feeling all the hurt associated with them.

On the other hand, Barbara's pain and anger were as palpable as the thrust of a knife. The therapist could resonate with her feelings. He anchored himself emotionally in her reactions. He could use the tension she was creating in the rest of her family with her anger and refusal to forgive. By validating her pain in the presence of the rest of the family, he confirmed her reality and amplified her voice within the family. The result was that they were compelled to contend with her. She spoke powerfully to one current of the therapist's feelings.

For the therapist, his hope was that Barbara's words would also resonate for Bernice by expressing feelings Bernice was having to hide from herself. Bernice's eyes and body language suggested that the issue of forgiveness took on greater meaning for her when

Barbara and Mary were dealing with each other about mother's part in the incest. The therapist felt he was offering Bernice something that might make a difference for her.

For the therapist, participation in the painful experience of Barbara and Mary confronting Mary's betrayal gave him full access to all of his internal struggle around forgiveness. Mary was to him the parent whose betrayal was most stinging. She was the natural parent and the same-gender parent. She understood, cared, and loved. That made the pain of the betrayal that much more acute. The family session offered Mary an encounter with everyone else's pain, and an invitation to confront herself and them with her guilt. Mary made herself accessible emotionally to John and her daughters. In the process, she reached the therapist. He could empathize with her guilt and regret. Who of us has not sinned? Who of us has not had a parent who hurt us; has not been a parent who failed our own children in some way?

What, then, did forgiveness represent to the therapist in his work with the family? It became a process through which he understood them, established a relationship with them, and fixed a pivot that gave direction to his work with them. However, it was also apparent that he passed through a significant personal process within himself around forgiveness to be able to work with the issue with the family.

THE THERAPIST'S PERSONAL BELIEFS

Now, this therapist's personal conviction about the beneficial effects of forgiveness predisposed him to open up a discussion about forgiveness when the stepfather introduced the subject. Regrettably, this is not the forum for this therapist to put forth all the associations with his personal life that forgiveness in a family context raised for him. However, he can at least try to distill his life experience into the philosophy about forgiveness underlying his encounter with the client family.

First of all, as a clinician he thinks himself responsible for addressing the psychological aspects of forgiving or not forgiving. He operates from the opinion that forgiving heals emotionally and not forgiving truncates emotional growth and the capacity for personal relationships.

From the perspective of emotions, not forgiving is about holding onto resentment—needing reparation from or punishment of the offender. Forgiveness is about letting go of the debt. The client who has been hurt no longer depends upon the offender emotionally to make up for or repair the injury. The client no longer waits for the payback. Emotionally he or she is free to give, love, and grow.

Getting to the place of forgiving requires taking certain steps, the first being to face the full extent of the wrong—the emotional hurt and the life consequences of the injury. Excusing, rationalizing, or denying diminishes the significance of the hurt. Facing that reality also means holding the offender accountable. It does not mean judging the moral state of the offender, i.e., how evil the person is. It does mean recognizing what the person did and the impact of the injury—the magnitude of the wound both to the one offended and to the relationship with the offender. The connection between them can be emotionally important to the one hurt, especially if the violator is a parent.

Facing the reality of the injury also requires facing one's own part in the event and ultimately being ready to forgive oneself without excusing what should not be excused. Some violations have victims who are totally helpless. Many more, especially in long-term relationships, involve some active participation. As much as we may want to protect the victim, we are condemning him or her to a secret guilt if that participation cannot be honestly faced, understood, and forgiven. This hidden guilt and hatred of self feed the splitting-off of personas. The acceptance of the frailty of our humanity frees us emotionally to love ourselves. Forgiving others is not possible without forgiving ourselves.

The therapeutic work of forgiveness continues with assisting the client to face the full meaning and impact of what happened. When it comes to the role of the offender, it means looking not only at what he or she did, but at what the offender meant and means emotionally to the client. That implies taking fully into account the emotions related not only to hurting back, but in particu-

lar to wishing to undo the injury and restore all that did feel good
and might have been in the relationship. This latter is often a secret
wish that binds the offended to the offender.

In order to face these realities, it may help for the victim to face
the offender. Talking to the offender may uncover not only the
reality of what happened and why, but also what is real and operating in the relationship today. The victim asks: Is this person sorry
or changed? Does he or she care about me and what has happened
to me as a result of the violation? This puts into the hands of the
client a reality to sift through in order to judge and decide about
the future. Looking into the eyes of the offender and speaking to
the injury may also give the client the chance to overcome an old
fear of that person, even an old emotional attachment.

What then follows is the work of examining all the emotional
implications of forgiving. Questions arise for the client: Will he or
she want to make up in some way for what happened? Is this a
debt that goes beyond a personal hurt and properly belongs to
some judicial authority? Should I acknowledge in some way my
role to free myself of my guilt? Is there a desire and possibility of
reconciliation on anyone's part? If so, is it appropriate and safe? If
not, can I root out of myself the emotional entanglements of the
need for love or for revenge, especially if the violator is a family
member? Inevitably there are many levels of emotion around forgiveness, often contradictory and hidden. Some are healthy and
some are self-defeating. Clients' emotions will range from not
wanting to accept the lonely responsibility for their own wounds
and scars to wanting back the offender to fill needs and hurts of a
deprived past. The outcome of their struggles about forgiving will
help determine whether they will gain emotional autonomy and
power and develop the capacity for trust and intimacy in other
personal relationships.

Still, there is a dimension of forgiveness beyond therapy—the
motivation born from a person's cultural, philosophical, and religious roots. A therapist can talk about the emotional freeing and
empowering effects of forgiveness. However, the motivation to forgive may also spring from the heart, wherein lies the ultimate goals
of an individual's life. What may be impossible to do for emotional
purposes may be doable for love of a transcendent God.

With our client family, the therapist did not get a glimpse of their spiritual motivations in just one session. What he did see left him concerned about Bernice's and Barbara's different emotional dispositions toward forgiving. He believed that emotionally driven needs of Bernice to reconcile and of Barbara to punish kept both trapped emotionally with the stepfather. Bernice will need help to face her pain about the breaking of trust in the relationship by her mother and stepfather before she can forgive and free herself from the past. Barbara has begun to think independently of her mother, sister, and stepfather. If, as a result of the consultation, she believes her mother's realization of her part in the incest and her regret over it, Barbara can choose to reconcile and regain a mother. It may be that she will never trust her stepfather again, no matter how much he changes. However, were she to move further toward forgiving him, she might let go enough so that, whether he were punished or not, she could proceed with her own healing. She could make peace with herself regardless of who is or is not on her side.

In this family session, the therapist took forgiveness as far as getting the family members further along the path of confronting what happened and stating where they were with each other. The therapist escorted them to where they could take yet another step toward choosing both what to do within themselves about forgiving and where to go in their relationships. They were at a new threshold. They could walk through the next door as they chose, separately or together.

11. Strength and Vulnerability

This is about a strong family facing life with a generous share of life's vulnerabilities. The core of the chapter is an edited transcript of a meeting with the family conducted not to help, but to get to know the family.

The family, which is not in therapy, receives services at an early intervention program that three-year-old Andre attends because of a neurological problem, neurofibromatosis. The family agreed to have the interview videotaped as part of the American Association of Marriage and Family Therapy's effort to develop materials for non-mental health service providers in early intervention. The purpose of the interview was to teach how to gather information for assessing a family not identified as pathological.

A DYNAMIC FAMILY

Andre and his four-year-old brother, Denis, belong to an African American family headed by a single mother of 23. The family lives on public assistance in one of Philadelphia's poorest neighborhoods. Andre's grandmother is deeply involved in the family.

The original focus was Andre, whose neurological condition seriously affects his learning ability and physical development. However, we find out that his congenital condition was likely related to his mother's, Jeannie's, sickle cell anemia. Her ailment, in turn, leads us to her sister's, Jeannette's, health problems and drug and alcohol addictions. All these difficulties have far-reaching implications for each and all in the family.

However, describing this family using the label "poor, single-parent family" would fail to capture this household. The family is part of an active, involved extended family and community. The challenge of the interview becomes discovering the full extent of the family's struggles, along with its complex web of strength and resources.

Jeannie is seriously affected by sickle cell anemia. She tires easily, is in constant pain, and suffers from clotting in her legs. She struggles to keep up with her active boys, is bright and articulate, and has some college and the ambition to return to school. There is a hope and strength in her. Both her children are by the same man, a man she loves but cannot live with. He remains actively involved with the boys and friendly with her.

Critical to the family picture is Jeannette, Jeannie's twin. While Jeannie is the one who does not lose heart, her sister, reportedly, is an angry, troubled young woman who abuses drugs and alcohol. Jeannette has spent much of her life in hospitals, also because of sickle cell. Jeannie has spent much of her life picking up after her sister, even when her own health and the rest of her family warn her to sop. Through much of this session she holds Jeannette's seven-month-old baby, Ruby (her sister being in the hospital), even as she spoke about how she is physically incapable of keeping up with her own children.

Jeannie's mother, Theodora, is an indomitable force who apparently discovered her power in church. However, because she is so capable, she may do too much for those around her—her family, friends, and church. Others around her may also be tempted to expect much of her. Widowed at a relatively young age, she was left with four children, two of whom have died, one while committing a holdup. Years after her husband's death, she had the twins. Jeannie, with her physical condition and care of her own children and Jeannette's daughter, leans heavily on her mother.

THE INTERVIEW

Present in the session are: Andre's mother, Jeannie; her mother, Theodora, who is in her late fifties; Ruby, Jeannie's twin sister's baby daughter, and, of course, Andre and Denis. In the course of the interview we will hear more about other siblings, godparents, and Andre's father, along with neighbors and fellow church members. This is a complicated family that is part of a living community.

The session take place in the living room of Jeannie's home. Jeannie and Theodora sit on the couch facing the therapist. Jeannie has Ruby on her lap. Jeannie's two boys, Denis and Andre, are playing on the floor between the therapist and the two women. The therapist has been introduced to everyone and in the process learns about Jeannie's twin.

THERAPIST   (*To Jeannie*) You have a twin?

THEODORA   She has a twin.

THERAPIST   Okay. Who is the older one?

THEODORA   She [her twin, Jeannette] is by a minute. She stole her [Jeannie's] birthright. 'Cause she [her twin] weighed 6-3 [and] she [Jeannie] weighed 4-12, and she [Jeannie] wasn't ready to come. So, they wound up having to take them. So when they were taking them, it put her sister a minute older than her. She [Jeannie] wasn't ready yet.

THERAPIST   (*To Jeannie*) Did you have a little trouble getting started . . . at birth?

THEODORA   Yeah, that's what made them have to take her. The other twin was working her way trying to get here and she wouldn't budge so then they had to wind up taking them.

The therapist stopped talking briefly with Jeannie and Theodora when the boys interrupted them. They were fussing over a block house they had originally started with the therapist's help. They wanted a little attention about what they had just completed. They got it.

THERAPIST   Did she have to stay in the hospital a while?

THEODORA   You know, she gained the weight very well. . . . [I] came home like on a Thursday and by that Saturday she weighed enough to come home. She did her eating and gained at night.

THERAPIST So she gained quickly.

THEODORA Yes, she did. And during all their growing up years, her sister stayed like maybe a pound and a half more than her, you know, during their growing up years.

THERAPIST (*To Jeannie*) And today, is she a pound and a half heavier than you?

THEODORA Today she is malnourished. She looks like a drug addict because—(*She does not finish the sentence. She starts a new thought.*) They have sickle cell.

THERAPIST Both?

THEODORA Uh huh, but the sister stayed the sickest and she never understood why Jeannie didn't stay sick. Jeannie's sicker now as she's gotten older than she did in her youth. In their youth Jeannette was always in the hospital.

THERAPIST So it's Jeannette and Jeannie?

THEODORA Uh huh, and she [Jeannette] was always in and out of the hospital. So she stayed upset and angry because she couldn't understand them being twins and she was the only one always wind up in the hospital. I don't know how she [Jeannie] stayed so well because she had the lower hemoglobin count, but still Jeannette was always the sicker one. She [Jeannette] was always the one who had the pains. She always had more trouble. Her [Jeannie's] sister is the one always in the hospital. . . .

THERAPIST But today?

THEODORA Today, she's [Jeannie's] had more trouble. But, then her sister's [Jeannette's] always in the hospital. . . . I have her [Jeannette's] first child which turned six in January and I've had her since she was about eight to ten months old.

THERAPIST So you've been raising her like your own.

THEODORA Yes. Yes.

. . .

THERAPIST Where is she [Jeannette] now?

THEODORA AND JEANNIE (*together*) She's in the hospital now.

JEANNIE That's why I have her [Ruby].

THERAPIST I see. But, she lives on her own?

THEODORA Oh yes. Yes, yes, yes!

THERAPIST It sounds like there is a little sadness there for you.

THEODORA It is, a lot of sadness.

. . .

THERAPIST She stole the birthright but ended up really paying a big price. Somehow or another, Jeannie, you have not had it so bad.

JEANNIE No, not until after I had my last baby. Well, after I had Andre, I started getting sick a lot.

THERAPIST I see.

THEODORA 'Cause she really didn't have no time—. She went away to college for a year—

THERAPIST Who did?

THEODORA Jeannie did.

THERAPIST Where did she go?

JEANNIE Bible college.

THEODORA And she was gone for a year and she got sick then, but the doctor said that she was traumatized 'cause she never, ever been away from home, and being that far she took sick, and she wind up having a sickle cell crisis which put her in the hospital there for about a week, but up until then, she never had to stay in the hospital.

. . .

THERAPIST Jeannie, you started to have trouble then when you were 18. Am I understanding that right?

THEODORA Yes, she had that sickness then and then after that she didn't get that sick enough to go to the hospital no more until after she had Denis.

THERAPIST I see. How much sickness has Jeannie had?

THEODORA Well, Jeannie was always a fighter and even going to school sometimes they had gym, they had all the exercises, running, hopping horses, and stuff and I would tell her, do you want me to write a note to the nurse, and she would say

no, let me try it, and if she has to limp and wear little soft
sneakers for two or three days after this, she would make sure
she did that so she could pass.

THERAPIST She's the tough one then, huh?

THEODORA Uh huh.

THERAPIST You kind of started life fighting anyway. You were only
four pounds or something and you had to fight your way up
from there. . . . (*To Theodora*) Theodora, you said that you
were in a group—

THEODORA Yes, a sickle cell parents group.

THERAPIST Who's we?

THEODORA All the parents.

THERAPIST From where?

THEODORA All the parents were in the sickle cell group from the
children's hospital.

THERAPIST Oh. Okay. I see. The children's hospital—

THEODORA The children's hospital had a sickle cell clinic. So what
happened, a lot of parents, in order to understand this, we
came together as a group. In order to be supportive of one
another, we were together as a group. . . .

JEANNIE I remember—

THERAPIST You remember?

JEANNIE Yeah.

THERAPIST . . . How long ago was this that you had this group?

JEANNIE Oh, we were young.

THEODORA Oh, I think I came out of it when they got about 14
or 15.

THERAPIST All those years?

THEODORA All those years.

JEANNIE Once you get a certain age you have to leave the children's hospital and go to [a general hospital].

THERAPIST (*To Jeannie*) So then, do you have good memories of
that group?

JEANNIE Yeah, it was fun 'cause for us, we had groups too, the sickle cell team. We had a group and we would meet, because for us it was hard for us growing up because people would label us. You know if they touched us, they would get what we had. So we would all come together on Saturdays, and when they didn't have their [parents'] meetings, we would have our meetings, and we would plan stuff because we didn't want to ask the parents to go on trips and stuff. We used to go to the Clement Park a lot, like every summer we would go to Clement Park.

THERAPIST So you made friends there, really, with other kids who had the same problem.

JEANNIE We still see them.

THEODORA Some of them still keep in contact. I haven't seen some of the parents in years. The kids, they still stay in contact.

THERAPIST I see. You don't live here with your daughter? Do you?

THEODORA I'm here on weekends.

. . .

THEODORA My church is here in the city.

THERAPIST Is it near here?

THEODORA 10th and Main.

THERAPIST Okay, so it's right around the corner.

THEODORA So I come in on Fridays. I bring her in after school on Fridays so that we can go to Sunday school and church, and then go back to Rosalynd on Sundays.

. . .

THERAPIST . . . (*To Jeannie*) Do you go too?

JEANNIE Uh huh. Since I was 10.

THERAPIST Oh, really? So then if you went to that church, then you must have lived here.

THEODORA Oh, I've been here since April 12th, 1969, when I moved into this house.

THERAPIST This house?

THEODORA This house right here.

THERAPIST All right. . . . So this was your original home.

THEODORA Yes, this was it. She's never lived noplace else. This was the only house.

THERAPIST All right. So now I'm really getting the picture here . . . this is really your *neighborhood*.

JEANNIE Yes, the people that I grew up with, most of the people that I grew up with are still here.

. . .

THERAPIST Has the neighborhood stayed enough the same so that you still know a lot of the people?

JEANNIE Yeah, a lot of the people, if they do move, wind up coming back.

THERAPIST To the church?

JEANNIE Yeah.

THERAPIST So the church really becomes like a magnet. Kind of holds people together then?

JEANNIE Yeah. 'Cause even people that have moved a distance, like one lady—she lives in Jersey. She comes from Jersey to our church.

THERAPIST Why does the church pull everybody back in? What is it about the church?

THEODORA I don't know. Our church, as this neighborhood changed when we moved in here in the area, it was an all white church, but the neighborhood changed—

THERAPIST Was this in '69, you said?

THEODORA I moved here in 1969, and that church got it's first black pastor in 1970 and with the neighborhood changing over, because when we first came in here they used to have gates, and they were locked, . . . and then after the black minister came here there were so many youth in the area and not in the church, he came out into the area—

THERAPIST He came out to the people.

THEODORA Yes, to the people to bring the children in and this became the children's home and the children in turn brought their parents in.

THERAPIST Okay.

THEODORA Because my children carried me in.

THERAPIST Really?

THEODORA Because I use to walk them to Sunday school and then go back after Sunday school to pick them up 'cause I definitely was not ready to join that church. That is not the church of my choice, but when they got on the choir, the choir director started calling me to make sandwiches and ask, "Will you come? The kids are having a tea." And then I got involved in that, and the next thing you know, I had joined the church and got involved in all the things they were involved in, the bake sales and all. I would bake cakes for their choir. I took their robes and got them washed up.

THERAPIST And this was—how old were you, Jeannie, when your mom was getting involved in the church?

JEANNIE When we asked her to come around to the church? Before we were baptized.

THEODORA Seven or eight.

JEANNIE Yeah, we use to come home and tell her everything about what the church was like and we would say, "Mommy, please come to the church. Please come to the church," and I think she got kind of tired of us every time we came home we kept begging her, . . . "Come on. Everybody else's parents are at the church." Mom would just walk and leave us there.

THERAPIST Your mom was a pretty independent sort. Right?

JEANNIE Yeah, so when she got around there, you can't keep her out. You can't keep her away from there.

THERAPIST So, once she makes up her mind, right? You said, "we." Did you and Jeannette go?

JEANNIE Yeah.

THERAPIST Both of you went.

JEANNIE Yeah, she was in the church back then. She was more involved than I was. She was outspoken and I was like—okay, I would agree with everything she'd say. If she wanted to go join the choir, I said okay.

THERAPIST So you were the more quiet one, then.

JEANNIE Yeah.

THERAPIST That's interesting. So you have been part of it all along. The church has really been a part of your family.

JEANNIE Yeah, because when I went away to college they had an offering and sent me money.

THEODORA To make sure when the kids go off to college that they don't forget about them.

JEANNIE And when we graduate from high school, I think is really nice, is they throw you a big party and give you an envelope with money in it. So that makes a lot of kids in the neighborhood want to go back to school because our church does help you.

THERAPIST I can hear it. It's really like family. I can see why people would come back, and you're not really that alone here because of that. . . .

. . .

THERAPIST You're all lucky because you have people that get to know you and you get to know them. They become part of your lives. So what do you do when you come in on the weekends? . . .

THEODORA I'm a Sunday School teacher. I'm also what they call a lay speaker. So I've been to school and I have my certificate. I am allowed to go out and if a minister has to be away and he needs somebody, he can go in the book, and my name is in the book.

THERAPIST Yeah, what do you do?

THEODORA I bring the word. ——

THERAPIST Okay.

JEANNIE Every year at our church, she does it in August.

THEODORA When our pastor goes away, he uses a sister minister and lay speakers so he doesn't have to go outside the church to bring someone in. So we all know when he goes away in August I have a speaking. . . .

. . .

THERAPIST (*To Jeannie*) What do you think of your mother's preaching?

JEANNIE She's good.

THERAPIST Yeah?

JEANNIE Yeah. . . . Usually me and my older sister and my aunt down the street, we all try to go to support her because in August, people go on vacation—like the church gets kind of small, but people in the church always tell my mom she brings the word.

THERAPIST She does.

JEANNIE Yeah, she does. I'm kind of proud.

THERAPIST Okay. Well, it sounds good!

. . .

THERAPIST (*To Jeannie*) . . . I was asking whether *you* were doing any of the teaching or anything else.

JEANNIE I teach Sunday school class when my little niece's teacher doesn't come. I'm like a fill-in. Whatever teacher doesn't come, I fill in and I take their spot. At Vacation Bible School I'm an assistant teacher. Whatever class they need an assistant teacher in, I do that. . . .

THEODORA Well, when they were younger, I first started out. I went as a counselor. I didn't know too much about being a counselor, but you grow into these things. You learn as you're out there with them.

JEANNIE But we had a different camp. The camp that we used to go to, it was overnight. We slept in these log cabins. We had swimming lessons and horseback riding lessons. My sister didn't like that too much though.

THERAPIST Oh. Okay. But you did.

JEANNIE Yeah.

. . .

THERAPIST Okay. So you've been volunteering as an assistant or a substitute, and do you like doing that?

JEANNIE Yeah. I like working with little kids. They're easier to work with.

THERAPIST I hear how active your mother is. She gets involved, and what I hear about you—you went to college for a year. Then you were sick and had a hard time, and so I don't know how ambitious you were about getting involved in things.

JEANNIE Well, at our church they know how she is, but they know if they call me and they need me to cook something, I'll cook it. If they need a cake, I'll make a cake. If they need me to come and help clean up—

THERAPIST Then you'll do it?

JEANNIE Yeah.

THERAPIST And you like doing it?

JEANNIE Yeah. I like the people. The people that call me and ask me are very nice and very friendly. I don't mind working with them.

THERAPIST Have you decided to go back to school? Are you doing anything about school?

JEANNIE I'm going to apply for community [college] in September. I'd like in September to take a couple of classes. I want to be an early childhood teacher.

THERAPIST Okay. So you do like kids.

JEANNIE Yeah. Well, when I went to college the first time I went to be a child psychologist.

THERAPIST Okay. So it still has to do with children. Did you actually finish that first year?

JEANNIE Yeah. I finished.

THERAPIST So, you have a year behind you. Okay. You did all right?

JEANNIE Yeah, well my English teacher—I got sick at the end. So I missed a lot of that. I had to take that when I came back, but when I came to her and took it, I got an A.

THEODORA But see, I thought she was going back to school. So we in turn put out that $300 to send her to summer school so she could catch up on that English and pass it, and then when September rolled around—

JEANNIE I didn't go back.

THEODORA She didn't go back.

THERAPIST Why not?

JEANNIE Well, they didn't understand that I was 14 hours away from home. I couldn't come home on vacation and it was different . . . there were black people, but predominantly it was a white college and the freshmen that came in made me feel like an outsider. The black kids that were there could go home. They didn't live more than one or two hours away and if I didn't find someone to go home with, I had to stay at the dormitory and I was stuck—and it was my first time and I was scared.

THERAPIST Right. Sure.

JEANNIE I was a mama's child. So, it was kind of hard, and I actually went there because of mama and my grandfather. They really wanted me to go away, and they wanted me to go to a Bible college.

THEODORA But you know, what I wanted was an escape [for her], because she always talked about getting away. She needed to get away and I felt that if you need to get away, this is what you need. You know, it's a beautiful spot, a beautiful spot.

THERAPIST I hear you.

THEODORA Because I went with her.

THERAPIST But the thing she's telling you is that "I'm a mama's girl. It was hard."

JEANNIE It was hard, and then, a lot of the kids there, they didn't have to work. I had to get a job on campus and start working. So it was kind of hard when they would go out and I would stay there in the dormitory.

THERAPIST I understand. . . . But now we're talking about five years ago? At this point, are you getting the itch to go back to school?

JEANNIE I had the itch last year, but Andre's been sick an awful lot since I've had him and there's nobody really. Mama's not here. There's nobody really and my sister down the street. She has three kids and I don't want to leave him with someone.

THERAPIST Now tell me, who's in the family? You have an older sister?

JEANNIE Yeah, I have . . . my brother Chris, my sister Camille.

THERAPIST Tell me how old everybody is.

JEANNIE Chris is 42.

THEODORA Chris would be 43.

JEANNIE Camille is 40.

THEODORA 41.

JEANNIE And Gen is—

THEODORA 39.

JEANNIE 39, and then Jeannette and I are the youngest, 23.

THERAPIST So, there are two different families.

THEODORA There are two different families. Gen was 15 when I had the twins. That part of the family, their father was dead. He died, he was like 33–34. He was in the Navy. He died of asphyxiation in Japan.

. . .

THERAPIST Wow, that must've been hard on you!

THEODORA Yes, because I had four kids.

THERAPIST That's what I'm thinking.

THEODORA I had four kids to finish raising 'cause I had a son that is dead. I have a son that got killed trying to rob a bar.

THERAPIST You've lived through a few things, haven't you?

THEODORA Oh yes. All this goes along with making me stronger.

THERAPIST Oh yes it does. Yes it does, and what year was that?

THEODORA '72 when he got killed.

THERAPIST '72.

THEODORA Uh huh, he had just turned 21 the 14th of February and he had said, "Ha, ha, Mom, you told me I wouldn't make it," and I'd say, "You haven't completed it yet," and then that Easter Sunday morning he was gone.

JEANNIE It was in the papers. My mom has the article.

THERAPIST Yeah. There are so many stories here.

THEODORA I was telling her—

THERAPIST What?

THEODORA That if I could be a writer, I could write for Harlequin Romance, I could write for all the times the Lord brought us through situations, if I was a writer.

THERAPIST You're doing it right now. Okay, so Jeannie, so you have your brother, a couple sisters. There's you and Jeannette. Now what I'm trying to get is a picture of. . . . Andre and I want to get a picture of the whole family. So you went to school. I understand what you described, now about the school and what it was like for you. You were a mommy's girl. Your sister wasn't, though. Jeannette wasn't.

JEANNIE She didn't get out of high school and all through high school she made it kind of hard for me 'cause when she had Antoinette, I was in the 12th grade and she would leave Antoinette with me when I got home from school. So I was working and going to school and trying to raise her daughter.

THERAPIST And she was out?

JEANNIE And she was out. So it was a wonder I kept my grades up to a 3.5 average, but I did have good grades, and she kind of hates me for that. She hates me because I got out of high school. My grade point average was pretty good and I did do the year of college, but if you listen to her, she graduated high school and she did the year of college. I didn't graduate.

. . .

THERAPIST Okay, so then you came back from college and got a job. Now, when did you have Denis?

JEANNIE I was 19. I was 19 when I had Denis in June of 1989.

. . .

THERAPIST And where is he [Denis's father] in your life now?

JEANNIE He's a big part of Denis's life. Andre—Andre is more to my mom. When I got pregnant with Rey, I didn't know until five months.

THERAPIST You said, "Rey"?

JEANNIE Andre. It was five months, and my mom didn't find out until I was seven months. . . . When she did find out, she was upset. She was very upset, but she's very supportive, too. She came into the city and she would cook me dinner for a whole week.

THERAPIST So you were living alone? Your mom was out. She wasn't here. But you were here. Were you here with your sister?

. . .

THERAPIST (*To Theodora*) Were you not happy about the pregnancy?

JEANNIE Because she saw me like Jeannette.

THERAPIST Oh, I see. . . .

. . .

THEODORA Everything seemed like it was going down the drain.

THERAPIST There are a lot of different reasons why you were unhappy. One was that you were counting on her; two, you
thought well, maybe she'll end up like Jeannette just having
babies and never have a family of her own.

JEANNIE But I worked.

THEODORA I knew that you worked, but the idea is that when
you're already sick and your body is not well and having a
second child. I admit, we had warned them that you can't
always have healthy children when you have sickle cell.
You're not guaranteed to have healthy children, and being
afraid that she would have a sick child and not be able to
handle it and then when I found out that he was sick, I knew
where I had to be in that picture 'cause I knew she was gonna
need my help. She was not going to be strong enough to do
it on her own. And truly, she's not because for everything
that goes on, if I'm not there, she makes sure she calls. If it's
possible, I'll find a way to get in if he needs me. I'm there for
him.

THERAPIST I just want to get one other thing clear here for myself.
Andre's father—is he the same father as Denis's?

JEANNIE Yes.

THERAPIST Now, is he involved with the boys?

JEANNIE Yes.

THERAPIST In what way?

JEANNIE Well, I'm not able to take Denis out to play because my
legs are not like they use to be. I can't chase him and run
him to the playground. He comes over and takes them to the
playground.

THERAPIST Is that from sickle cell?

JEANNIE Yeah, well, they had already told my mom that my legs are going to start messing up. They are.

THERAPIST What happens with your legs?

JEANNIE I get blood clots, and I can't walk.

THERAPIST You get blood clots?

JEANNIE I can't walk and I can't get out of bed. It hurts real bad to get out of bed, but I don't want to go to the hospital. I refuse to go to the hospital 'cause I don't want to get addicted to the drugs. The last time I went to the hospital the doctor gave me morphine pills to bring home. I threw them in the trash.

. . .

THERAPIST You're so young to be having these kinds of problems with your legs. What is it like for you?

JEANNIE Sometimes it's upsetting because you see other people. I see other young people having children and they can go out and take their kids to the zoo, and they can do it by themselves. I know I can't. So it hurts. Sometimes I can't pick up Andre or I can't give Denis a hug, and Denis will get upset. He'll say, ''What's wrong, Mom?'' It's kind of hard to explain.

THERAPIST Would you be in pain?

JEANNIE Yeah, and the last time I got sick I had to call my mom and my sister, and they had to come over because I was real sick and I was scared.

THERAPIST Scared of what?

JEANNIE I don't know. My stomach was hurting and my head. I couldn't get out of bed. I couldn't walk, and I was scared I was going to have to go to the hospital and they would keep me. So, instead of doing that, my mom came in and my sister came in. It took them a while, but they got here.

THERAPIST You say your sister. Which sister?

JEANNIE My sister, Gen. She can't do for me like she wants to 'cause she's working, but if I need her she'll get here one way or another.

. . .

THERAPIST You guys have really gone through a few things, haven't you? Denis's father comes how often?

JEANNIE Whenever he can. Lots of times. It's on the weekends. He's good for coming to meet me 'cause I can't. Nis likes to run and is very hyperactive.

. . .

THERAPIST So his father meets you every weekend?

JEANNIE Yeah.

THERAPIST Just for one day, or for two days?

JEANNIE No, sometimes he takes them for the whole weekend.

THERAPIST Takes them?

JEANNIE Yeah.

THERAPIST Oh, I see. And Denis likes that?

JEANNIE Yeah. His bond is with his dad because when he was younger I wasn't home. I worked. When I was living with his dad's mom, I worked and his dad stayed home and took care of Denis.

THERAPIST And Andre doesn't have the same kind of bond to him?

JEANNIE No, his bond is with me and my mom 'cause after I had Andre me and his dad went through a lot of stuff and we both—

THERAPIST So you guys were together for a while.

JEANNIE Yeah, since Denis was about one, and then I got pregnant with Andre. So we went through lot of stuff.

THERAPIST Three years? How many years were you together?

JEANNIE: Were we together? We've been together since 1988, yeah, about four years.

THERAPIST Four years. Why did you break up?

JEANNIE I was tired of working and taking care of him and Denis. It was too much for me, and he was kind of violent in his own way. He was in an abusive family. His stepfather was abusive, and that's the only way sometimes that he could relate. So I didn't want to be bothered. So I called my mom up and asked her if I could come home, and she let me come home.

THERAPIST When was that?

JEANNIE In '90 I came back home.

THERAPIST That must've been—I mean, it sounds like you feel you did the right thing.

. . .

THERAPIST Wasn't it hard for you to break up?

JEANNIE Yeah.

THERAPIST It's a long time you and he were connected.

JEANNIE Yeah, we went through a lot. . . .

THERAPIST Are you over him now? Is it finished or is there still something—. Oh, okay. I see. I got the look from your mom. It's not finished.

JEANNIE No! I mean, I love him.

THERAPIST That's what I was asking.

JEANNIE I do love him.

THERAPIST But—

JEANNIE But, my kids come first.

THERAPIST And you can't all be together? Because—he won't be the kind of father you want—or what?

JEANNIE Our personalities are—they clash. You have to kind of push him and me. I'm independent because of my mom. I'm a go-getter. If you're supposed to get up and take care of your family, then that's what you're supposed to do.

THERAPIST So you ended up having to take care of him.

JEANNIE Yeah.

THERAPIST That's what you're telling me. So you love him, but you can't really live like that. Not as a family.

JEANNIE No.

The issue was identified, but in line with the purpose of the interview, the therapist did not want to work with it. He had covered Andre's context. He proceeded to ask about Andre directly.

THERAPIST That's right. I understand that. When did you find out that Andre had neurofibromatosis?

JEANNIE He was six months old and we took him for a stomach virus and they saw a bunch of spots and that's the start of it.

THERAPIST I see.

JEANNIE But there's a lot of things that go with it. It can cause cancer. It can cause leukemia. It can cause your child to go blind. They can lose their hearing. They can be dwarfs—like Andre is extremely small for his age. They can be slow.

THEODORA Learning disabilities.

THERAPIST Does he have learning disabilities?

JEANNIE Yeah, learning disabilities. He has teachers that come out. . . . Like one thing Denis might go through now, Andre might not go through for another year or so. So he'll always be slower.

THEODORA He's got such tiny hands. We've spent so long trying to teach him. Now you see a child of three does a beautiful job of feeding himself, but he has a very hard time. The spoon is so big, he gets tired. He'll stop eating and say, ''feed me.'' Because even holding a spoon is kind of rough on him 'cause if you look at his hands, his hands are very tiny.

. . .

THERAPIST . . . What kind of learning disability does he have?

JEANNIE Before his teacher started coming out, he would have violent fits because he could not communicate with us. He would bang his head on anything that was around, and it got real bad. My mom was ready to buy him a helmet 'cause we got scared.

THEODORA Because I was on her. I said you've got to get him checked out. This is not normal. First, I thought it was autism. I thought he was autistic because I know they have a tendency to sit and bang because we would be downstairs and he would be knocking his head against the crib bars.

THERAPIST Really?

JEANNIE We'd be downstairs and you'd hear this bang, bang, bang.

. . .

THEODORA And these were things that bothered me, and I stayed on her and said that I can't do it, you've got to do it and you've got to find out, but something is not right, this is not right. Then we went to a meeting at the children's hospital where all the people come together and that's when we found out all this real information of the things that could go wrong and the things that can happen.

THERAPIST So when did the teacher start coming out?

JEANNIE It's been a couple of months now. When I first tried getting him into the program it was hard. It was a long process. They had to test him to make sure that he had a learning disability, and when they first started coming out here he was still having the fits. They would have to hold him. Then maybe the third or fourth time they came out, he was okay.

THEODORA He was hurting because he couldn't communicate.

THERAPIST Did the teacher help him to communicate?

JEANNIE/THEODORA They helped him be able to talk.

. . .

THEODORA Oh, I hear the baby.

THERAPIST Did you want to take care of the baby?

THEODORA (*To Jeannie*) Do you want to go get her?

THERAPIST We can stop. You've got a job to do.

(*Brief intermission*)

In this final phase of the interview, the therapist tries to help. Jeannie presents the problem that she must resolve to move ahead with her life. Theodora agrees that is the immediate issue. The therapist supports what they already know they must do. He suggests some options, and gives recognition to Jeannie's power to determine the outcome for herself.

JEANNIE: Well, with Ruby I didn't want to raise another baby because of Andre being sick, and then to raise another sick baby, it's hard.

THERAPIST Is she sick?

JEANNIE She was a drug-addicted baby.

THERAPIST Oh!

JEANNIE She was addicted to the drugs that her mom was taking. Her mom was sick, and they were shooting her up with morphine and Demerol so it was hard.

. . . ₵

THEODORA . . . This is her [Jeannette's] last baby. She was in the hospital for a month or so.

JEANNIE None of us had seen her when she was first born. I didn't see her until they left her here with me for almost a month.

THERAPIST Okay. So you've got Ruby now?

JEANNIE Yes, DHS [Department of Human Services] put her in my custody.

THERAPIST I see.

THEODORA You see, I told her it was too much. She [Ruby] needs check-ups. I don't like her eyes, and I'm a good one for going over babies. It's the grandmother/mother instinct. She's definitely going to need her eyes checked 'cause she has to cross them completely in order to zero in on you. Her feet are completely turned in and these are things that need to be looked into. She [Jeannie] can't really look into them with having to run with Andre. She hasn't been able to keep up with her own sickle cell.

JEANNIE I haven't been to a doctor appointment for my sickle cell in five months.

THEODORA Every time she gets ready to make an appointment something happens with Andre, and she has to cancel hers out, so that throws her off for not having her check-ups like she needs to.

THERAPIST What's the solution?

THEODORA I don't like seeing your children get lost in the system. But I'm from the old school. Self-preservation is the first law of nature. You have to take care of yourself and if you have something left over, you can give to somebody else. Right now she don't have nothing left over. I come in here and I watch— we talk for five minutes and she's asleep. That's because she knows that I'm here and I can keep control over everybody. No sooner, before we can talk and she's out of it. This means that she's completely run down.

. . . ₵

JEANNIE I've always been there for Jeannette. Jeannette knows this and she abuses me—she really does.

THEODORA She's never been able to tell her twin "no."

JEANNIE If she needs money, I'll go take it to her. If she needs anything, I'll go give it to her, but if I ask for anything the answer is "no."

THEODORA It's completely different. Whatever Jeannette says, Jeannie must do it and must be there. It's always been like that, and I realize this. So, I just have to stay out of it.

THERAPIST So what's going to happen?

. . .

JEANNIE I'll just be tired.

THERAPIST But it's not just tired we're talking about here.

JEANNIE I don't want to put her into the system.

THERAPIST I understand.

JEANNIE Foster homes aren't like they used to be. I want to be able to see her.

THERAPIST It's not possible for her to be in a foster home and you see her?

THEODORA I don't know. She hasn't inquired.

JEANNIE She [Ruby] has a sister that's two. She's with her other grandmother and she [grandmother] is trying to get custody. I don't want custody of Ruby. If I really have to, then I will go and get custody, but I really don't want to put her in a foster home.

. . .

THERAPIST Is there no one in the church who could be a foster [family]?

JEANNIE No, and in that church the people that would get her would want to keep her.

THERAPIST Would that mean that you couldn't visit her? That you couldn't have a relationship with her?

JEANNIE I don't know. I guess it depends.

THERAPIST Because it sounds like the church is like a big family. Even if they were to keep her, I can't imagine that they would say no, that you can't see her.

JEANNIE But her mom would have to sign the papers saying that she was going to give her up, and she's not ready to do that.

THERAPIST Okay, so you've got another big one to work out here.

JEANNIE Her mom will call, and she'll get real nasty on the phone and say, "You're trying to take my daughter from me." . . . I told her that if she would be the mother she's supposed to be, none of this would happen. She has to use a walker and it's kind of hard for me to see my sister like that 'cause I remember us going to school and playing jump rope and being active. Now she's sickly looking and you just don't want to look at her.

THEODORA Jeannie has to realize that she has herself and Andre. . . . I got so angry last week when she told me about Andre, and I told her to give up and let Ruby go into the system and we'll pray about it. You've got to take care of your own.

THERAPIST What do your sisters say?

. . .

JEANNIE They know I can't handle it.

THERAPIST And you know you can't handle her. You just can't say "no" to Jeannette.

THEODORA She just can't say "no" to her twin.

THERAPIST You may want to think about it. It looks like it's heading in a way where you'll be forced to make a decision, and before you get to that point you may want to ask for and get information. Talk to the people in the system. Find out what the possibilities and options are, what arrangements can be made. Could you see her or not? Just in case it gets to the point that you can't keep her.

. . .

THERAPIST (*To Jeannie*) Do you want to go back to school?

JEANNIE Yes. My mom knows this. I told her and Jeannette awhile ago. I was supposed to go back this summer, this month I was going to summer session, but when they brought Ruby here it was too late to sign up.

THERAPIST . . . You're going to have to make the decision, and Jeannette's not going to make it easy for you. Jeannette doesn't have her life together, and if you take on her problems—and that *is* what you're doing—

JEANNIE I've been doing that for 23 years.

THERAPIST If you take on her problems, you're not going to be able to move ahead and take care of what you have to take care of. You know that I'm not telling you anything you don't already know. . . . But you have a couple of things to solve in your life, and the immediate one right now is Ruby. You also have to solve the one dealing with the boys' father. This will affect your life, too. You have some big decisions to make.

JEANNIE We just got Denis started in school in September. Now it will be easier for me to go to school because Andre's godmother said that she would watch him while I was at school. When I get home, I'll go get him and pick Denis up.

THERAPIST Everyone comes to a certain point in their life where they have certain decisions to make and your whole future depends on that. You can block yourself and stay stuck or you can move on. You're in charge of those decisions, not Jeannette, and not your mother. She knows you're in charge of those decisions. . . . It's been wonderful talking to you both. You're a real inspiration. . . .

DISCUSSION

Indeed, they are an inspiration. However, Jeannie has her troubles not only with Andre's health, but her own. She also has problems with her sister Jeannette. Standing between her and solutions to her life's problems is the weakness in her degree of commitment to what she knows is right for her. When threatened with conflict and loss of love, she is capable of compromising away what she knows to do. She wants to be liked. Nevertheless, she has always been strong, and she can hear that she has power to choose the better path for herself.

With the tough choices she faces, Jeannie is not alone. She has supports not only from her family, but also from her church. It is clear that the church has been central to and formative in Jeannie's life. For her, it is a place of worship. It is also a place in which to learn a philosophy of life and to receive encouragement to live it. It is a place where she belongs and has a role.

Spiritually, the family has an approach to hardship that draws strength from pain. Theodora has a traditional Christian philosophy that, "All this goes along with making me stronger." They are also not alone: "The Lord brought us through situations." Jeannie seems to share the belief. The interview works within the rich resource of Jeannie's and her mother's spirit.

This is an African American neighborhood and an African American church. Historically, it is part of a long-standing tradition in the black community. This is an activist neighborhood church. It remains strong and ready to do for the families and individuals who belong. Jeannie and her mother both belong and participate. Because Jeannie has her church community, she has options not available to many poor families. The interviewer encourages her to consider families in the church as possible placements for Ruby, if Jeannie finds she can no longer care for her. Then Jeannie and Theodora would not have to sever their ties with the baby.

The bread of support in Jeannie's life is right where Jeannie lives—in her family, church, and community (Jeannie also knows how to use the welfare and medical systems). Given the resources that are part of Jeannie's life, the interviewer can find help within her own world. He does not have to think of creating a network of support for her. Jeannie has options that are realistically within her reach, not only because they are there, but because she is capable of making use of them.

The interviewer is not overwhelmed by the hardships Jeannie faces. She is not surrendering to the hardships. She is realistic and finds meaning and purpose and love in her life just as it is. Both she and her son are incurably ill. She is responsible for her children even with her illness, but she does not retreat. She strives to be there for her twin also—the saddest figure in this human drama. Jeannie's struggle is how to be available to her sister and her niece and not be crushed herself in the process. As difficult as the choices are, Jeannie remains in charge of her choices. She has within herself, her family, and her community the strength she needs to choose rightly and wisely.

A Postscript on Diversity

Jeannie's story brings home dramatically the issue of diversity. The issue comes to mind when thinking about Jeannie and her family. She talked about the difficulty of attending a white college even if there were blacks there. She had grown up in a black world. Those she loved and trusted were in a black world. Living away from home, in a college that felt like white society, was alien, lonely, and frightening.

We see the world she lived in—the church of which she was a part, and the neighborhood she never really left. She has been sick all of her life and dependent upon an all-too-competent mother. Jeannie developed her own competence, but not her independence. It was too much for Jeannie to leave, all at once, her mother, her church, and her ethnic culture to live in the alien world of a culturally white college. However, was this a move into the white world or into general society with all its complexities? Is this a question of either/or? Should there not have been a bridge between the two worlds, built by both those worlds, for the Jeannies of this society?

I do not believe that Jeannie's story can answer this big question. However, it would be hard to leave her story without being impressed by the life and strength that her church, with the racial and cultural community it represented, gave to Jeannie and her mother. I personally doubt that they would have overcome their hardships as they have without being part of the world created by that church and the spiritual, social, and community resources it provided. Poor, minority groups need successful community eco-systems that include family, friends, schools, social agencies, hospitals, and church. They need solidarity of their race and culture to establish and maintain identity and self-esteem, from which spring the power and freedom to choose for self in a society that can overwhelm. However, what is that particular world without a vital connection to the mainstream of society with all its problems?

I believe we speak here to the essence of diversity. Diversity is not about "us versus them." Neither is it about easy agreement among different cultural, ethnic, and racial groups. And neither is it about easy community living among the different groups. It is a bold, rich, and complex tapestry. It has to do with being different in values, traditions, and speech, and the same in human need, suffering, and love. It has to do with living in separate neighborhoods, and together in the larger common community of nation.

Diversity of culture, ethnicity, and race gets its significance and specialness in the context of our universal identification as human beings.

Jeannie is an African American. Jeannie is a Woman. Jeannie is also Everyperson.

Epilogue

The book ends on a personal note, as well it might since its origins are quite personal. It began somewhere in Spanish Harlem a seemingly long time ago during the Depression. Its seeds are in a note, surprisingly well preserved, from a visiting nurse telling an expectant mother that she can get free milk and bread at the local Democratic Club.

Today people like my mother—of Latino, African American, Native American, and white European origin, all poor and in some pain about their lives—look for some answers from professional counselors. These professionals themselves will discover with just a moment's reflection some of the same human struggles in their own lives. Perhaps they can even recall experiences with poverty in their own earlier years. If the wounds do not have exactly the same sources, they are at least in like flesh and souls.

Our therapy can seem presumptuous before the depth of personal struggles these families bring and the social conditions that so test their powers. These are people working for their bread to survive and looking for the nourishing strength of love for their souls from their families, their communities, and their God. This more-or-less commonality with us, their therapists, gives us a ticket of entrance into their lives. If we can risk some memories, emotions, and mutuality, we can join them in the human experience. Then we can presume to use our professional learning and skills because we have also used ourselves.

This book describes one therapist's clinical encounters. It is a shame that I have not been able to tell all that I thought and felt personally during these interviews. As therapists we all bring so much of ourselves into our encounters with people and families—and reveal so little to our colleagues. We are telling more these days, but no matter how much we tell, there is always more that we don't tell. It seems that our life experiences and personal thoughts and emotions are among our most important resources in our work. Yet, they are always to some degree a secret resource. The real tragedy is when we aren't honest with ourselves, and so deny our clients.

Recently, we do seem to be looking for ways to talk out loud about our personal selves in ways that help us understand ourselves and help our therapy. Murray Bowen, Virginia Satir, and Jim Framo have all offered us some avenues for personal reflection and expression about our family lives that serve as tools to make us more thoughtful, sensitive, and insightful therapists. Moreover, Monica McGoldrick, Celia Falicov, Nancy Boyd-Franklin, Elaine Pinderhughes, and many others are helping us think about how our cultural, ethnic, and racial heritages enrich our therapy.

We live in a troubled and contentious world, where our values have emerged as vital dimensions of our relationships and work with our clients. America has moved away from its cultural, moral, and religious traditions. The standards and structures of the past have been largely invalidated by what is happening philosophically, socially, and politically in society at large. Instead of evolving from and building upon the past, we seem intent on refuting it. We are now in the midst of a social upheaval that centers on the rights, separateness, and self-fulfillment of the individual. This is not a simple turn in thinking. It is full of contradictions. It is both a social/secular philosophical movement and a spiritual/religious search. At the same time that this society moves away from traditional social structures and religions, it invents new lifestyles and new spirituality. At the same time that people appear to be making themselves the center of their universe, there is a move to look beyond to a transcendent source of life and meaning. The turmoil of pursuit and debate is intense and is spilling over into all corners of our lives. We seem to be arguing everywhere about whether and how to give expression to these philosophical, spiritual, and religious sentiments in our lives—family, neighborhood, school, politics, etc. We, in our profession, are certainly talking about the place of social values and spirituality in our work.

At the moment, with the movement into constructivist thinking, family therapy is questioning reality, morality, and the traditional bonds of the human community. Is there a reality, a truth, a God? Is there a natural and/or divinely sourced order and morality? Are we bound to one another in a common destiny, responsible for one another? On the other hand, are our images of what we perceive and relate to outside ourselves "inventions" (Efran, Lukens, & Lukens, 1988)? Are we operating from a "vision of many competing discourses and discursive communities that clash and contradict each other, and from which we select a fictive self" (Goldner, 1993, p. 158)? How subjective are the "intersubjectively and intrasubjectively confirmed constructs and meanings about problems and . . . solutions" (Prest & Keller, 1993, p. 141) that we bring into therapy? Are there no objective boundaries that we can draw around the self, the family, and consequently, the community (Efran et al., 1988)?

These are questions fundamental to our therapy. If we split off "a separate world of language, divorced from any notion of a relevant social and material realm" (Fish, 1993, p. 228), we destroy the basis for social and personal morality. There is no enduring basis in essential reality for justice or injustice, right or wrong. Since "both problem and cause are simply a set of constructions about reality" (De Shazer & Berg, 1988, p. 42), we have no moral basis for therapeutic goals outside of what therapist and client construct together in the moral and social vacuum of the office.

Therapists communicate values in therapy, such as their views about justice in the abuse of power in personal relationships and the rightness or wrongness of yesterday's or today's family structures. Therapy perforce reinforces or invalidates people's sense of ethnicity, culture, and spirituality. Therapists can lend importance or insignificance to what gives meaning and purpose to clients' lives. They can work with or around people's values. In one man's opinion, "ordinary" people "wish to make moral judgments, but their culture does not help them do it" (Wilson, 1993). As therapists, we are a part of that culture that reaches most deeply into people's lives, empowering or disempowering them and their values, morality, and culture.

This dilemma is in front of us as therapists all the time, whether we wish to acknowledge it or not. People define themselves through values. They view themselves and the world through their ethnicity, guide their lives through their morals, and perceive meaning in their existence through their spirituality. In today's society any pretense of consensus about values has left us. As therapists we come together with people in critical life circumstances, where we may well be their last recourse to find validation and support for their culture, morality, and spirituality.

Overtly or tacitly our clients come to us with these questions. Questions about values, morality, and spirituality may not be explicitly articulated but are alive in their complaints. These questions give meaning to the pain, struggles, and choices people face. Without values people have no reason to take one path versus another. As therapists, we would not have a role in their lives. We who are escorts, scouts, and guides would have nowhere to look, no new vision, no new meaning to pursue.

It is the poor who are most pervasively experiencing the effects of a society whose compass is pointing in so many directions at once. The poor are trapped in a society over which they have little say. They have little power to shape it, give meaning to it, design how it serves and supports their lives. They cannot rise above the turbulence of a society through the power the well-to-do possess to purchase and create their own worlds. Yet, they depend upon that society to provide possibility and opportunity.

Nevertheless, the poor, like the rest of us, can transcend. In our profession it is unconscionable that we do not do whatever possible to provide the bread of survival to the disadvantaged. That is part of our general mission, even if it is not specifically the job of every therapist. However, the other side of that effort needs to be the nourishment of the human spirit. It is the human spirit that will take the poor above social circumstance and give encouragement to their lives. The poor need government, business, and professionals to create opportunity and possibility. They need themselves—their communities, families, and beliefs—to strengthen them to endure the hard things they cannot change, to contend for what can and should change, and to overcome their own discouragement and anger in order to thrive.

Traditionally, the poor have had their families, neighborhoods, cultures, and religions. Somehow, they did not seem as poor then. They certainly were not as despairing, isolated, and violent as they are today in America. The new poor are up against philosophical, cultural, and social conditions that are potentially crushing. They are structurally isolated from society. General economic prosperity or recession does not by itself reach deeply enough into their lives to make a fundamental difference. They are trapped in a world that has little access to society at large. Conditions have persisted for so long that they are not easily changed; even when doors are open to them, they cannot, as a group, just pass through.

The deterioration of communities, the weakening of families, and the intellectual, moral, and psychological undermining of the individual are not overcome in a day. The negative attitudes that much of society has developed toward the poor, particularly toward the critically stressed groups, will also not readily dissipate. There will always be some from these groups who will break through and succeed, just like those who survived the concentration camps. However, as communities these poor need more than doors unlocked. They need an active hand to join theirs.

The damage of chronic stress to their communities, families, minds, and souls has so hardened their situation that they need well planned, consistent assistance from society. That help needs to take into account the full ecosystem—individual, family, and community. That ecosystem includes the economics, the political, and the cultural, with all that implies about race, ethnicity, and spirituality. On the other hand, the poor need themselves, their own leadership and strength, to push through. Some will push harder than others. Some will join hands with their helpers. Others will not. The poor are like everyone else. They have choices. Here, the spirit becomes the ultimate resource to overcome the barriers within themselves and within society.

THE HUMAN SPIRIT AND THE POOR

Today, questions about the human spirit appear much more pressing for the poor. When people are low in milk and bread, need for the spirit somehow becomes more urgent, important, and necessary. Economic, political, and social circumstances do not of themselves combine to give or take away meaning and purpose. The source of hope, the resource the poor can claim for themselves, is the spirit of community cooperation, family loyalty, personal self-respect, and religious belief. When they come to share their lives with us in therapy, the poor bring these resources with them, whether as seedlings or as flourishing assets. Given what life has been like for them, they may not know what they have. It is for us to recognize their strengths, cultivate their potential, and join them in partnership to contend.

However, for us to address our clients about the spirit, we need to look first at ourselves. We need to recognize what gives meaning and purpose to life for us, just as we have in the past learned to explore our unconscious and our families of origin. We need to think about how our own views about life help or hinder our understanding and ability to relate to people and their struggles. How we think about values, morality, and spirituality may be primitive or elaborate, closed or open, harmonious with our lives or in conflict. Our philosophical and spiritual views can serve to connect or block us from others. There is work we must all do with ourselves to gain insight about the spiritual component of our lives and how it affects our views and relationships with others.

When it comes to our work, however, spirituality is an arena where we need our clients. It will require that we see ourselves not as proprietary experts on the subject, but as companions on a journey, *their* journey. We do not own the expertise about the spirit. As therapists, we are not the new priesthood. We all have our own personal philosophical, social, and spiritual perspectives. We have varying degrees of commitment to our values. We have, in effect, our respective "religions." However, the poor come to us sometimes clothed only with their ethnicity, culture, and spirituality. It is not for us to dress them with our apparel.

Today's therapeutic models often carry banners for social causes and philosophies that reflect the world of the intellectual and the academic. They espouse their current philosophies and social causes. The poor ethnic or racial minority client often comes with very traditional customs, lifestyles, and religious beliefs. There is often a natural antagonism between the liberal professional and the traditional client. Professionals may well feel that traditional values and social structures oppress their clients. However, in trying to save them, we may rob from their souls.

We certainly do not have to agree with our clients' perspectives on life. However, neither do we have to work with them if we do not respect their belief systems and lifestyles. If we choose to enter their lives, we need to work with their values, morals, and spirituality. We can offer alternatives, if we can do so without demeaning their identities, traditions, and beliefs, and if we can make it so that they can easily say "no" to us. We can offer more of who we are to them, if we can also be open to feel and think with them in their world, as well as join them in the common human experience within the boundaries of therapy. Then they can take from that experience, whether alone or with family and community, what they may need, and may choose new answers for their lives. We have much to give in the therapeutic encounter if we can put that joining in the larger context of life—of their family, community, and spirituality. Our openness to their spirit will allow them to pursue further meaning and purpose in their work with us. Our work is whole when the practical touches the transcendent, the bread joins the spirit.

Bibliography

Aponte, H. J. (1974a). Organizing treatment around the family's problems and their structural bases. *Psychiatry Quarterly, 48,* 209–222.

Aponte, H. J. (1974b, March). Psychotherapy for the poor: An eco-structural approach to treatment. *Delaware Medical Journal, 46,* 134–144.

Aponte, H. J. (1976a). Underorganization in the poor family. In P. J. Guerin (Ed.), *Family therapy: Theory and practice* (pp. 432–448). New York: Gardner.

Aponte, H. J. (1976b). The family-school interview: An eco-structural approach. *Family Process, 15*(3), 303–311.

Aponte, H. J. (1979a). Family therapy and the community. In M. S. Gibbs, J. R. Lachenmeyer, & J. Sigal (Eds.), *Community psychology: Theoretical and empirical approaches* (pp. 311–333). New York: Gardner.

Aponte, H. J. (1979b). Diagnosis in family therapy. In C. B. Germain (Ed.), *Social work practice: People and environments* (pp. 107–149). New York: Columbia University Press.

Aponte, H. J. (1982). The cornerstone of therapy: The person of the therapist. *Family Therapy Networker, 6*(2), 19–21.

Aponte, H. J. (1985). The negotiation of values in therapy. *Family Process, 24*(3), 323–338.

Aponte, H. J. (1986). "If I don't get simple, I cry." *Family Process, 25*(4), 531–548.

Aponte, H. J. (1987). The treatment of society's poor: An ecological perspective on the underorganized family. *Family Therapy Today, 2,* 1–7.

Aponte, H. J. (1989, Winter). Please join me in a short walk through the South Bronx. *AFTA Newsletter, 37,* 36–40.

Aponte, H. J. (1990). "Too many bosses": An eco-structural intervention with a family and its community. *Journal of Strategic and Systemic Therapies, 9*(3), 49–63.

Aponte, H. J. (1991). Training on the person of the therapist for work with the poor and minorities. *Family systems application to social work: Training and clinical practice* (pp. 23–40). New York: Haworth.

Aponte, H. J. (Summer, 1993). The persons of the mentor and the learner. *AFTA Newsletter, 52,* 19–20.

Aponte, H. J., & VanDeusen, J. M. (1981). Structural family therapy. In A. S. Gurman & D. P. Kniskern (Eds.), *Handbook of family therapy* (pp. 310–360). New York: Brunner/Mazel.

Aponte, H. J., & Winter, J. E. (1987, Spring). The person and practice of the therapist: Treatment and training. *Journal of Psychotherapy and the Family, 3*, 85–111.

Aponte, H. J., Zarski, J. J., Bixenstine, C., & Cibik, P. (1991, July). Home/community-based services: A two-tier approach. *American Journal of Orthopsychiatry, 61*, 403–408.

Attneave, C. L. (1969). Therapy in tribal settings and urban network intervention. *Family Process, 8*(3), 192–210.

Auerswald, E. H. (1968). Interdisciplinary versus ecological approach. *Family Process, 7*, 202–215.

Bellah, R. N., Madsen, R., Sullivan, W. M., Swidler, A., & Tipton, S. M. (1991). *The good society*. New York: Knopf.

Boszormenyi-Nagy, I., & Ulrich, D. N. (1981). Contextual family therapy. In A. S. Gurman & D. P. Kniskern (Eds.), *Handbook of family therapy* (pp. 159–186). New York: Brunner/Mazel.

Bowen, M. (1972). Toward the differentiation of a self in one's own family. In J. Framo (Ed.), *Family interaction: A dialogue between family researchers and family therapists* (pp. 111–166). New York: Springer.

Boyd-Franklin, N. (1989). *Black families in therapy: A multisystems approach*. New York: Guilford.

Brosman, M. (1990, May/June). Home-based family therapy not same as office practice. *Family Therapy News*, 4.

Bryce, M., & Lloyd, J. C. (Eds.). (1981). *Treating families in the home: An alternative to placement*. Springfield, IL: Charles C Thomas.

Cassano, R. (1989). Multi-family group therapy in social work practice. Part 1. In R. Cassano (Ed.), *Social work with multi-family groups* (pp. 3–14). New York: Haworth.

DeMuth, D. H. (1990, Summer). The social consciousness of family therapy: A time of change. *AFTA Newsletter, 40*, 10–13.

de Shazer, S., & Berg, I. (1988, September/October). Constructing solutions. *Family Therapy Networker, 12*, 42–43.

Efran, J. S., Lukens, R. J., & Lukens, M. D. (1988, September/October). Constructivism: What's in it for you? *Family Therapy Networker, 12*, 27–35.

Elkaim, M. (1979). Broadening the scope of family therapy or from the family approach to the socio-political approach. *Psychologic und Gesellschaftskritik*, 9–10; 82–101.

Fish, V. (1993, July). Poststructuralism in family therapy: Interrogating the narrative/conversational mode. *Journal of Marital and Family Therapy, 19*, 223–232.

Fleishman, J. (1994, January 9). A close-knit society imperiled. *The Philadelphia Inquirer*, pp. A-1, A-10.

Freud, S. (1937). Analysis terminable and interminable. In J. Strachey (Ed.

and Trans.), *The standard edition of the complete psychological works of Sigmund Freud* (Vol. 23, pp. 216–253). New York: Norton.

Garcia-Preto, N. (1982). Puerto Rican families. In M. McGoldrick, J. K. Pearce, & J. Giordano (Eds.), *Ethnicity and family therapy* (pp. 164–186). New York: Guilford.

Goldner, V. (1985, November/December). Warning: Family therapy may be hazardous to your health. *Family Therapy Networker, 9*, 18–23.

Goldner, V. (1993). Power and hierarchy: Let's talk about it! *Family Process, 32*, 157–162.

Graham, S. R. (1980, Winter). Desire, belief and grace: A psychotherapeutic paradigm. *Psychotherapy: Theory, Research and Practice, 17*, 370–371.

Haley, J. (1980). *Leaving home*. New York: McGraw-Hill.

Hare-Mustin, R. T. (1978). A feminist approach to family therapy. *Family Process, 17*, 181–194.

Hoffman, L. (1981). *Foundations of family therapy*. New York: Basic Books.

Hoffman, L. (1990). Constructing realities: An art of lenses. *Family Process, 29*, 1–12.

Illich, I. (1972). *Deschooling society*. New York: Harper & Row.

Illich, I. (1977). *Medical nemesis*. New York: Bantam Books.

Kaplan, L. (1986). *Working with multiproblem families*. Lexington, MA: Lexington.

Kerr, M. E. (1981). Family systems theory and therapy. In A. S. Gurman & D. P. Kniskern (Eds.), *Handbook of family therapy* (pp. 226–264). New York: Brunner/Mazel.

Keith, D. V., & Whitaker, C. A. (1977). The divorce labyrinth. In P. Papp (Ed.), *Family therapy: Full length case studies* (pp. 117–131). New York: Gardner.

Knitzer, S. L. (1982). *Unclaimed children*. Washington, DC: Children's Defense Fund.

Laqueur, H. P. (1973). Multiple family therapy: Questions and answers. In D. A. Bloch (Ed.), *Techniques of family psychotherapy: A primer* (pp. 75–85). New York: Grune & Stratton.

Lawson, W. B. (1985). Chronic mental illness and the black family. In M. T. Fullilove (Ed. for the Black Task Force), *The black family: Mental health perspectives* (pp. 95–104). Department of Psychiatry, San Francisco General Hospital, UCSF School of Medicine.

Living alone can be hazardous to your health (1990, March 5). *Business Week*.

Marder, D. (1993, May 8). Dead teen's friends say he was dressed to kill. *The Philadelphia Inquirer*, pp. A-1, A-10.

Minuchin, S. (1970). The use of an ecological framework in the treatment of a child. In E. J. Anthony & C. Koupernick (Eds.), *The international yearbook of child psychiatry: The child in his family* (pp. 41–57). New York: Wiley.

Minuchin, S. (1974). *Families and family therapy.* Cambridge, MA: Harvard University Press.

Minuchin, S., & Fishman, H. C. (1981). *Family therapy techniques.* Cambridge, MA: Harvard University Press.

Minuchin, S., Montalvo, B., Guerney, Jr., B., Rosman, B., & Schumer, F. (1967). *Families of the slums.* New York: Basic Books.

National Commission on America's Urban Families (1993, January). *Families first.* Washington, DC: Author.

National Commission on Children: Interim Report (1990, March 31). *Opening doors for America's children* (p. 33). Washington, DC: Author.

O'Neill, M. (1993, May 6). In Japan, nostalgia is a best seller. *The Philadelphia Inquirer,* p. A-22.

Paul, B. B., & Paul, N. L. (1985). Outpatient multiple family group. In M. P. Mirkin & S. L. Koman (Eds.), *Handbook of adolescents and family therapy* (pp. 161–172). New York: Gardner.

Piaget, J. (1970). *Structuralism* (C. Maschler, Trans. & Ed.). New York: Basic Books.

Pinderhughes, E. (1989). Understanding race, ethnicity, and power: The key to efficacy in clinical practice. New York: Free Press.

Prest, L. A., & Keller, J. F. (1993, April). Spirituality and family therapy: Spiritual beliefs, myths, and metaphors. *Journal of Marital and Family Therapy, 19,* 137–148.

Rabkin, R. (1970). *Inner and outer space.* New York: Norton.

Rassoch, J. W. (1981). Multiple family therapy. In R. J. Corsini (Ed.), *Handbook of innovative psychotherapies.* New York: Wiley.

Rich, S. (1989, November 5). Despite U. S. prosperity, one-fifth of children poor. *The Philadelphia Inquirer,* p. A-5.

Rotunno, M., & McGoldrick, M. (1982). Italian families. In M. McGoldrick, J. K. Pearce, & J. Giordano (Eds.), *Ethnicity and family therapy* (pp. 340–363). New York: Guilford.

Schorr, L. B. (1989, November/December). Let's stop recycling poverty. *Family Therapy Networker,* 13–14.

Speck, R. V., & Rueveni, U. (1969, September). Network therapy—A developing concept. *Family Process, 8*(2), 182.

Tavantzis, T. N., Tavantzis, M., Brown, L. G., & Rohrbaugh, M. (1985). Home-based family therapy for delinquents at risk of placement. In M. P. Mirkin & S. Koman (Eds.), *Handbook of adolescents and family therapy* (pp. 69–88). New York: Gardner.

Weiner, T. (1991, March 3). U.S. leads way in violence, report says. *The Philadelphia Inquirer,* p. A-3.

Wilson, J. Q. (1993). *The moral sense.* New York: Free Press.

Wittaker, J. K., Kinney, J., Tracy, E. M., & Booth, C. (1990). *Reaching high-risk families: Intensive family preservation in human services.* New York: Aldine de Gruyter.

Yalom, I. (1985). *The theory and practice of group psychotherapy.* New York: Basic Books.

Index